Against Innocence

Against Innocence

Gillian Rose's Reception and Gift of Faith

Andrew Shanks

scm press

The Author has asserted his right under the Copyright, Designs and Patents Act, 1988, to be identified as the Author of this Work

British Library Cataloguing in Publication data

A catalogue record for this book is available from the British Library

978 0 334 04136 8

First published in 2008 by SCM Press
13–17 Long Lane,
London EC1A 9PN

www.scm-canterburypress.co.uk

SCM Press is a division of
SCM-Canterbury Press Ltd

Typeset by Regent Typesetting, London
Printed in the UK by
CPI William Clowes, Beccles, NR34 7TL

Contents

Winterreise: for Gillian Rose, 9 December 1995
Afternoon

Still, where you were concerned, we always
arrived too late; too late, myopic, short of sleep,
with fingers stumbling to decipher messages
you left for us, engraved in a hard surface.
It was a distant relative of yours who drove
his lawyer's reed into the black Sinai basalt
till the calligraphy of little streams broke out
to age the hopeless rock as if with history,
as if with words; another kinsman, distant or not too distant
writing in falling sweat on stone, body to ground, something
his friends never quite managed to read . . .

Rowan Williams, *Remembering Jerusalem: Poems*[1]

In Memoriam: Gillian Rose

There is a kind of sanity that hates weddings
but bears an intelligence of grief
in its own kind. There are achievements
that carry failure on their back, blindness
not as in Brueghel, but unfathomably
far-seeing . . .

Geoffrey Hill, *A Treatise of Civil Power*[2]

Foreword

There is a clinging to Jesus that shows itself in the longing to be utterly sure of our rightness; we want him there, we want him where we can see him and manage him, so that we know exactly where to turn to be told that everything is all right and that he is on our side.

Rowan Williams, Easter Sermon, Canterbury Cathedral, April 2003

Some books seem to be about one thing but are actually about something else. This is one of those books. Andrew Shanks and I began *Against Innocence* as a joint project. Both of us shared a passion for Gillian Rose's work and a common mind that her philosophy was both tremendously important and shamefully neglected. Yet in the preparation of this book we found ourselves in the midst of an ever widening disagreement that meant it could only be written by a single author.

What follows is a spirited defence of what one might call the theology of the peace negotiator or mediator. Simply put, the mediator pursues a theology that refuses to accept that a disagreement can ever reach a point where there is no benefit to be gained from further conversation. Put a different way, it is a refusal to accept that two seemingly irreconcilable positions are indeed irreconcilable. The mediator is the supreme pragmatist, employing all the philosophical strategies up his or her sleeve to keep opponents round the table, to keep them talking.

The philosophical substructure of this theology of mediatory conversation is Hegelian; indeed, I would want to call it dialectical –

though the three thinkers that matter most in this book, Shanks, Rose and Rowan Williams (all Hegelians of sorts), refuse to equate the drivers of Hegel's thought with the crab-like progress of thesis, antithesis and synthesis. Instead, Williams perfectly describes the Hegelianism of the mediating peace negotiator when he writes: 'Reflection requires that the plain opposition of positive and negative be left behind. Thinking is not content with the abstraction of mutual exclusivities, but struggles to conceive of a structured wholeness nuanced enough to contain what appeared to be contradictories.'

As it turns out, this 'struggle to conceive of a structural wholeness nuanced enough to contain what appeared to be contradictories' is a pretty accurate summary of the Archbishop's strategy in dealing with the warring parties of contemporary Anglicanism. Indeed, rarely has there been a more convinced exponent of the theology of the peace negotiator than Rowan Williams. Which is why, although he only gets a couple of direct mentions, the Archbishop dances around the subtext of this book on almost every page. Without mentioning it at all, what Andrew Shanks has produced is a brilliant and subtle apologia for the Archbishop of Canterbury's strategy in dealing with the culture wars within the Anglican Communion over homosexuality.

Gillian Rose didn't just convert to Christianity. She converted into Anglicanism. Specifically, she was received into the Church of England. And this is not insignificant, for the Church of England is, above all else, a peace treaty between antagonistic theological visions – as a shorthand, between the basic theological archetypes of the (Protestant) Roundhead and the (Catholic) Cavalier. The Church of England was forged out of the bloodshed between these hostile visions, with both sides reluctantly agreeing to suspend their sense of being exclusively in possession of the truth in order to achieve a peaceful coexistence. This is why Anglicanism is the natural home of the peace negotiator.

Of course, there are various strategies for peace negotiation, some more effective than others. Much of the time, particularly in the Church, it simply means a process whereby people with competing visions are shut away in a room with a flipchart and a facilitator. Mostly, this doesn't produce any significant meeting of minds. Rather, it produces a lot of angry and frustrated Christians who feel they have wasted their time in a directionless quagmire of well-meaning but pointless conversation. In contrast, the sort of peace negotiation suggested by Rose and Shanks has a definite strategy: it attempts to dismantle our desire for innocence. For what is recognized by the true mediator is that innocence – or the 'longing to be utterly sure of our rightness', as Williams puts it – is exactly the motivation that leads people to reject compromise and continue with the theological fisticuffs. Thus the target for much of the theology in this book is the stubborn desire for the sort of moral purity that refuses negotiation. For the mediator it is better to inhabit the uncomfortable world of compromise, even if this suggests the possibility of betraying one's deepest convictions. Better that than the cheap innocence premised upon the refusal to entertain negotiation, conversation or compromise.

To put it at its starkest: peace is better than truth. Of course, this is not a description that advocates of this position would recognize. In typically Hegelian fashion, they reject the suggestion that peace and truth stand in opposition to one another. This is why, when the Archbishop is charged with sacrificing truth for unity, as he often is, his comeback has consistently been that unity is a means by which truth is made visible, that we come to truth through the process of uniting conversation. In other words the 'struggle to conceive of a structural wholeness nuanced enough to contain what appeared to be contradictories' applies even to the apparent antithesis of truth and peace.

This is beginning to sound all rather abstract. In fact, it isn't at all. Here is how the 'against innocence' theology might impact upon a particular process of thought – let's say my own. Ever since the gay priest Jeffrey John was rejected as the Bishop of Reading because of his sexuality, the red mist has descended upon many parts of the Church. For many, it was a declaration of war, made all the more galling by the fact that this betrayal was perpetrated by someone who once had progressive views on homosexuality. Back in 1998, as bishops from around the world met at the Lambeth Conference and voted through a condemnation of gay sex as incompatible with Scripture, Dr Williams – who abstained from the vote – wrote an open letter to gay Christians promising to work for their full inclusion in the life of the Church. It was a promise he would fail to keep. Like many, I remain eye-poppingly angry about all of this. It is a subject on which I find it hard to imagine any sort of compromise. For me, the issue of justice for gay people in the Church is utterly non-negotiable.

And it is here, just as I have worked myself up into a lather of righteous indignation, that the 'against innocence' theology gets to work. For the mediator offers the suggestion that the indignation I have expressed is really a form of self-righteousness – more about me than it is about anything else. Moreover, it protects my own moral innocence by blinkering me to the full consequences of my position. The innocence of the angry activist is a refusal to accept that even the noblest cause can have unwanted and deeply unfortunate consequences. The mediator has a point: things are as they are. It is some of the poorest people in the world who will suffer most from the collapse of the Anglican Communion. Which is why Rowan Williams is prepared to bracket out his own progressive instincts on homosexuality – what I earlier referred to as a betrayal. From Shanks's perspective, it is not at all a betrayal, but something generous and self-sacrificial. The Archbishop has given up a false show of innocence in order to negotiate peace. On this reading, his handling of the gay crisis is a heroic act of the supreme mediator prepared fully to face the tragic reality of division. In contrast, the activist is playing 'let's pretend', refusing to accept that others suffer for his/her self-righteousness, and unwilling to give up reputation in order to seek some sort of settlement. It's a pretty hefty charge.

Rose's work is an encouragement to pay attention to the philosophical condition of human fallenness. Human beings are haunted by complexity, compromised by mixed motives, and debased by threads of complicity with cruelty and untruthfulness. We constantly seek to represent ourselves with various fictions of our own innocence – the innocence of the activist, of the silent or prayerful, of the victim – thus failing to recognize that we all own shares in the ways of the world. This isn't so much a counsel of despair; rather, it's a fearlessly honest description of what it takes to love our neighbour.

There is one further thing that Rowan Williams's approach to peace negotiation owes to Rose's general philosophy and that is its insistence on the importance of law in the formation of public ethics. For Rose, the significance of law grows out of an attack upon postmodernity which, she argues, represents an abandonment of the public sphere. It's a fascinating line of thought. The Holocaust so traumatized western culture – and especially and obviously the work of Jewish intellectuals who were prominent in the creation of postmodern ethics – that the ethicists of the mid-part of the twentieth century attempted, almost subconsciously, to construct an ethics without any reference whatsoever to the actual necessity for violence or force. It was an understandable reaction to the violence of the death camps and, in its way, another manifestation of the desire for innocence. Yet this had the effect of generating a form of ethics characterized by a refusal of obligation or constraint. Instead, postmodern ethics became shaped by an insubstantial and convoluted language – a particular target was Levinas's talk of 'the face' and 'the other' – that refused to be grounded in practical application. It couldn't be grounded in practical application, because practical ethics always implies some form of coercion, some use of force. For practical ethics – the sort of ethics that one needs to run a city for instance – a sense of the proper use of force is essential. Postmodern ethicists were too concerned with their own innocence from violence to make the sorts of moral judgements that are necessary in the public sphere. Thus, in effect, they betrayed the city.

Rose notes that this refusal of practical ethics by Jewish thinkers is especially ironic given the centrality of law in Jewish religious thought. For, according to Rose, it is to the ethics of law that we must look first in order to see our way past the unhelpful innocence of the postmodern ethical cul-de-sac. It is through the application of just law that ethics is made substantial and real. Yes, law involves constraint, implies consequences for law-breakers, and so forth. But, precisely because of this, it is the proper moral vehicle for those who would bring an ethical vision to bear on the world. It is the right way of doing the sort of ethics that will risk making a difference.

This, I suspect, is one of the intellectual tributaries that has led Rowan Williams to place so much emphasis on covenant as the answer to the problems of the Communion. Good law offers a safe space for different viewpoints to learn from each other. As Williams once put it in a lecture to the Centre for the Study of Jewish–Christian Relations in Cambridge: 'Covenant promises one world, not a totalising conformity enforced by central power, but a mutual recognition of the debt of honour and love, and a search for ways in which the good of each and the good of all may coincide.'

Perhaps there is no more obvious a representation of the broken middle than the Church of England and its dysfunctional progeny, the Anglican Communion. The fact that I felt unable to complete this book with my friend Andrew Shanks is one tiny consequence of this brokenness. Yet for Rose, the fact that something is broken does not make it unserviceable. Which is why this book sounds a note of hope. Even stupid and sinful people can be used as bearers of the good news. Even brokenness can reflect the glory of God. And that means there is hope for us all – agitators and mediators alike.

Revd Dr Giles Fraser

Acknowledgements

I would like to thank, first, Giles Fraser, for his general brio and enthusiasm in helping launch this project. Then: Barbara Laing of SCM Press – for immediately seeing the point. I am also particularly grateful to Lynn Rose and Simon Barrington-Ward for correcting biographical errors, and pointing me in new directions. Anna Rowlands, in her Ph.D. thesis, has already begun to develop a proper, extended theological reading of Gillian Rose's work, and I have benefited a great deal from consulting her. Thank you to John Millbank, and to Nick Walker, for their expert help – I only hope they will not think I have gone too far astray, in the end. And thank you, as well, to the two poets whose tributes to Gillian Rose I have put as epigraphs to my argument, for their permission: Geoffrey Hill and Rowan Williams.

Manchester Cathedral
2008

1

A Deathbed Baptism

❧

On 9 December 1995 the philosopher Gillian Rose was baptized on her deathbed. In his sermon for Christmas Day the following year the then Archbishop of Canterbury, George Carey, told the story:

This time last year you may have seen the obituary of Professor Gillian Rose, who died of cancer at the age of 48. A brilliant philosopher, she sought all her life for meaning. She lived life to the full; she had lovers and many friends. She was at the top of her tree as a philosopher and thinker. She was tough minded, rigorous and sharp. She told her friends that she was 'too Jewish to be Christian and too Christian to be Jewish'.

A deep friendship grew between herself and Simon Barrington-Ward, the Bishop of Coventry. Starting from their common interest in Hegel, and her own wide reading in theology, she shared with him, as with other spiritual allies, her own ethical and theological explorations. Then, two years before her death, she was told she had cancer. It spread swiftly throughout her body, but her indomitable mind refused to accept the finality of life. She carried on thinking and one day, to everyone's surprise, asked Simon if he would baptise and confirm her and give her her first communion. Characteristically she wanted to make a party of it. She invited some professional philosopher friends to her baptism – Jews, Christians and atheists alike, who were all

1

coming to Warwick University for a conference she had long planned. But it was too happy an ending to conclude in that way. Just a few hours before the agreed time, the hospital phoned to tell the Bishop that Gillian was slipping into a last sleep. He rushed to her bedside and was just in time to baptise and confirm her. She could only make her responses with a squeeze of the hand and then she went to meet her Maker, her Saviour and her true Lover.

But Gillian's party went ahead. The Bishop told of Gillian's baptism and her friends, believers and atheists alike, wept and rejoiced for a friend whose journey was over.

ఌఌఌ

Well, it sure was a theatrical, as well as tragic, way to go.

The Archbishop did not personally know her. But he had heard the story from Simon Barrington-Ward a little while before, at a small gathering of bishops, and it had evidently moved him deeply. It is not quite true to suggest, as he does, that her request for baptism came 'to everyone's surprise', although it certainly did surprise some. And it is surely also somewhat misleading to suggest, as George Carey's account appears to, that all her friends, when they heard what had happened, simply 'wept and rejoiced'. By no means all of them rejoiced at the news of her baptism![1] Of course, her Christian friends were glad – among them George Carey's successor at Canterbury, Rowan Williams, who knew her well and was intellectually close to her.[2] Others, however, were troubled, even suspicious that she had perhaps been manipulated, in her dying weakness, by unscrupulous clerics. Indeed, I can well imagine that, in the light of that suspicion, some people might misread the Archbishop's retelling of the story here, essentially, as a mere boast: 'Look what a catch we got!'

Such suspicions, though – as I will seek to demonstrate – spring from a basic misunderstanding. In actual fact, this baptism was not at all the outcome of some sudden, last minute 'conversion'. On the contrary, it represented quite a natural symbolic conclusion to the whole trajectory of Rose's thought.

And, as such, I think it really was worthy of an archbishop's tribute. Thus, let us consider this baptism in its character as a gift to the Church. Every baptism is such a gift. Only, very few baptism-gifts are quite as complex, problematic and, I think – if properly understood – _disturbing_ for us to receive as the gift of Gillian Rose. Very few are quite as richly promising, either, as a contribution to our ongoing corporate reflection on the true nature of faith.

A few months before her death Rose had published a short auto-biographical memoir, entitled _Love's Work_, framed by her experience of cancer.[3] This is the best-known of her writings. It is more or less an act of defiance, in the face of death. When first informed that she had cancer – she tells us – her immediate 'jaunty' response was to say to the hospital consultant who had made the diagnosis, 'I am the happiest, healthiest person I know.' Whereupon he had replied, 'Well, you are going to be very severely tried.' ('I like him for putting it like that,' she comments, 'it leaves me be.'[4])And she describes the ensuing trials with great candour, but also quite without any trace of self-pity.

She allows us various glimpses here into her love affairs. And she writes about some of her more eccentric friends, taking a gleeful delight in their eccentricities. Then, too, she shows us something of her family background.

On both sides her ancestors were Polish Jews. She speaks of Passover _Seder_ nights at her maternal grandparents' home. Linguistically, she writes, these grandparents of hers 'move easily between Yiddish, Polish, Russian, Hebrew and French (the last of these languages specially acquired for their frequent holidays at the gaming tables of Cannes and Nice), [but] are indifferent and heavily accented speakers of English'.[5] They had emigrated from Łódź when they married, because both their families disapproved of the match; first to Germany, then to London. Her grandfather's family meanwhile had also emigrated, but not her grandmother's. And so, with the single exception of one remote cousin, they all perished as victims of the Shoah, some fifty of them, 'the children bayoneted first in front of their parents'. – 'My mother said, "Grandma would kill German babies." "Why would Grandma kill German babies?" "Because the Germans killed Jewish babies."?'[6]

Gillian Rose was born Gillian Stone. But she changed her name by deed poll when she was sixteen. Her parents had divorced, acrimoniously; she was bitter against her father, so she rejected his name and adopted her stepfather's instead. 'Stone' became 'Rose'. Back in Poland, though, her father's parents had in fact originally been called 'Riddell'. They had become 'Stone', as a gesture of becoming-English, only after their arrival in Manchester. And 'Rose', likewise, was an Irish-style abbreviation of 'Rosenthal'. Both her fathers were medical doctors, and both were, as she puts it, 'disaffected Jews', spiritually uprooted from their ancestral tradition. Then, however, just as she left home to become an undergraduate at Oxford, her mother's marriage to her stepfather also broke up. She was – she tells us – so traumatized by the drama of this that she reacted by lapsing into agoraphobia, a condition that recurred throughout her twenties. And with her stepfather's authority broken as a result – in the same way that her father's had much earlier been – she eventually began to look beyond their shared disaffection from religion.

Yet there was for her no easy way back. Some years later, wanting cheap accommodation within easy reach of the British Library, where she was pursuing research into the Neo-Kantian tradition of philosophy, she bought a flat in Stoke Newington, and found herself surrounded by a community of Lubavitcher Hasidim, the most evangelistic of Ultra-Orthodox Jews. Here was the world of ancient Central European Jewry, fiercely preserved in defiance of so many centuries of Gentile persecution, Judaism at its cosiest, at its most theatrical, and most set apart from the surrounding world. The pale-faced men in their dark, late-eighteenth-century garb, the women with their uniform wigs, and the clusters of children that piety requires them to bear, as many as possible, in order to defeat the ever-menacing forces of destruction. A community of such unswerving loyalty to its ever-beleaguered tradition – locked tight into the intense corporate privacy of its nightmare memories and messianic hope. 'One day', Rose remarks,

looking out of the window of the flat, I saw a wedding party arrive at the block of flats on the opposite side of the road. Not an Hasidic wedding, an ordinary English wedding. What struck me at once was the lightness of the vision: slender, young brides-maids in short, white, muslin dresses with loose, bare limbs, the adults attired in the pastel hues of matrimonial finery, and the commingling of the sexes in easy, high spirits, all on their way from the church ceremony to the jollifications of the reception. My disinterested perception of this happy procession was brusquely interrupted by the loud irruption of a sub-human howling, the source of which was unlocatable. It was howling as if from a dark, dank cave, where some deformed brute had been chained and tempted since time immemorial. The howling did not cease even after the last of the wedding party had dis-appeared from view.

It was I who was howling, in utter dissociation from myself, the paroxysm provoked by the vivacious contrast between the environing judaism and this epiphany of protestants, the customary, laborious everydayness broken by the moment of marriage, the cloaks of the clandestine pious cleaved by the costumes of those weightless, redeemed beings.[7]

In a sense, all of her thinking is a sublation of that howl. Imagina-tively connected with, and yet also cut off from, both worlds, by her history and her inner solitude, she is driven to protest against their disconnection – and so to protest against such disconnectedness wherever it is found, between worlds of every sort.

Again, Rose is a philosopher who had had to battle her way through (mild) dyslexia – an especially troubling condition, she remarks, for one brought up in such a bookish culture as she was. Nothing came easy to her in the reading of books. In her judgement of ideas she is, above all, allergic to what comes easy.

Nor does she ever make things easy for her readers! Her writing is often quite exasperatingly dense and allusive. And yet it is lit by sudden moments of startling originality, and by a blazing insistence on moral complexity. This is philosophy without inhibitions: a quite uninhibited love of Truth, at its rawest.

The first of her books is a study of the Neo-Marxist German Jewish philosopher Theodor W. Adorno. She actually claims to have taught herself German by reading Adorno: 'I was attracted by the ethical impulse of his thought, but also by the characteristics of his style, the most notoriously difficult sentence structure and the vocabulary full of *Fremdwörter*. This embarkation also betrays a further motivation: an inexorable inner need to experience my dyslexia in daily intercourse with the signs and syntax of Adorno's forbidding universe.'[8]

As for the 'ethical' attraction here: she was attracted to a form of philosophical reflection pervasively haunted by the memory of the Holocaust, and a systematic identification of wisdom with maximum sheer unsettledness of thought. Yet, at the same time, Adorno's thought also breathes a spirit of the most sardonic irreligion. There is not much discernible egalitarianism left in Adorno's residual Marxism – but what essentially does remain, always there in the background, is Marxist atheism.

This, then, is the starting point of her intellectual journey.

Another admirer of Adorno's work is Martin Jay; a leading chronicler of the Frankfurt School in general, to which Adorno belonged.[9] And Jay is the author of an intriguing little essay on Rose. As one who has stayed put at what had also been her starting point, he reflects here on her eventual reception of faith. To people like himself, Jay writes – indeed, to many of her closest friends – the news of this final decision of hers, to enter the Church, 'came as a thunderbolt'.[10] All the more so, since her initial move beyond Adornoesque atheism, in the early 1990s, had seemed to be, far rather, towards a fresh sort of progressive, philosophic Judaism.

Jay writes of her, as a friend, with wry amusement. Encountering her in the context of an academic conference, 'I was reminded' – he remarks – 'as I had been before, of Lord Melbourne's reaction to Macauley: "I wish I were as cocksure of anything as he is of every-thing"'. And he goes on: 'Rose's extraordinary self-confidence, fondness for gnomic pronunciamentos, and hedgehoglike ability to incorporate every possible position into her own worldview meant that productive dialogue with her was, in fact, difficult.' Nevertheless, he regrets that her work remains, as he sees it, unduly neglected as a result. In his words:

> Although she was by all accounts an inspirational, if tough, mentor – ten doctoral students dutifully accompanied her when she moved from Sussex to Warwick – and had a number of devoted friends and intellectual soulmates, including the philo-sophers J. N. Bernstein and Howard Caygill, her influence seems to have been relatively modest.[11]

For the fact is, her work does not fit any current intellectual fashion, and the dedicated followers of intellectual fashion have evidently never quite known how to respond to her.

To be sure, Jay is one of those troubled by what he calls the 'gesture' of her baptism:

Although a nonobservant Jew unperturbed by any disaffection from the tenets of Judaism, I cannot avoid an involuntary shudder at the news of a positive decision to convert to another religion. I am unable to throw off the troubling memory of nearly two thousand years of eager attempts to convert Jews to Christianity, either through persuasion or coercion, attempts that are intimately related to the sorry history of antisemitism. Although there are many explanations why in certain circumstances Jews willingly purchased this 'entry ticket to European culture', as Heine famously called it, none fails to leave a bad taste in my mouth.[12]

On the other hand, he is by no means suggesting that she herself was insensitive to such considerations. He entirely shares the visceral irreligiousness of Frankfurt School 'critical theory'. And yet, the basic, generous point of his essay is to insist on the unique challenge of Rose's work – precisely by virtue of its *whole* trajectory – to the prevailing prejudices of his own intellectual world. Thus, he writes: these days, 'when alterity, heterogeneity, nonidentity, difference, and otherness have become the tired buzzwords of our fractured culture, it is Rose who paradoxically represents a form of genuine strangeness, unassimilable to any school of thought'.[13]

Or one might, perhaps, put it like this. Rose originally emerged, as a philosopher, within the thought-world of atheist postmodernity. (Is not Adorno a postmodern Marxist?) And then she, step by step, proceeded to break free from the limitations of that world. What atheist postmodernity, in itself, professes to affirm above all else is just the most radical free-spiritedness. But nothing, indeed, could better illustrate such free-spiritedness in action than the way in which she, finally, repudiated atheist postmodernity. That is the 'paradox'.

From the standpoint of atheist postmodernity any reception of religious faith is, straight away, essentially under suspicion of being a mere flight from difficult reality, an expression of inner weakness, a bid for consolation and comfort. However, as Jay acknowledges, this scarcely seems to be the case here. Far rather, the impulse at work is surely none other than a resolute determination *to try and open up honest conversation between and within divided worlds.* For that is how Rose most fundamentally understands intellectual vocation in general.

Thus, on the one hand – as a consummate intellectual – in being baptized she was for the first time becoming part of a genuinely catholic moral community. That is to say, a form of community precisely designed to bring intellectuals into the deepest possible conversation with the salt of the earth.

And, on the other hand – as a secular philosopher and a thoroughly Jewish Jew – her becoming, at the same time, *also* a Christian meant that she was, so to speak, situating herself at the point of confluence between all three main streams of traditional Western European spirituality. She did not choose to be baptized in order to take refuge in an exclusive orthodoxy. But, quite to the contrary, she was, so far as she could, symbolically adopting the role of universal mediator. Was her option for baptism a betrayal of her Jewishness? Notwithstanding all the ugly history of Christian antisemitism, she at any rate did not see Christianity and Judaism as rival paths.

࿇

The epigraph to *Love's Work* is a saying that comes from a saint of Mount Athos, the Russian monk Staretz Silouan (1866–1938):

Keep your mind in hell, and despair not.

In fact, according to Silouan himself, these are words that he once heard spoken to him, by a disembodied voice, at a time when he was plunged into deep depression. He was praying. And he understood this to be a direct response to his prayer, from Christ.

In the course of Rose's book the saying recurs three times. With regard to her cancer, she invokes the wisdom of the Staretz against the self-help literature of 'alternative healing'. So she describes the obligatory sickly-sweet serenity that is there identified with true well-being, even in the midst of disease, as 'the counsel of despair which would keep the mind out of hell'. And she goes on, 'The tradition is far kinder in its understanding that to live, to love, is to be failed, to forgive, to fail, to be forgiven, for ever and ever.'[14]

In quite a different context, recalling the end of a love affair, she writes:

> Resist the telephone! Even though help is only a few digits away. For the first time, I say "No" to any alleviation, to the mean of friendship, to the endlessly inventive love of my sisters. *I don't want to be justified.* Keep your mind in hell and . . . I want to sob and sob and sob . . . until the prolonged shrieking becomes a shout of joy.[15]

No revenge – not even the revenge of being reassured that one is in the right. She will allow herself no such consolation.

And then too she speaks about her mother's response to what had happened to her family at the hands of the Nazis: all those murders, with 'the children bayoneted first in front of their parents'. She comments on this with harsh loving compassion – although also I think with, frankly, rather puzzling unfairness! Her impression, she writes, is that

> nowadays, my mother denies this; she denies that it happened and she denies that her mother suffered from it, so deep is her own unresolved suffering. This denial and unexamined suffering are two of the main reasons for her all-jovial unhappiness – the unhappiness of one who refuses to dwell in hell, and who lives, therefore, in the most static despair.

This is perhaps best taken as an oblique, general comment on a whole generation, in a collective state of shock; it is certainly a judgement framed in terms of the most exorbitant moral ideal.[16]

'Keep your mind in hell, and despair not' is indeed a basic formula for the ideal truth inherent in Christlikeness. 'Take up your cross', says Jesus to his disciples, 'and follow me'. For that is how God is revealed – first and foremost, on the cross. Properly interpreted, the symbol of the harrowing of hell captures the very essence of revelation. Above all, God's love is just what shines through the mixture of profound respect and compassion evoked in those who witness that quality of resoluteness, in the afflicted, which Jesus on the cross represents, and who do not turn aside, but let themselves be truly confronted by it.

Rose does not begin *Love's Work* by telling her readers that she, the author, is dying of cancer. This fact only emerges at the beginning of chapter 6 – after five chapters in which, as she herself puts it, she has 'continually wooed' the reader, with her quirkily told tales of family, friends and lovers. Here, however, that 'wooing' abruptly gives way to confrontation: 'Suppose', she writes, 'that I were now to reveal that I have AIDS, full-blown AIDS, and have been ill during most of the course of what I have related. I would lose you.'[17]

Well, it is not AIDS, but ovarian cancer. Not liable to be quite so great a shock to the reader, perhaps – but, still, a challenge. Do we really want to read about this? So she taunts us almost; explicitly confronts the universal human instinct, in us, to shrink back, and turn away from the afflicted.

'Keep your mind in hell, and despair not.' Let me add some further theological comments of my own at this point. What Staretz Silouan is talking about is the subjective experience of God-forsakenness, which may or may not be masked by some degree of emotional anaesthesia. But now consider hell as the condition of *objective* alienation from God, in rigidly impenitent sinfulness. Here, by contrast, the anaesthesia is surely both automatic and total. For one cannot truly *feel* the reality of one's sin, and fail to repent. The traditional imagery of the last judgement shows us what we *ought* to feel, when the true moral reality of our lives is unveiled; or what we *would* feel – were it not for original sin, preventing us. To be alive is to be in God's presence, in principle this is heaven, it should be bliss, yet, being fallen creatures, we lack the necessary taste to appreciate it. And at the same time we remain more or less locked into sin. In principle this is hell, and ought to be torment. But, as we are fallen, impenitence anaesthetizes us. Manipulative church ideology misrepresents heaven as an immediately intelligible reward for virtue. And it misrepresents hell, likewise, as an immediate threat of punishment for vice. However, let us be honest: to talk of heaven and hell is to gesture towards depths of difficult reality that remain forever beyond us. We are in heaven, now, and we do not recognize it. And in so far as we are simultaneously also locked into hell, we do not feel that either. Hell, in the objective sense, is thus no punishment, as punishment is usually understood; it is nothing but a sheer unfelt emptiness, where God should be. To be damned is merely to feel – in the most trivial, numbed sort of way – forever *innocent*.

How, then, are we to be saved? Divine revelation, as a therapeutic response to the desensitizing Fall, operates by confronting us with eloquent spectacles of pain; precisely, the inspirational example of those who, with the utmost resolution, hold fast to the truth of heaven even in subjective hell.

Although Rose was not baptized until the very end of her life, her thought is, in fact, essentially consonant with the pathos of divine revelation, at this level, right from the beginning. Always, she is critical of intellectual structures in so far as she suspects that they may tend to shelter delusions of innocence. She is a prophetic philosopher, a philosophical prophet. Absolutely a philosopher in her intellectual sophistication and radical repudiation of anything at all sectarian, she is nevertheless far more than just an ivory-tower dweller. Indeed, she represents the very boldest possible sense of intellectual vocation: contemplating the overlap between heaven and hell. Intellectually immersed in purgatory.

She is a universal mediator, constantly intent on challenging the delusions of innocence that most of all damage proper communication between the inhabitants of divided worlds, by keeping everything superficial.

2

Against 'Holocaust Piety'

In 1990 the new Polish government established a Commission for the Future of Auschwitz. How to make the place a truly fitting memorial to what had happened there? Under the previous regime, it was felt, the commemoration had been distorted by the imperatives of Communist Party propaganda. So a fresh beginning was to be made. And Gillian Rose was among those invited to act as a consultant to the process.

Yet she is notable, not least, as a sharp critic of what she calls 'Holocaust piety'.

At one level her critique of this 'piety' springs from a profound mistrust of the motives at work where Holocaust commemoration has been institutionalized as a sort of 'culture industry'. In the early 1990s, for instance, an issue arose: what was to happen to the last remaining, original, wooden barrack from Auschwitz-Birkenau, in view of the fact that, left where it was, it would soon rot away entirely? She expresses her horror – and the horror of her fellow consultants – when they heard that a bidding war had erupted between the various Holocaust Museums in the USA, each of them desperate in their rivalry to obtain this precious barrack. As she puts it: 'The Holocaust has become a civil religion in the United States, with Auschwitz as the anti-city of the American political community.'[1] It turns out that the devotees of this civil religion have a positively medieval appetite for relics. And, just as in the case of the medieval cult of saints' relics, one has to ask, what exactly has happened to the memory at stake here?

That bidding war serves as a grotesque illustration of the way in which Auschwitz has come to serve as the symbolic 'anti-city of the American political community'. And likewise in Britain: when, in 2001, the government inaugurated the national observance of 27 January each year as 'Holocaust Memorial Day', this was surely all about Auschwitz being configured as the anti-city of the British political community. (27 January is the anniversary of the liberation of Auschwitz.[2]) Rose is by no means arguing that there should not be Holocaust Museums or Holocaust Memorial Days. Only, she is concerned that the commemoration should not be reduced to the level of a propaganda exercise; or, perhaps more precisely, an exercise in pre-propaganda, designed to soften people up for the propaganda of the current political establishment. Of course we must be grateful that our rulers are not Nazis! But in its crudest forms 'Holocaust piety' is nothing but a systematic sentimentalizing of that gratitude, a strategy for turning it into tearful self-congratulation.

And then the same 'piety' also comes in more sophisticated, ostensibly dissident forms – with which, however, Rose is just as unhappy.

Her most sustained discussion of 'Holocaust piety' as such comes in an essay, written for a conference in 1994, entitled 'Beginnings of the Day: Fascism and Representation'.

The, at first sight, typically cryptic title is an allusion to Kazuo Ishiguro's novel *The Remains of the Day*, and its film adaptation, both of which she admires, and briefly discusses in the course of the essay. She associates these works with Hegel's famous remark about 'the owl of Minerva', as the emblem of true philosophic wisdom: 'The owl of Minerva spreads its wings only with the falling

of the dusk.'[3] Thus, she wants here to affirm the Hegelian understanding of philosophic wisdom, as arising out of an essentially
chastened appropriation of the past; such as she also finds in
Ishiguro's narrative. The appeal of Fascist and other sorts of totalitarian propaganda rests on the exact opposite attitude: one in
which we, the addressees of the propaganda message, are encour-
aged to adopt the sentimental role, with regard to historic trauma,
of purely innocent voyeurs. This is the attitude that belongs, in
Rose's terminology, to 'the beginnings of the day'. For it offers us a
taste, at least, of something like the innocence of Eden. So it seeks
to seduce us. Propagandists sentimentalize history, as a way of
confirming, and reinforcing, our given prejudices. As propagandists, they can have no other ambition.

But then, the point is, that same general species of sentimentality
is also characteristic of a great deal of ostensibly anti-Fascist art.
The prime example she cites is Stephen Spielberg's film *Schindler's
List*. Indeed, there could scarcely be a finer expression of what one
might perhaps term '*naive*' Holocaust piety than Spielberg's film.
(Rose is, in this case, much less critical of the original book,
Thomas Keneally's *Schindler's Ark*.[4]) Thus, *Schindler's List* is a
sentimental film in that it invites us to view the horrors it portrays
through the innocent eyes of a saviour. To be sure, Oskar Schindler
is a flawed hero; but his flaws are such that they simply make it
easier for us, the viewers, to identify with him, and so share in his
ultimate innocence. We are not asked to identify, emotionally, with
anyone who, in any way, shares the actual guilt of the criminal
regime. And that, above all, is what Rose finds missing here: that
kind of chastening.

Instead, we are presented with what she calls 'the sentimentality
of the ultimate predator'. As she puts it:

> In a nature film, we could be made to identify with the life cycle
> of the fly as prey of the spider, and we could be made to identify
> with the life cycle of the spider as prey of the rodent. We can be

16

made to identify with the Peking Opera singer who is destroyed by the Cultural Revolution, and we can equally be made to identify with the rickshaw man, for whom the Cultural Revolution was 'the beginning of paradise'. It is only the ultimate predator whose sympathies can be so promiscuously enlisted.[5]

As 'sentimental predators', we may rather enjoy being invited to sympathize with forms of grief we run no risk of sharing. But, on the other hand, our sentimentality shrinks back from works of art designed to make us confront our own predator nature: the various forms of violence in which we are actually complicit; or our general proneness to collude, ourselves, with even worse things, were the occasion to arise. Naive Holocaust piety essentially reflects the 'sentimentality of the ultimate predator' in this sense.

Only, if in our remembrance of these horrors we are to get beyond the level of naive Holocaust piety, what follows? The real originality of Rose's argument lies in the way she goes on to juxtapose two basic alternatives to naive Holocaust piety: either

1 a more sophisticated, *philosophical* mode of Holocaust piety; or else
2 beyond all 'piety', what she calls 'Holocaust *ethnography*'.

❧

Sophisticated, philosophical Holocaust piety differs from the naive mode, such as informs *Schindler's List*, by virtue of its being much less populist, much less overtly sentimental. And yet it is still a type of 'piety' in the derogatory sense Rose intends. That is to say, it remains, at least to some extent – in her view – a response of sanctified self-indulgence. Thus, whereas naive Holocaust piety is a form of self-indulgence in populist sentimentality, the more sophisticated version issues in a self-indulgently generalized sheer *disgust* with all forms of modern popular culture, or serious political ambition in the modern context.

Confronted with the horrific memory of the Holocaust one is at first struck dumb. And philosophical Holocaust piety is, in essence, a project of staying with that struck-dumbness. It rhetorically invokes the ineffability of the horror in order to justify a certain sort of contempt for the garrulous world – but this is a contempt that all too easily tends to become infected with the self-indulgence of mere intellectual snobbery. Inasmuch as genocidal totalitarianism is a product of modernity, the memory of its crimes is seen here as discrediting all things modern, tainting every sort of characteristically modern enterprise by association. And so it tends to become politically quite disabling.

One of the prime exponents of such 'piety' is, precisely, Adorno. As other examples, in the essay 'Beginnings of the Day', Rose cites 'Holocaust theology, Christian and Jewish', Lyotard and Habermas.[6] Elsewhere, again, she speaks of Zygmunt Bauman's work in the same terms.[7] She considers that Derrida falls into this category; especially as he misinterprets Walter Benjamin,[8] while perhaps the most extreme example she discusses is the work of Maurice Blanchot.[9]

The thinker, on the other hand, that she most admires – and considers *the most decisively anti-totalitarian* – is Hegel. Against these philosophical 'Holocaust pietists', who are all more or less rejecting of Hegel, Rose basically wants to uphold the Hegelian brand of cosmopolitan modernist hope.

For there is, after all, no immediate element of propaganda ideology in Hegelian modernism, and neither is there any desire for sentimental edification. Yet Hegel is nevertheless preoccupied with the philosophical requirements of large-scale popular solidarity building, to promote the interests of what he calls 'Spirit': the many-layered impulse towards a world of maximum equality, minimum coercion. What philosophy has to contribute to the solidarity-building work of Spirit is, above all, a logically coherent and persuasive narrative foundation for the energizing, inspirational hope on which that work depends. In other words: stories seeking to ground such hope in historic reality, so far as possible demonstrating its potential realism. And so this is what Hegel, for his part, labours like a philosophic Hercules to supply.

In a sense, however, the most comprehensive formula for the destructiveness of Fascism is that it sets out to destroy the modernist impulse of Spirit, according to this definition. The great rabbi-philosopher Emil Fackenheim famously urged that, after the Holocaust, the Jewish people were now confronted by a new 614th commandment: Thou shalt not hand Hitler posthumous victories by giving up on your Jewishness, either in despair or through indifference. Rose is critical of Fackenheim – he is in fact, for her, the chief representative of 'theological Holocaust piety' in Jewish form. (Johann-Baptist Metz, she thinks, plays a similar role among Christians.) But her basic argument against this whole species of thinking is, in effect, a variant of his. Fackenheim's argument is addressed to Jews as such; hers is addressed to philosophers as such. Yet it has the same structure: Thou shalt not hand Hitler posthumous victories by abandoning the sort of hope that, in its purest philosophic form, Hegel preeminently represents.

Not all of those whom Rose regards as philosophical 'Holocaust pietists' are merely dismissive of Hegel. Adorno in particular, although he has no time for Hegel's Christianity, is a respectful critic. And Fackenheim presents his own philosophical work very largely as a critical Jewish outgrowth from Hegel's. But, even in these cases, the nightmare memory of the Holocaust is essentially understood by 'Holocaust piety' as tending to deflate modernist hope of every kind, very much including the Hegelian variety. The basic trouble with such thinking, from Rose's point of view, is that, because it is so mesmerized and dismayed by the memory of the horror, at a certain level it actually succumbs to the murderers' destructive intent. Thus, it represents a disastrous loss of faith, by the most thoughtful people, not only in modernist propaganda ideology, but also in the non-propagandist political promises of Spirit; a most unfortunate failure to discriminate between the two.

In 'Beginnings of the day', she also, provocatively, juxtaposes philosophic 'Holocaust piety' to the thought of Heidegger.[10] Now, of course, Heidegger was no 'Holocaust pietist'! On the contrary: he scarcely ever uttered a philosophic word about the Holocaust. And indeed, in view of his having once been an active member of the Nazi Party, his silence on the topic, after 1945, is I think quite rightly notorious.

Yet the fact nevertheless remains that, above all in his later work, Heidegger stands for a very similar fundamental repudiation of Hegelian hope to that which Rose criticizes in the philosophy of 'Holocaust pietism'. His doctrine of 'Being' is actually, in a sense, the most formidable erasure of Hegel's doctrine of 'Spirit'. Thus, the later Heidegger, recoiling from his spell of Nazi activism, is the thinker who has constructed the very boldest alternative philosophic grand narrative to Hegel's. He constructs a grand narrative of traumatized despair, designed to vindicate the most absolute withdrawal, by philosophers, from any sort of large-scale solidarity-building enterprise, whatsoever, in modern conditions. In that way he represents exactly the same tendency that Rose also criticizes in 'Holocaust pietism'; only, carried to its ultimate extreme. Adorno, especially, spits venom at Heidegger. But are they not, after all, akin? Adorno comes from quite a different point of the political compass, and has a very different style; unlike Heidegger, he does not work creatively in the genre of grand narrative. *For all practical purposes*, however, his 'melancholy science' has much the same inhibitory effect as Heidegger's grandiose disillusionment. Rose does not wish to be any less serious about the memory of the Holocaust than the protagonists of 'Holocaust piety' are. It is just that she mistrusts the latent kinship between their 'piety' and that of Heidegger, towards 'Being'.

What is ultimately at stake here, she argues, is the elementary difference between two species of 'mourning' for the Holocaust:

'inaugurated' and 'aberrated' mourning.[11] 'Inaugurated mourning' is grief launched on a trajectory towards eventual healing. But 'aberrated mourning' is the sort of grief that goes round and round in circles; locked into mere futility. Her suspicion of philosophic 'Holocaust piety' is that it is, in reality, nothing more than a sanctification of aberrated mourning.

Again, compare the rationale of Hegel's grand-narrative grounding for hope. The overall story that Hegel is telling is all about the historic emergence, to articulate self-awareness, of 'absolute Spirit'. That is, the impulse towards a world of maximum equality, minimum coercion – rendered 'absolute', operating at full strength. But what constitutes the strength of absolute Spirit? It is surely nothing other than the strength that enables one to 'keep one's mind in hell, and not despair'. 'Spirit' is, not least, Hegel's term for that element in humanity that, even in the most tragic circumstances, is still capable of resiliently rising above the tragedy, neither lapsing into moral anaesthesia, nor sinking into gloomy self-pity. And, as a history of divine revelation identified with the self-unfolding of Spirit, the Hegelian grand narrative therefore takes shape very much as a '*divine comedy*'.

It is true that there are not many actual jokes in Hegel's work. However, at the beginning of her essay 'The Comedy of Hegel and the *Trauerspiel* of Modern Philosophy' Rose cites his general definition of 'the comical', as a quality of Spirit: 'an infinite light-heartedness and confidence felt by someone raised altogether above his own inner contradiction and not bitter or miserable in it at all'.[12] And she salutes the indomitable element of comedy, in that sense, at the heart of Hegelian wisdom. There is nothing callous, frivolous or cruel about this point of view, no mere refusal to acknowledge the everyday reality of hell. But, for Rose, what Hegel represents is simply true philosophical hope *at full stretch*. This is a vision of heaven emerging right out of the depths of hell – and overcoming hell not at all by denial, but nevertheless in laughter. Hegel's philosophy of history is a uniquely radical systematic mobilization of hope, not only against the introverted despair of melancholia, but also against the extraverted despair of raging fanaticism; both the two soul-sicknesses out of which – where the soil is ready – totalitarianism grows.

Rose seeks to reaffirm this project, now in reflection on the very worst catastrophes of the twentieth century. So she writes:

> As a propaedeutic to politics, I offer *the comedy of absolute spirit* as *inaugurated* mourning . . . This comic approach – I cannot resist the provocation – would also offer a deeper and more drastic alternative to the current sacralising, commercialising and elevating into *raison d'état* as well as Providential anti-reason of the Holocaust in America and Israel.[13]

❧

Against 'Holocaust piety', in both its naive and philosophical forms, Rose advocates 'Holocaust ethnography'. In 'Beginnings of the Day' she defines this as a mediating reflection on 'the representation of Fascism and the fascism of representation'.

'The representation of Fascism and the fascism of representation' – this is a tight-packed portmanteau formula. But let us try to unpack it a bit. The term 'representation' is being used in two quite different senses here, and the term 'fascism' in three senses.

In speaking of 'the representation of Fascism', first, she has in mind what philosophic 'Holocaust piety' would piously forbid: the specific sort of 'representation' that belongs to a hope-giving grand narrative. 'Holocaust ethnography', as Rose uses the term, begins from a basic repudiation of this taboo. Therefore, its basic task is to consider how the actual history of mid-twentieth-century genocidal totalitarianism ought to be represented, or accounted for, in such a setting. All coherent modern cultures, as such, are held together politically by some more or less explicit sort of grand narrative, or set of competing grand narratives. And is it not, in general, far better for philosophy to be patiently engaged in trying to reshape the prevailing grand narrative, rather than just backing off, as postmodernism does, in aloof disgust? Rose, at any rate, is no postmodernist. (She is, if you like, a pioneering post-postmodernist.) How, though, is the obscenity of the Holocaust to be at all plausibly accommodated within this sort of hopeful, solidarity-building narrative? 'Holocaust piety', pre-emptively, escapes the problem. 'Holocaust ethnography', by contrast, will confront it, in all its undoubted difficulty.

And then, in so doing, there is also a second problem it has to confront. Namely: 'the fascism of representation'.

'Fascism' in this latter context has become a very broad term for everything psychologically predisposing people to collude with Fascist, or other totalitarian movements; and hence also, by yet a further extension, everything tending to get in the way of our properly learning the moral lessons of the nightmare. (In Adorno's jargon, it is whatever, in any way, caters to the tastes of the universal 'authoritarian personality'.[14]) 'Representation', likewise, has a much broader meaning than before: it simply means any kind of artwork. By 'the fascism of representation' Rose means a fundamental problem intrinsic to the very enterprise of trying to grasp, and communicate, what most of all needs grasping and communicating with regard to these memories, in any artistic format whatever.

The basic test that Rose wants to apply to every artistic representation of Fascism, and its catastrophic consequences, is how far it leaves us not only horrified and brought to tears, but truly shaken, by a dawning awareness of our *own* actual implication in 'fascism', more generally. Anything less, she argues, is in the end mere 'voyeurism'. One way or another, however, art has to charm us; even if it teases us with horror, it must always do so with a certain charm. Otherwise it ceases to have the attraction of art. And of course it is much easier for art to remain charming if it allows us, as we respond to its depictions of horrific crime, to continue feeling

23

comfortably innocent, ourselves. Inevitably, as a result, the requirement of charm tends to render the artistic representation of Fascism voyeuristic. In so far as it is subject to this pressure, the very process of artistic representation thus becomes 'fascist': complicit in the latent 'fascism', in the broad sense, of those to whom it is addressed. That is the problem.

Nor is this only a problem in the case of a popular, almost propagandistic work such as *Schindler's List*. Granted, it is more crudely apparent there. But Rose is also critical, for example, of Claude Lanzmann's great documentary film *Shoah*, on the same grounds.[15] One might well find this surprising, in view of the sheer, sustained, searing power of Lanzmann's representation of the Holocaust. In stark contrast to *Schindler's List*, *Shoah* does at any rate have the virtue of being completely unsentimental. Yet, Rose is still looking for something more. For, after all, in viewing *Shoah* one is still always in the role of an appalled *judge*; it never puts the viewer, as such, in among the *judged*.

And so too in the case of Primo Levi's famous memoir of his time in Auschwitz.[16] Levi's writing is great art. But Rose contrasts it with the writing of Tadeusz Borowski, a Gentile Polish inmate of Auschwitz who recorded his memories in a devastating collection of short stories, *This Way for the Gas, Ladies and Gentlemen*.[17] As she remarks:

> Borowski represents himself, a deputy Kapo, as both executioner and victim, and deprives the distinction 'of all greatness and pathos'. While Borowski never denies his ethical presupposition – for otherwise not one sentence could have been written – he makes you witness brutality in the most disturbing way, for it is not clear – Levi always is – from what position, as whom, you are reading. You emerge shaking in horror at yourself, with yourself in question, not in admiration for the author's Olympian serenity (Levi).[18]

Borowski is by no means a model of well-balanced philosophic wisdom. His writing is also streaked with the bitterest sort of vindictive despair. But there are appalling moments when these tales completely transcend art, in the sense that art is designed to charm. They bear raw witness to a level of truth – about hell – beyond all art.

Rose imagines 'a film in which the representation of Fascism would engage with the fascism of representation. A film, shall we say, about the life story of a member of the SS in all its pathos, so that we' – good anti-Fascists though 'we' are! – 'empathise with him, identify with his hopes and fears, disappointments and rage, so that when it comes to killing, we put our fingers on the trigger with him, wanting him to get what he wants'.[19] In other words: a film that fundamentally challenged, 'in the most disturbing way', our natural desire to feel innocent.

Although she does not mention it, the book that might provide the basis for such a film has actually already been written. It is Gitta Sereny's account of her interviews with Franz Stangl, the one time Commandant of the Treblinka death camp, shortly before his death, in a West German prison, in 1971.[20] The artistic charm of this book derives from our being able to identify with Sereny herself, as interviewer. But it is, I think, a model of actual artistic engagement with, in Rose's phrase, the 'fascism of representation'. For we are, at the same time, also, quite seriously invited to identify with Stangl.

Thus, it quickly becomes clear that, even though he was caught up into such monstrous crimes, Stangl himself was by no means a monster by nature. And one sees how he was gradually drawn in. As a policeman in Austria before its incorporation into the Nazi *Reich*, he had been involved in the arrest of Nazi activists; he was all the more compliant, after the Nazi take-over, because he therefore felt like a marked man, and was also afraid for his wife and children. An efficient operative, he was first recruited into the euthanasia programme, then transferred to work in the death camps, along with many of his former colleagues, as a sort of natural progression. One sees that in other circumstances he would have been quite an ordinary, decent, rather likeable man. Despite everything, he continued in fact to be warmly loved by his devout Roman Catholic wife and by his children. And so, in reading Sereny's account, one is drawn to imagine oneself in his shoes. We are shown this man, in his old age, genuinely it seems struggling, baffled, to come to terms with the enormity of what he had been part of; what it had made of him. How can we both imaginatively identify ourselves with a man like Stangl, and then also honestly connect with his leading role in the inferno of Treblinka? *Artistically*, there is no way. We just cannot do both at once. Inasmuch as art is, by its commitment to charm, trapped in human fallenness, it is impossible. Here we are brought up short, balked by the 'fascism of representation'. That is, by the moral limitations intrinsic to the very enterprise of art as such.

There is indeed no artistic way of *directly* effecting such a connection. All art, as such, can do is point towards the problem, as it were, from afar. And this is where Rose turns to *The Remains of the Day*, both novel and film, as a model. She admires Ishiguro's novel, and its film, for the charming way they elicit our compassion for a man who is – albeit at several removes from the ugly reality – complicit in the politics of Fascism. The servant of an English lord; trapped by his rigid devotion to the traditional, feudal ethos of his world. In a great English country house – the immediate setting could scarcely be more remote from the reality of Auschwitz. Yet it so happens that the man's employer is a leading campaigner for the appeasement of Nazism. The butler's loyalty betrays him into unquestioning complicity in this cause. In this regard, as in other more intimate ways – but everything is interconnected – it leads him to betray what we can see to be his true calling, to a quite different, freer-spirited life. And this self-betrayal then comes to symbolize all the various other betrayals by which we, all of us, tend to be misled into collusion with fascism, broadly understood.

'The representation of Fascism and the fascism of representation', Rose concludes, 'contrasts equally with classic and revisionist Marxism, and with Orientalism, the politics of identity'.[21] In this sentence 'the representation of Fascism and the fascism of representation' functions as her portmanteau formula for an ideal approach to political philosophy.

Philosophical 'Holocaust piety' looks upon the Holocaust as a sublime moment of disillusioning enlightenment, that fundamentally explodes, once and for all, any representation of the world in terms of grand-narrative framed political hope. Rose, for her part, refuses to accord the murderers so much power, not only to murder but also to close down the thinking of future generations. And so she seeks to reopen the question of how the Holocaust is to be represented – how the whole history of Fascism is to be represented – in all its ultimate meaninglessness, as she sees it, at this level.

Yet, at the same time, she is by no means an indiscriminate apologist for grand-narrative framed political hope. She contrasts the version she wants to defend with the Marxist and 'Orientalist' versions.

'Orientalism' is a curious name to give the 'politics of identity', in view of the way that Edward Said in particular has converted it into a name for forms of scholarship springing from, and meant to help give legitimacy to, Western cultural imperialism. But what Rose evidently has in mind is the exact antithesis to that: the thinking of movements engaged in resistance to Western cultural imperialism, and appealing to traditional cultural identities as a basis for that resistance. As Marxist grand narrative culminates in a hope for the eventual global triumph of the proletariat, so 'Orientalist' grand narrative culminates in a hope for the eventual global triumph of a particular, currently oppressed culture. Its most conspicuous version is *salafi* Islam. But there are also Hindu and Buddhist equivalents.

The basic trouble, however, with both Marxism and 'Orientalism', in this sense, is that they are ideologies commonly promoted by propaganda. And then the method of communication has impacted on the actual content of the message; they have, in practice, become more or less propagandist ideologies. But what is propaganda? It is precisely *the most ruthless exploitation of artistic charm*, in order to trigger a certain unthinking response in people. Propaganda works by presenting us with the most charming possible picture of what the world might be, and what we might become. Or of what now needs defending against attack.

As a hermeneutic of suspicion focused on the 'fascism of representation', Rose's thinking cultivates a fundamental mistrust of artistic charm in any form, for what it may be covering up. Thus, she rejects propagandistic Marxism and 'Orientalism' not for their entertaining of such grandiose political ambitions, or for the corresponding bravado of their grand narratives – on the contrary, she approves of this. But, rather, she rejects them because she mistrusts their charm. In so far as they are propagandist ideologies, they are, after all, of the same species as Fascism itself. For Fascism is actually definable as a total addiction to propaganda: politics altogether reduced to a mere quest for the most spectacular propaganda effects, by appeal to *whatever* popular prejudices, in the given social context, appear ripest for that purpose.

Marxism, as a propagandist ideology, allows its protagonists to feel innocent, and propagandist 'Orientalism' does the same. Both sorts of movement encourage their followers to think of themselves either as innocent victims, or else as innocent defenders of victims. This is a crucial aspect of their solidarity-building charm. But Rose has no desire for a solidarity of the innocent. Instead, what she is looking for is really the absolute opposite. One might say that it is the solidarity of the shaken. For her the ideal basis for solidarity is a shared experience of having been shaken – in the sense of being rendered acutely aware of the corporate sins of one's world, not only in objective terms but also in terms of one's own personal complicity in them.

And is not this why, in the end, she turns to religion? It is because she wants a strategy for large-scale solidarity building that will not only be effective, but also as free as possible from propaganda. But the only real alternative to propaganda, for this purpose, is a certain form of religion.

Thus, what propaganda contributes to the large-scale mobilization of solidarity is a succession of quick, prejudice-triggering, simple emotional hits. Inasmuch as religion, by contrast, is an emotional mobilization of potentially large-scale solidarity *wrapped in prayer*, it is in principle, surely, doing quite a different job. For true prayer is all about connecting with reality in ways that propaganda, as such, cannot. That is to say, it is a contemplative discipline, precisely designed to slow one down; to make one stop and think; to undo the mischief of over-simple messages; above all, to shake one out of one's delusions of uninvolved innocence. Obviously, not all prayer accomplishes this. All too often propaganda and prayer are yoked together, on the disastrous misunderstanding that the one is properly a supplement to the other, both in the service of the same truth. Indeed, religion will no doubt always tend to be more immediately effective, as a form of solidarity-building, where it is supplemented with its own brand of propaganda. Nevertheless – *in itself* it remains something else.

What Rose, in effect, turns to is the ideal of an altogether propaganda-free form of religion; an evangelistic form of catholicism (with a small 'c') whose whole sense of purpose would be to serve as a comprehensive *therapy against propaganda*. And her thinking-through of 'the representation of Fascism and the fascism of representation' has, I think, fundamentally to be understood in the light of that already apparent religious ideal.

3

The 'Question of Law'

❧

Some people's idea of morality simply stems from their wanting to be just, to do justice to others. Other people are driven, instead, by a desire to be recognized as innocent. Most of us, most of the time, are a mixture of both. Our morality stems from both sorts of motive, so intertwined that we are all too easily oblivious of the difference. But is not the desire to be innocent, properly under-stood, the great distraction, turning us away from the authentic desire to be just? If we want to be just, we must first of all give up wanting to be innocent. In terms of Christian theology, this is surely the true meaning of 'original sin'. What the story at the beginning of Genesis represents is the sin that consists in clinging to one's desire for innocence. Quite apart from any particular troubling memories or sense of guilt, true faith in God implies a primordial renunciation of our infantilizing nostalgia for Eden. The more intense one's faith, the more intense is also one's sense, not necessarily of guilt, but of participation in sin.

Rose herself was not, by trade, a theologian. But, as her eventual baptism serves to indicate, her thought may essentially be regarded as a way in to theology. ('I am really a theologian in disguise', she once wrote.[1]) And, as such, it is first and foremost a prolegomenon to the systematic understanding of original sin. Thus, she is in effect systematically exploring the implications of the basic distinc-tion between the desire to be just and the desire to be innocent, in the most uncompromising way.

Nor does this only apply to strategies for the commemoration of the past – as, above all, in the case of the Holocaust. It equally applies to strategies for the organization of the future. Her reflections on 'Holocaust piety' actually emerge out of the background of her more systematic meditation on what she calls the *'question of law'*.[2] So now let us turn to consider that.

✦

First, though – a word about my interpretative approach here. Rose is a highly original thinker, and she is saying some genuinely thought-provoking things. But it has to be admitted that her books are also very heavy going. Part of the trouble is that she is a systematic thinker who, however, largely leaves it to her readers to infer the system for themselves. Her thought is, indeed, for this reason in particular need of commentary. Again and again, in reading her, one is left struggling to see the wood for the trees. Or, rather, it is not just a wood; to read her is indeed to be plunged into a whole ferocious jungle of ideas. As a guide, she runs through the jungle at tremendous speed. She keeps slipping out of sight, then reappearing in the most bewilderingly different places. Following her, one has to have a very high tolerance for feeling lost, much of the time.

My aim is to try and provide a general map of her thought. But in order to do so I have found myself compelled to make pivotal use of certain terms and expressions which are not in fact hers, but mine. In the previous chapter, the notions of artistic 'charm' and the 'solidarity of the shaken' are glosses I have introduced, in order to try and clarify her argument, as is the comparison between true religion and 'propaganda'. The elementary distinction between the 'desire to be just' and the 'desire to be innocent', immediately above, is another. And now let me develop it further: how might one define the core insight at work in her systematic discussion of the 'question of law'?

The way I would like to formulate it is to say that here is a thinker who, with unprecedented radicalism, systematically identifies the highest wisdom with *the virtues of the good, mediating peace negotiator*. Although this is not a phrase she herself uses, it seems to me perhaps the best way of expressing the matter.

Thus, her most momentous book is entitled *The Broken Middle*. That phrase, 'the broken middle', is the primary Rosean formula for the location of true wisdom.[3] But another name for 'the middle', in the sense she intends, might precisely be *the place of the peace negotiator*, seeking to mediate between disputatious others, to understand them and gain their confidence. The peace negotiator, not in the sense of aiming at a mere coercive suppression of violence; but where 'peace' means the achievement of a genuinely unforced, cheerful accommodation between all interested parties, without exception.

Rose was indeed, by all accounts, anything but a pacific or diplomatic character, in the ordinary sense. She could be both charming and explosive. She was a quite exceptionally restless and demanding person. In certain contexts her restlessness – her not being quite of this world – actually had the potential to become quite destructive.

Of course, such people can be very dysfunctional – and yet is there not, at the same time, a certain rare capacity for insight that belongs to just that personality type, when infused with philosophic genius? It is what comes of a basic refusal ever to let sleeping dogs lie. Where cultural conflicts are just suppressed, or politely dowsed down in an easy-going spirit of mutual tolerance, rather than being freely and openly negotiated – that is, where the 'brokenness' of the 'broken middle' is ignored – this suits the complacent beneficiaries of the established order, and the intellectually lazy. Rose's idea of philosophy is that it is a systematic project for highlighting latent conflicts. Yet, that does not mean: in the form of a call to war. For her idea of philosophy equally springs from a fundamental refusal to think in terms of an 'innocent us against guilty them', the mentality of group-belligerence. Rather, it is a prophetic project of bringing to light the very deepest conflicts by which one's culture is fractured, in order then to mediate between the opposing parties, so to speak, as a *referee*. That is, a referee systematically interpreting, and applying, *the law of good debate*. In relation to all the most intractable issues of moral, political and religious debate within one's given culture, the true philosopher, as she understands the role, is not a partisan advocate. The philosopher is not in the first instance called to negotiate on behalf of any particular party to the dispute, but rather to try and make the contest, in itself, as beautiful and as revealing as possible.

Rose's whole thinking essentially hangs together as a meditation on the 'question of law', in that broad sense. In other words: the question of what it takes, the ideal rules of engagement required, to bring all and sundry together, most helpfully, into true conversational give-and-take. And above all those people who are most different from one another in cultural conditioning and experience of life; whose perceptions of the world are therefore most different. How, without any appeasement of bullies, to bring people together in conversation from which no topics are excluded because of their being too hurtful or too infuriating; conversation, moreover, premised on an absolute readiness for self-criticism, issuing in practical self-transformation? By the 'question of law' is meant the whole question, what sort of institutions this requires, with what sort of ethos.

The aim here is by no means 'peace' in the sense of 'peace and quiet'. But it is *shalom*, peace as justice. There is nothing conciliatory about this sort of mediation. On the contrary, what Rose loathes is just any sort of 'us-against-them' thinking, for which the ideal 'us' remains internally conflict-free. The highest wisdom, for her, is what aspires to, and enables, a maximum holding-acceptance of inner conflict, both on the part of groups and of individuals. Yet, the point is that, where equitable peace is not immediately possible, strategically to place oneself in 'the middle', so defined, can only mean to live in 'brokenness'. For it is to experience the sheer excess of compelling – yet often quite incompatible – moral demands made upon one by the representatives of various different interests, by which one is for ever being pulled backwards and forwards. And the result is bound to be a systematic destruction of innocence. This 'middle' is the place where our wanting to be recognized as innocent is necessarily 'broken', just because here we are exposed to everyone's judgement, and our claims to be innocent will never satisfy everyone.

Compare that other notable convert, St Paul. He, famously, speaks of having made himself 'all things to all people' (1 Corinthians 9.22). The context for this is the struggle within the first-generation church over the conversion of Gentiles. Ought Gentile converts to Christian faith first become Jews, subjecting themselves to all the traditional requirements of Jewish law? Some said yes; others, like Paul himself, said no. Paul wanted to make conversion as easy as possible for Gentiles, but he also wanted to keep the nascent Christian community from splitting apart over the issue. And therefore, as he puts it,

> Though I am free with respect to all, I have made myself a slave to all, so that I might win more of them. To the Jews I became as a Jew, in order to win Jews. To those under the law I became as one under the law (though I myself am not under the law) so that I might win those under the law. To those outside the law I became as one outside the law (though I am not free from God's law but am under Christ's law) so that I might win those outside the law. To the weak I became weak, so that I might win the weak. (1 Corinthians 9.19–22a)

He is quite open about it; he clearly sees no sacrifice of integrity in so doing. But on the contrary he says, 'I do it all for the sake of the gospel, so that I may share in its blessings' (9.23). This really is a most striking biblical vindication of mediating openness, or magnanimity.

However, Paul's mediating enterprise was quite limited in scope: when he speaks of being 'all things to all people', what he actually means by 'all people' is just 'all Christians, or potential Christians, as such'. Consider, now, what it might mean to try and be, with real integrity, 'all things' quite literally 'to *all* people', all those whom one ever encounters. Anyone who attempts this is clearly liable to be torn apart by mutually antipathetic sympathies. And that is what it means to occupy what Rose calls the 'broken middle'. It is to join what Hegel once described as 'the bacchanalian revel' of Spirit.[4] Hegel's metaphor is meant to conjure up the sheer impossibility of ever genuinely fixing spiritual truth into any sober, settled form of correctness. But the original god of such 'revels', Bacchus, or Dionysus, was not only the god of wine; he was also 'Dionysus Zagreus', which means 'Dionysus torn in pieces'. He was a fertility god, dying and rising again, in the usual way of fertility gods. Only, his dying was singularly violent: according to his myth, as a child he was ripped apart, limb from limb, by the Titans. To occupy the 'broken middle' is to be unreservedly open to the ideal demands of peace negotiation, at every level of moral concern, with all comers; accepting the inner torn-apartness that such openness necessarily implies. Indeed, *it is to recognize this as the very essence of the truly sacred.* And so it is also to be quite uncompromisingly opposed to everything that tends to inhibit such openness, in general. But might one not see the central image of the Christian gospel, the image of God on the cross, precisely as a symbolic representation of that opposition, pushed to its ultimate extreme? What Hegel, for his part, calls the 'bacchanalian revel' of Spirit he also, elsewhere, speaks of as the 'speculative Good Friday'.[5] He is talking here about the fundamental sacredness of the will to true peace-negotiation, in the most open, *shalom*-oriented sense – as revealed in a symbol of its absolute denial, by the regime of Pontius Pilate, a regime which simply wanted to impose 'peace and quiet' without negotiation. For what does that denial amount to? Nothing less, we are now shown, than the murder of God! The trajectory of her thought – it seems to me – renders Rose more and more radically Hegelian. Her option for the 'broken middle' is pure neo-Hegelianism, at this deepest level.

❦

And so how might one summarize the overall *shape* of her systematic argument?

Rose sets out to explore what she calls the *'equivocation of the ethical'*. By this she means the often confused-together interaction of two quite different basic species of mediating negotiation, with regard to morality in general.

Both species of mediating negotiation involve ethical challenges to 'the ethical', in the specific Hegelian sense of *Sittlichkeit*. That is to say, the ethos of the most strongly coherent sort of moral communities; those that are held together, not by material self-interest or coercion, but by a deep, genuine respect for particular moral authority figures, and an intensely felt, conservative rootedness in a particular historic tradition.[6]

- The first species has to do with the challenge to *Sittlichkeit* inherent in the spirit of what one might perhaps call 'self-expressive nonconformity'. This is, again, admittedly not a term Rose herself uses – but let us use it as a rough designation for the activity of individuals with a nonconformist sense of personal calling, a principled suspicion of any, as they would see it, intrusive moral consensus, as such, whatever its content.
- The second species has to do with the challenge that emerges from the domain of secular politics, in so far as the loyalty-claims of religious, ethnic or class-based *Sittlichkeit* are confronted by the much looser rival loyalty-claims of the modern, culturally pluralist state. The challenge – let us say – of 'secular humanism'.

What Rose calls the 'broken middle' is, in the most general terms, none other than the space to be opened up by our properly negotiating the resultant 'equivocation', or double disputedness, of the 'ethical'. It is what breaks open to the extent that both these two species of conflict are well negotiated: with no relevant voice ever either suppressed or ignored, and yet with a real will to mutual understanding and ultimate agreement.

Here then are the two prime aspects of what she calls the 'question of law'. The 'law' in question is both the moral law, framing the whole area of dispute between *Sittlichkeit* and self-expressive nonconformity, as defined above, and the law of the state, framing the whole area of dispute between *Sittlichkeit* and secular humanist politics. The 'question', at its simplest, is, 'What do we most fundamentally all need to agree upon, as a basis for our life together in society at large?' And, in a nutshell, her answer is something like: 'Let us found our life together, first and foremost, on the principle that good law is whatever best fits with, and serves to encourage the spirit of ideal conversational openness – recognized as sacred.'

Thus, what is to be reckoned truly sacred? Properly to negotiate the 'equivocation of the ethical', from Rose's point of view, requires that we decisively repudiate three primary types of misidentification here:

1 the error of the sheer advocate of self-expressive nonconformity – at its intellectually most sophisticated this takes the form of what Rose herself calls 'nihilism', philosophy charged with the most corrosive contempt for non-philosophy, but, at a more popular level, it also appears in the widespread current exaltation of 'spirituality' over 'religion', where the sacred is reductively identified, simply, with whatever serves to reinforce individual 'spiritual' autonomy as such;

2 the error of the sheer advocate of secular humanist politics as such, that what is truly sacred is just the moral independence of the state from any form of established religion or the like; and

3 the error of the sheer advocate of *Sittlichkeit* in some particular
   form, that the truly sacred is just whatever most of all defines
   the special distinctiveness, from all others, of their own moral
   community.

For these notions – although they may each be associated with a
good deal of truth – are all, in themselves, far too narrow. They are
erroneous just because of their mutual exclusiveness, their primordial closure to the most demanding sort of negotiation. And in
systematic terms, therefore, Rose's thinking largely takes shape as a
polemic on these three fronts. In all three cases she is attacking that
most elementary of obstacles to peace-making virtue, the tendency
to set up, in one's mind, an innocent 'me', or 'us', against a guilty
'them'. First it is innocent self-expressive nonconformists versus
guilty conformists; then, innocent secular humanists versus guilty
reactionaries, intent on defending corrupt structures of authoritarianism; and finally innocent true believers versus guilty un-
believers, or heretics.[7]

    In Chapter 1 I quoted her autobiographical account of how one
day, looking out of her window in Stoke Newington – and observing a wedding party arrive at the block of flats opposite – she
suddenly found herself howling. What prompted the howl was her
desolate sense of the chasm dividing the relatively individualistic
and secularized world of those ordinary English wedding guests
from the hyper-intense *Sittlichkeit* of her Hasidic neighbours. The
whole of her thought, I remarked, is in a sense a sublation of that
howl. For she is lamenting what both sorts of world lose as a consequence of not entering into proper, sympathetic communication
with one another: the proneness of the one to unchallenged rigidi-
ty, the proneness of the other to equally unchallenged spiritual
superficiality. True civilization must surely involve not only the
warm togetherness and rich shared imaginative resources of
Sittlichkeit at its best, but also the relaxed attitude to cultural and
political differences, in general, promoted by secular humanism at

its best. And, at the same time, it must equally encourage the unpredictable creativity of self-expressive nonconformity at its best, as well. One might, I think, well say that for Rose the vocation of the true philosopher is to be a systematic mediator between these three very different species of imperative.

She was, in the end, received not just into Christianity, but into the Church of England; baptized an Anglican.[8] Membership of the Church of England is not easily construed as an innocent historic identity. Hence the rather suspicious eagerness of so many of us Church of England people to discount our denominational belonging, and proclaim ourselves to be nice, innocent, simple 'Christians' instead. For here, of course, is a church that, in its schismatic origins, was expressly founded to be an agency of despotic rule. Thank God – and thanks also to our Nonconformist, Roman Catholic and secularist opponents – over the centuries our white-knuckle grip on power has gradually been prised open. But, still, those origins continue to constrain us. Bound together, in the first instance, not by any strongly distinctive moral or doctrinal stance, but simply by traditional privilege, we have evolved into a broad Church. Thus, this is an institution which has tended to allow its members to relate to it very much on their own moral or doctrinal terms; some, indeed, with an intense sense of belonging to one of the various competing partisan tendencies within the Church, others however altogether more loosely. Anglican *Sittlichkeit*, therefore, lies wide open to the challenge of self-expressive nonconformity, not only from outside the Church but also from within. And, moreover, our being an established church has also left us just as immediately exposed, in a modern state, to the challenge of secular humanist politics, as we are both invited to play a civil religious role, and resisted in that role. Granted, these two challenges may very often take the form of temptations, perhaps to some extent they always do: on the one hand, the temptation of a merely unthinking omni-tolerance; on the other hand, temptations to collusion with the mere conceit of the secular establishment. Yet, nevertheless, if, by way of an ideal, one is looking precisely for a true church of the 'broken middle', then everything surely depends upon our not being *over-protected* from the danger. We must learn to resist the temptations possibly associated with the challenge of self-expressive nonconformity and secular humanism by being, to the fullest possible extent, exposed to them.

The institutional culture of the Church of England serves to maximize such exposure. If only we could clearly grasp the resultant advantages! But what would that involve?

Right at the heart of the Church's corporate life is an act of historic commemoration:

> The Lord Jesus on the night when he was betrayed took bread, and when he had given thanks, he broke it, and said, 'This is my body which is for you. Do this in remembrance of me.' In the same way also the cup, after supper, saying, 'This cup is the new covenant in my blood. Do this, as often as you drink it, in remembrance of me.' (1 Corinthians 11.23–5)

So, as a community, we remember our origins, and the dogma of the incarnation also then infinitely amplifies the gravitational pull of the memory, drawing into orbit around it everything else in our corporate past which still remains alive for us, still morally troubling, still in need of working through. At its truest, Christian theology is a systematic discipline of openness in the negotiation of difficult memory. It seeks to do justice, ideally, to the very widest possible range of different human perspectives on the disputed past, so as to draw out (such openness being the only way it can in fact be drawn out) the latent element of divine revelation there. And Rose's thought may, essentially, be read as a preparation for this basic task.

4

'Thinking the Absolute'

❦

Rose is a difficult thinker in much the same way that Hegel also is.

Thus, the difficulty essentially derives from her extraordinary ambition: in her work as a whole, she is attempting a direct articulation of what Hegel, in the *Phenomenology of Spirit*, calls '*das absolute Wissen*', 'absolute knowing'.

But – it will perhaps be objected – how can anyone claim to articulate such a thing as 'absolute knowing'? Is this not an insanely arrogant claim, a sort of absolute intellectual hubris?

No, it is nothing of the sort. On the contrary, it is precisely the proper humility of thought – towards its infinite vocation.

Hegel, for his part, adopts the term 'absolute knowing' for what he is aiming at, in the first instance, as a polemical counter-thrust to Kantian theological agnosticism. His basic suspicion of such agnosticism is that it is merely an arbitrary closure to conversation. All too soon the agnostic just shrugs his or her shoulders, and calls a halt to conversation about God, saying, 'I do not know, we cannot know' – as if that was all there were to be said. On the contrary, Hegel wants to insist, there is always far more to be said, both for and against traditional faith, which agnosticism, whether pious or impious, is defensively evading. 'Absolute knowing' is first of all an absolute refusal of agnostic defensiveness. It is an absolute determination to hold open the kind of risky conversation which agnosticism, by contrast, seeks to close.

But note the strong flavour of *paradox* in this notion of 'absolute knowing'. It is a theological notion. However, when he speaks of the 'absolute', Hegel is in fact fundamentally subverting the common-sense understanding of theological knowledge. He is intent on overthrowing the common-sense assumption that theology is, intrinsically, a form of metaphysics – in the sense that the truth it is looking for is a form of *correctness*. The truth of 'absolute knowing' is not a form of correctness about God.

In other words, it is not the sort of truth that directly inheres in a set of accurate propositions as such. Metaphysics is a matter of abstract propositions; that is, propositions considered in abstraction from conversational context. However, the truth of 'absolute knowing' is the sort of truth that is precisely a quality of whole conversations. It is truth as the work of Spirit, *Geist* – divine Spirit indwelling human conversation, and forever struggling to open it up. As Rose puts it: 'The *Phenomenology* is not a success, it is a gamble.'[1] The passage that it traces to 'absolute knowing' is not a pathway to metaphysical success. It is an unfolding gamble on being opened up to others, in conversation. Metaphysics, strictly speaking, looks for truth in abstract propositions without reference to conversational context – Hegel, on the other hand, arrives at his notion of 'absolute knowing' precisely by way of a systematic consideration of conversational context, a critical survey of contrasting contexts for the work of Spirit, different mentalities, considered in terms of the hindrances they each represent to true conversational openness. For that is what he means by a 'phenomenology of Spirit'. When common sense reacts with outrage to the notion of 'absolute knowing', it is because it assumes that this is the name of some purportedly ideal metaphysical theory. In fact, though, a 'phenomenology of Spirit' – inasmuch as it aims not, in the first instance, at truth-as-correctness, but rather at truth-as-openness – is, essentially, a trans-metaphysical enterprise. One might perhaps say that it is philosophy on the way to theology-beyond-metaphysics.[2]

Indeed 'absolute knowing', properly understood, is not a theory at all. It is not a theory, but a sense of vocation. To enter into it is to recognize the absolute summons of what might be called perfect Honesty, a turn of the will towards ever greater conversational openness. Misunderstood as the name of a theory, of course it sounds like a claim to have arrived at some final satisfaction of the appetite for metaphysics, that is to say, a claim to have reached an end of the need for thought about the nature of God, a ceasing of exploration, a static result – which common sense then, of course, quite rightly declares to be impossible. But in fact it is the exact opposite. The whole point of the Hegelian notion actually lies in its subversion of common sense, to the extent that common sense is enslaved to metaphysics. This is why common sense cannot grasp it. What is 'absolute knowing'? It is the paradoxical self-knowledge of Socrates – 'I know only that I know nothing' – opened up to systematic ongoing reflection on the history that opens up that knowledge. This is no mere theological agnosticism, of the sort that closes down conversation – on the contrary. But it is, precisely, a knowing of the ultimate 'nothingness' of purported metaphysical 'knowledge', as such, when it comes to what really matters. That is to say, it is a recognizing of the absolute irrelevance, to salvation, of any sort of orthodoxy uninformed by the vocation to perfect Honesty. The word 'absolute' derives from the Latin *absolutus*, past participle of *absolvere*, to 'release' (*solvere*, 'loosen' or 'dissolve'; *ab*, 'from'). And the *Phenomenology of Spirit* is a systematic study of spiritual release, or salvation: the release of Spirit – the impulse to truly open conversation – from a whole series of different inhibitions; the power of which, in each case, inheres in their having become an integral part of common sense. In Rose's terms, it is a systematic survey of all that is broken up in the 'broken middle'. And 'absolute knowing' is, quite simply, a name for that breaking-process considered as a whole. So it is not a static theoretical conclusion – but, precisely, an explosive release of spiritual desire. It is, first of all, absolute shakenness, out of the safe inertia of thought-less common-sense prejudice. Then, in political terms, it is that shakenness made the absolute basis, purely and simply in itself, of an ideal solidarity. And finally, with regard to religion, it is an acknowledgement that such solidarity constitutes the proper absolute *essence* of the sacred.

Some interpreters, recoiling with common-sense incredulity from the notion of 'absolute knowing', have charitably sought to rescue as much as possible from the Hegelian heritage while jettisoning just this, and what is immediately bound up with it. Marxists in particular have spoken of rescuing the radical Hegelian 'method' (meaning something like the sheer grand-narrative energy of Hegel's thought) from the discredited 'system', with its absolutist claims. But Rose, in *Hegel contra Sociology*, emphatically repudiates any such approach. 'Hegel's philosophy', she argues, 'has no social import if the absolute cannot be thought.' (She actually repeats the point four times, at different points in the book.[3]) And her whole interest here is in that 'social import' – which she wants, so far as possible, to promote.

The 'social import' of Hegelian wisdom depends upon 'absolute knowing' being 'thinkable' – the vocation to an ideal conversational openness being fully acknowledged – by a large enough constituency to make a real difference in the world. This imposes a twofold task upon thinking: on the one hand, to devise strategies for the maximum dissemination of such 'knowing'; on the other hand, to ensure that it really still is *absolute* knowing' which is being disseminated, in all its true absoluteness, and not some diminished simulacrum. Hegel's famously overt 'system' is his pedagogic strategy for the maximum dissemination of the ideal, by both academic and religious means. Again, Rose, by contrast, is a much less *overtly* systematic thinker. Her thought chiefly addresses the other task, of insisting on the proper absoluteness of the absolute.

Thus, Rose's work is, generally speaking, a good deal narrower in scope than Hegel's own. In the *Phenomenology* Hegel sets out to survey the struggles of Spirit at every different level of human experience. First he considers the relation of the self to the material world; then the immediate reflection of the self, as such, back to itself; then the relations of the self to a society of other selves, abstractly conceived; then the self-reflection of whole ethical communities, considered as historical phenomena. But Rose focuses almost entirely on this last level, where phenomenology borders straight onto theology. Her primary concern is with 'absolute knowing', specifically, as an inhabiting of the 'broken middle': an absolutely resolute commitment to mediation, in response to the historic fractures of ethical community.

However, that is already a major part of Hegel's concern, also. The brokenness of the 'broken middle', as such, is most directly the theme of chapter 6 of the *Phenomenology*: in this chapter he compares various ways of occupying what Rose calls the 'middle', a whole range of basic different strategies for managing moral conflict. Or, rather – with allusive illustrations spanning the whole of European history, from Ancient Greece to his own day – he observes how, in different cultures, the management of conflict has fallen short of the true peace-negotiative ideal. In that sense, he looks at the manifold 'brokenness' of the middle. The survey begins with societies governed by a strong, single and maximally homogeneous form of *Sittlichkeit*. Even this breaks up, when the values of the state come into conflict with the values of the family, the sort of conflict classically illustrated by Sophocles's tragedy, *Antigone*. And then Hegel goes on to consider how moral conflict management has been addressed in ever more complex societies. He brings before us a procession of increasingly individualistic and/or irreligious worldviews, further and further removed from being simply immersed in a strong *Sittlichkeit*. We are invited to consider the attitudes associated with Roman law, as a project of bringing order to a multicultural empire; the attitudes associated with life at a royal court; the attitudes characteristic of the emergent bourgeoisie; the attitudes at work in the Enlightenment, and in modern Pietism; the attitudes that came to expression in the French

Revolution; the attitudes typically expressed in late eighteenth- and early nineteenth-century novels. The whole argument is infused with the latent ideal of 'absolute knowing', and, in that aspect, it traces a path of purgation. From the simple *Sittlichkeit* of classical antiquity, Hegel leads us, through a contemplation of *Sittlichkeit* under all sorts of stress, towards the possibility, now at last, of a renewed *Sittlichkeit*, precisely opened up as never before towards 'absolute knowing'. And so, in the following chapter, he goes on to a study of comparative religion, oriented towards the question of how that renewed *Sittlichkeit* might be given religious form.

I will come back later to how Rose discusses certain particular figures within this chapter of the *Phenomenology*.[4] But there is a sense in which her whole thought – inasmuch as it is all framed as a meditation on the 'broken middle' – has its roots in the ground that Hegel, for his part, is just beginning to cultivate, especially here.

Her being a thinker of 'absolute knowing', however, means that Rose also has to wrestle, *mutatis mutandis*, with the same basic species of communication-problem that bedevils the *Phenomenology*. For how, after all, is one to communicate something that is, by its very nature, as elusive as this ideal? In the first place, 'absolute knowing' is an absolutely universal vocation, applying to all people, in every sort of intellectual context. Therefore, it needs to be illustrated by a great diversity of examples, the more diverse the better. Hegel, in the *Phenomenology*, attempts to link together into a seamless argument all the various different examples he gives, but it scarcely works; they are, quite simply, too diverse. There is indeed a clear progression in the book from level to level, but otherwise it must be said that the links are very artificial. Never mind – it is the diversity itself that counts.

Rose's work, above all *The Broken Middle*, differs in that, unlike Hegel, she abandons all pretence of seamless argument. The argument of *The Broken Middle* jumps, in mind-boggling fashion, from topic to topic. Fragments of philosophy, theology, political theory, historiography and biography, anthropology, literary criticism and theory of architecture are thrown all higgledy-piggledy together. The underlying coherence of her thought is systematically covered up by a surface show of randomness.

Moreover, it is crucial that the illustrations should very clearly be seen to be no more than illustrations. The argument of the *Phenomenology* is full of veiled allusions. This veiling is not just obscurantism. It is intended as a reminder that what is really under discussion is not this or that particular historic event, thinker or movement. But that, rather, the real topic is always the universal call of 'absolute knowing', as this relates to the most general possibilities of human experience – which the events, thinkers and movements alluded to are simply meant to exemplify.[5] And it is the same in Rose's work. Only, another way her approach differs from Hegel's in the *Phenomenology* is that she is always much closer-up to the examples she discusses. She develops her own position by way of quite a detailed consideration of other thinkers, and specific historical contexts; as indeed Hegel also does in other works. Yet, if one then compares Hegel's *Lectures on the History of Philosophy* there is a further difference. He is concerned not only to measure other thinkers up against the ideal of 'absolute knowing' but also, at the same time, to provide his students with a helpful basic introduction to, and exploration of, their thought. Rose however, in most of her work, has no interest in providing helpful introductions. Her first book, *The Melancholy Science*, is an introduction of sorts to the thought of Theodor W. Adorno.[6] In her subsequent writing, though, she only ever deals with other thinkers in order to evoke the demands of 'absolute knowing', as directly as possible. She is not interested in giving us, her readers, information, for information's sake, but she wants to coach us in an attitude. And, as an educator, she is implacable. Her ambition for us knows no limits. In *The Broken Middle*, for instance, she discusses Hegel, Adorno again, Kierkegaard, Maurice Blanchot, Franz Kafka, Sigmund Freud, Thomas Mann, René Girard, Rahel Varnhagen, Rosa Luxemburg, Hannah Arendt, Emmanuel Levinas, Franz

Rosenzweig, Emil Fackenheim and various others. Yet none of this discussion is likely to be much use to those who are unfamiliar with these thinkers, or who are looking for basic assistance in understanding them. On the contrary, it is the other way around; one constantly needs to go back to these thinkers' own texts in order to understand what Rose is saying. Her book reads like an accumulation of marginal notes compiled originally for herself alone, on those texts – abstruse musings, studded with arcane witticisms. Fully to understand her, one would have to have already read all the various other writings on which she is drawing. Her whole interest is in the way these other thinkers have borne witness to 'absolute knowing' as a knowing of the 'broken middle', or the way they have fallen short of such witness. *The Broken Middle* is not, in the first instance, about their thought; it is simply about this sort of witness, in general, and what it implies.

Rose's writing is an evocation of 'absolute knowing', truth as a conversational ideal. So it aims at the staging of a vast conversation; in which the figures immediately considered are chosen as representatives of the most diverse constituencies. The wisdom to which it aspires is none other than a supreme mastery in the art of holding a multitude of the most contrasting points of view, all at once, in one's head. It is a matter of sensing their multifarious connections, implicit as well as explicit; and criticizing them always, essentially, only for their apparent, impatient closures to sympathetic conversation, where such conversation is seriously offered. This is difficult writing, not at all because it is inept, but because it is an attempt, in the most direct way possible, to *enact* the intrinsic difficulty of 'absolute knowing'. Rose is forever hurrying us along, lest our attention get snagged on just one aspect of the whole, when what alone matters to her is the whole, as a whole. Everything is therefore discussed at breakneck speed, a whole turbulent mêlée of thoughts racing by, bewilderingly.

The argument of *The Broken Middle*, in particular, is so altogether focused on the ultimate ideal indicated in the title that everything else in it, as a result, appears to be quite out of focus. One gets something of the same blurred effect in Adorno's highly mannered writing, the subject of her first book. Only, Adorno's thought is vitiated by his all too complacent complete lack of feel for religion. For Adorno, the essential mark of ethical truth is that it always involves a maximum sheer restlessness of thought; he tries to develop a philosophic style of writing directly corresponding to the simple intransigence of that principle. And Rose does the same. It is just that she has a much fuller, because more religious, sense of the proper difficulty of the 'broken middle', which leads her away from Adorno – first, back to Hegel, and then, without abandoning Hegel, also back to Kierkegaard.[7]

But *can* the 'absolute' ever be thought – properly – by sufficient numbers to have a real 'social import'? The actual historic fate of Hegel's thinking certainly highlights the obstacles. He has so often been, it would appear, quite wilfully misunderstood, wilfully caricatured – both by hard-line secularists and by conservative Christians, both parties fundamentally repudiating his project of trying to make peace between them. Lacking any immediate sympathy with his project, these critics have had no interest in actually comprehending what Hegel means by 'absolute knowing', and so have just assumed that it is some sort of rather hazy, but at any rate madly presumptuous, metaphysical claim. And then, on this basis, both parties, together, have concocted, in Walter Kaufmann's phrase, the 'Hegel myth'.[8] The once widespread notion that Hegel was a nationalistic political reactionary belongs entirely to the myth; as does the curious notion that he was a mere apologist, in principle, for whatever is historically successful, as such.[9] It is true that he was against any sort of essentially self-indulgent, self-righteously utopian hostility towards practical politicians, and that he belonged to the generation of those whose original, idealistic enthusiasm for the French Revolution had been traumatically chastened by the spectacle of the Jacobin Terror. However, 'absolute knowing' implies an absolute critical restlessness not only in relation to the utopian or revolutionary critics of the status quo, but just as much, also, in relation to its mere upholders. Proponents of the 'Hegel myth' sometimes describe his thought as 'totalizing', so hinting at latent affinities to totalitarianism. Nothing could be more misleading! Would-be mainstream Christian critics sometimes speak of him as a heretical, 'Gnostic' thinker. It is true that he was intrigued by that most intriguing of figures, Jakob Boehme, to whom the label 'Gnostic' arguably does apply – and to that extent there is, indeed, slightly more to this charge than there is to the other, quite empty accusation of 'pantheism'.[10] But, surely, to be a 'Gnostic', in the classic heretical sense, one has to be a sectarian. And no one could be less sectarian than Hegel is. He is anti-agnostic, in the sense that agnosticism is a mere refusal to engage with theology; yet no one could be less Gnostic, in the classic sense.[11]

So is it then, perhaps, the inevitable fate of any serious advocate of trans-metaphysical, systematically reconciliatory 'absolute knowing', as such, either to have their thought distorted in this way, or else – as is, at present, much more the risk in Rose's case – merely to be ignored and forgotten?

Maybe it is. The philosophic story Hegel has to tell is a story of progress, inasmuch as it traces the emergence of the possibility of his own insight. But it is by no means a story of guaranteed triumph.

❧

Rose is a Hegelian – who, however, also admires Kierkegaard. Hegel and Kierkegaard together: in intellectual terms, her eventual option for Christian baptism seems very largely to derive from her reading of these two Christian philosophers. Her work may be divided into two periods, divided by a gap of several years. The first period, up to 1984, saw the publication of *The Melancholy Science,*

Hegel contra Sociology and *Dialectic of Nihilism*: these works, considered as a group, are first and foremost a vindication of Hegel and his worldview. But the second period, beginning with *The Broken Middle* (1992) differs, essentially, in that she had now become just as much concerned to vindicate Kierkegaard and his worldview. And to reconcile that worldview with Hegel's.[12]

On the face of it, this is indeed a curious conjunction, for of course Kierkegaard always presented himself as a scathing critic of Hegel. He is actually one of the prime initiators of the 'Hegel myth'. And yet, the point is that they are both tireless philosophic explorers of the 'broken middle'. Both are, in Kierkegaard's phrase, forever 'making difficulties everywhere'; refusing any easy opinionatedness, essentially in order to open conversation up. Only, Kierkegaard is primarily concerned with a different species of conversation from Hegel. His wilful misunderstanding of Hegel is no doubt unfortunate. But such was the overwhelming presence of Hegel in Kierkegaard's intellectual world that it seems this wilfulness of his was a subjective necessity, the only way he could effectively assert the alternative validity of his other priorities.

Thus, we come back here to the basic dichotomy between the two spheres of negotiation: the political sphere, dealing with the challenge, to traditional *Sittlichkeit*, of the secular modern state, and the pre-political or existential sphere, dealing with the challenge of self-expressive nonconformity.

Hegel's primary creative concern is with the former. Hence the particular shape of his interest in History, his construction of grand narrative: in practical terms, Hegelian grand narrative is all about setting the context for ongoing negotiation between the institutional Church and the institutions of the secular modern state. It is framed as a global history of 'freedom' – in the sense that the cause of 'freedom' is what institutions, generally, are meant to serve; the basic proper legitimation-principle for institutions, both ecclesiastical and secular. But Kierkegaard by contrast is not interested in mediating between Church and state. Instead, he wants to speak direct to self-expressive nonconformists *as* self-expressive non-conformists, in a Christian context. And so he mocks Hegel's 'professorial' concern with the negotiation of political History. No academic himself, not in the pay of any state institution, but a gentleman of independent means, he revels in his resultant independence.[13]

Nevertheless, Kierkegaard is just as radically a peace-negotiating mediator – in his own different way – as Hegel is. His use of pseudonyms is a method of systematically setting out divergent points of view, as demanding reconciliation. And the initial terms of his general reconciliatory project are set out in *Either/Or*. Here he counter-poses two elementary opposite standpoints.[14] On the one hand, in this work, the essayist 'A' (who also edits the 'Diary of a Seducer') represents a purely 'aesthetic' point of view; a belief in quite unfettered self-expressive nonconformity. On the other hand, 'Judge William' represents an initial, but all too facile attempt to reconcile the element of truth in this with 'ethics', the demands of Protestant *Sittlichkeit*, focusing especially on the desirability of marriage. In the end, the entire Kierkegaardian project is framed as a systematic renegotiating of the same issue, on an ever deeper 'religious' level. Or, to put it in Rosean terms: precisely, with an ever greater acceptance of spiritual brokenness.

By its very nature all philosophy may be said to be a devising of strategies for intellectual transcendence, an attempt to rise above the mere clash of opposing partial truths at the level of 'opinion'. Thinking at the level of 'opinion' is thinking entirely trapped within a given viewpoint, belonging to a particular historic time and place. Philosophy by contrast seeks to penetrate to the eternal: the most comprehensive possible overview. For Plato's Socrates this is essentially a process of 'recollection', a turning backwards, to uncover what one's experience has already, in fact, potentially taught one, but what, for lack of questioning, one has not yet understood. Kierkegaard, on the other hand, calls it *'repetition'* – by which he largely means the same as St Paul meant by being 'born again'. (It is just that the notion of being 'born again' has acquired all sorts of quite narrowly circumscribed churchy, or even sectarian, anti-philosophical connotations which Kierkegaard seeks to evade by speaking of 'repetition' instead.) And in *The Broken Middle* Rose also adopts this Kierkegaardian term for her own purposes.

'Repetition' differs from Socratic 'recollection' by virtue of its decisive orientation forwards, as well as backwards: to aspire to 'repetition', in the Kierkegaardian sense, is to be inspired by a fundamental commitment to hope, understood in orthodox Christian fashion as a primary virtue in itself. And Kierkegaard then further opposes the sort of mediation he calls 'repetition' to 'mediation' in the Hegelian sense of the term.[15] Thus, his fictional 'Hegel' is a thinker who operates exclusively at the level of seeking to resolve theoretical puzzles, without any sort of inner self-transformation being involved at all. So he portrays 'Hegel' as a thinker with no real understanding either of 'repetition' or, for that matter, of Socratic 'recollection', inasmuch as both of these are radical processes of inner self-transformation. This fiction is, indeed, sheer gratuitous slander! Although Hegel does not anticipate the Kierkegaardian terminology, when he speaks of 'Spirit' he is surely talking, precisely, about the power that enables true 'repetition'.

In the persona of 'Johannes Climacus', Kierkegaard also re-opens St Anselm's old question: *Cur Deus homo*, Why a God-man?[16] For what exact purpose might it be supposed necessary for divine revelation to take the form of incarnation? And the answer suggested revolves, fundamentally, around the contrast between Christian faith and Socratic recollection. The salvation in question here resembles the enlightenment brought about by Socratic recollection – so 'Johannes Climacus' argues – inasmuch as it involves a no less radical calling into question of ordinary unthinking common-sense conformism. But the affirmation that the teacher is God incarnate is also meant to invest such questioning with an infinite intensity of pathos, which Socratic recollection by contrast lacks. Why a God-man? Simply in order that the imperatives of true thoughtfulness, represented in that form, should be invested with the most intense religious passion. Both ways, the Socratic and the Christian, are bound to be constantly offensive to idle, unthinking common sense; both are, in that sense, commitments to paradox. Only, Christian repetition differs from Socratic recollection – it represents '*absolute* paradox' – in the sense that it is 'absolutely' impassioned.

Compare this notion of 'absolute paradox', however, with Hegel's notion of 'absolute knowing': what is the real difference? Both are equally trans-metaphysical notions of divine truth. The pathway that Hegel traces towards 'absolute knowing' might very well be described as a pathway of ever deepening paradox, inasmuch as every turn represents a fresh offence to idle, unthinking common sense. Hegel, in the *Phenomenology*, begins with the most abstractly universal forms of human experience, and then gradually progresses in towards the historic specificity of Christian faith, philosophically interpreted. Kierkegaard – not only as 'Johannes Climacus' but also, above all, as 'Vigilius Haufniensis', 'Frater Taciturnus' and 'Anti-Climacus' – starts with the phenomenon of Christian faith, and then contrasts it with the most immediate other existential options.[17] But, in the end, 'absolute knowing' is surely just 'absolute paradox' approached another way.

'Absolute knowing'/'absolute paradox': both of these are formulations for the final liberation of the very fullest peace-negotiative magnanimity, from the last restraints of idle, unthinking common sense. Rose's own distinctive formula for the same is that it is the operation of *aporia* and *agapé*. *Aporia*: the collapse of all given understandings of the ethical before the irreducible singularity of each individual's own first-hand experience. *Agapé*: overflowing love, beyond all self-interested reason.[18]

Kierkegaard theorizes the experience of *aporia* and the claims of *agapé* in the most confrontational fashion. When in 1855 he suddenly collapsed in the street, and died, he was in the midst of a savage one-man pamphlet campaign against the Danish Lutheran

Church. A latter-day prophet Amos, he was urging his fellow citizens, for Christ's sake, not to go to church – until the Church openly confessed how great a gulf there was between its own governing spirit, that of comfortable, established 'Christendom', and the original spirit of gospel truth. All of his writing originates as the self-expression of a radically alienated individual, as such. And in retrospect this ending may well be seen as its natural culmination.

Hegel, by contrast, always writes very much as a philosophic horse-whisperer – trying, so far as possible, not to spook those two skittish beasts, church and state. There could scarcely be a greater difference in tone. But does that mean that Hegel, for his part, merely endorses the ordinary failure of common-sense 'Christendom' properly to respect *aporia*, or give space for *agapé*? By no means! Every turn in the pathway traced by the *Phenomenology* is, in fact, either a deepening of respect for *aporia* or else an opening up of space for *agapé*.

Kierkegaard testifies to *aporia* and *agapé* in one mood, Hegel in another. But for Rose the validity of such testimony does not depend upon its mood. In terms of her personal idiolect, both Kierkegaard and Hegel are equally ambitious in their 'agon of authorship', as giving voice to the 'equivocation of the ethical'. And what she seeks to affirm is, quite simply, such ambition in itself.

❧

Kierkegaard's 'agon of authorship' might indeed very well be defined as a systematic working through of the confrontation between traditional Christian theology and the spirit of modern self-expressive nonconformity.

Again, this latter term is mine, not Rose's – and neither is she herself a theologian. In *The Broken Middle* she compares Kierkegaard, not with any other Christian theologians, but with Kafka and with Freud. The comparison with Kafka, however,

surely serves to highlight the specific difference which Kierkegaard's theology makes when it comes to dealing with the demands
of self-expressive nonconformity at the very highest pitch of intensity. And the comparison with Freud, then, further helps open up
the Kierkegaardian theological analysis of self-expressive nonconformity, in terms of its trans-theological implications, more
generally.

It is, I think, a very interesting interpretative strategy – only, as
usual, she goes so fast! So now let us retrace her basic argument,
going just a little more slowly.

Kierkegaard/Kafka

Kierkegaard resembles Kafka, biographically, inasmuch as both of
them were men whose sense of vocation was largely worked out in
terms of a painful turning away from the prospect of marriage.

Thus, in September 1840 Kierkegaard proposed to Regine Olsen,
and was accepted. He was 27; she was 18. But there followed, for
him, a year of anguish: he loved Regine intensely, yet increasingly
felt that he was not fit for marriage, it was not his true calling.
Finally – to her dismay – he broke the engagement. And his writings, from then on, are full of more or less fictionalized retellings of,
allusions to, and reflections upon, this traumatic event.[19] Kafka,
likewise, was twice engaged to Felice Bauer, first in 1914 and then
again in 1917. But on each occasion, for reasons explained at length
in the letters he wrote to her, he broke off the engagement. And he
also put something of this experience into fiction, in 'Wedding
Preparations in the Country'.[20]

Both men attribute their unfitness for marriage, partly, to a deep
predisposition to melancholy; associated, in both cases, with their
relationship to their fathers. Kafka's father, a moderately successful
Jewish businessman in Prague, appears to have been an extremely
caustic, domineering character. Or so, at any rate, he is portrayed
in Kafka's autobiographical 'Letter to his Father', written in 1919

but never delivered; a letter which is a bitter indictment.[21] Kierkegaard, by contrast, had a deep veneration for his father. But Michael Kierkegaard had also been an intensely melancholy man. A strict and rigid Pietist with, as his son put it, a 'glowing imagination', he was convinced that the premature deaths of five of his other children were evidence of a divine curse laid upon the whole family, which he attributed to his own sin. He had become a very wealthy merchant, but came from poor origins; as a child he had tended sheep on a Jutland heath, and there, one lonely day, had solemnly cursed God. In his own view he, and his, had been under a reciprocal curse ever since, a curse redoubled by other sins, for which he could not forgive himself. And his son shared this belief. In his *Journal* Kierkegaard writes of the horror he felt at the prospect of having to initiate Regine into this terrible aspect of his family background.[22]

But (Rose urges) let us not just get stuck on the biographical details. For Kierkegaard himself, pondering the reasons for his personal decision, despite everything, to remain single, this experience becomes the occasion for a very much more wide-ranging philosophical meditation on the meaning of singularity in general. His own story is, for him, one might say, a microcosmic representation of the whole conflict between the proper claims of *Sittlichkeit*, established ethical consensus, and the no less proper demands of conscientious self-expression.

In Kafka's case the demands of self-expressive nonconformity take shape as an obsessive-compulsive vocation to write – which, in the end, he decides is too much of a burden to impose on Felice. Kierkegaard's dilemma is similar, except that his literary vocation is also infused with passionate religious faith. This is the obvious difference between them. Kafka's writing is largely an evocation of hell, a nightmare existence completely devoid of the presence of God. But Kierkegaard, in presenting the claims of *Sittlichkeit* and the demands of conscientious self-expression, systematically sets out to invest both impulses with the plenitude of Christian hope.

The *Sittlichkeit* of Kierkegaard's bourgeois Lutheran world made marriage the universal norm. His not marrying Regine was of course, immediately, a scandalous offence to that world's ethical common sense. But, at another level, in retrospect he himself also agrees with his conventional critics: on 17 May 1843 he confides in his diary, 'Had I had faith, I should have remained with Regine'.[23] That is to say, his leaving her was, at least partly, an outcome of his lacking sufficient faith in God's forgiveness of sins, both his own and his father's; in this sense, as he comes to recognize, true Christian hope fully chimes in here with the claims of *Sittlichkeit*. Yet, on the other hand, he also continues to think that the decision was, again at least partly, a matter of his holding fast to his own exceptional, God-given, self-expressive individual vocation. And, in general, he seeks to argue that true Christian *Sittlichkeit* must include a profound openness to the possibility of such exceptions.

In the little book *Fear and Trembling*, which Kierkegaard wrote under the pseudonym of 'Johannes de Silentio', this whole species of possibility is entitled 'a teleological suspension of the ethical'.[24] By the 'ethical', here, is simply meant what *Sittlichkeit* prescribes, at its best. Thus, he is not talking about an upsurge of protest aiming at the reform of some corrupted form of *Sittlichkeit*; but about a 'suspension' of what are freely acknowledged to be the proper rules. The classic symbol for this is the story of the *akedah*: God's testing of Abraham recorded in Genesis 22. God has promised Abraham great things for his posterity, and in order that these promises may be fulfilled, Abraham and Sarah in their old age have miraculously been granted the gift of a son, Isaac. But now God tests Abraham by commanding him to take Isaac, bring him to Mount Moriah, and there kill him, as a human sacrifice. This is not only a basic offence against true *Sittlichkeit* in that it is the murder of a son by his father. The whole purpose of *Sittlichkeit*, in any form, is to ensure the survival of the moral community, as such, and in killing his only son Abraham will indeed be ensuring the exact opposite. Moreover, he loves Isaac. Nonetheless, God has spoken, and so, telling no one of what his purpose is, he proceeds to obey. Not until the very last minute, when he has bound Isaac and laid him on the altar, and has raised his knife, does God – in the form of a suddenly appearing angel – intervene to stop him, after all. *Fear and Trembling* is largely a meditation on this story. 'Johannes de Silentio' underlines how Abraham differs from such other legendary figures as Agamemnon, Jephtha or Brutus, who also found themselves compelled to sacrifice children, but, in their cases, in tragic, unexpected, dutiful fulfilment of publicly made vows. The observance of a publicly enacted vow is something that *Sittlichkeit* itself demands. By contrast, Abraham's act of faith really is a pure 'suspension' of the ethical. That, for 'Johannes de Silentio', is Abraham's unique symbolic greatness. And then 'Johannes' appends various other legendary or folkloric tales, all about problematic love affairs, which illustrate the dilemmas involved in Kierkegaard's own 'teleological suspension of the ethical', in relation to Regine. He continues to insist on the radical *uniqueness* of Abraham, as a model of supremely paradoxical, and therefore supremely true, faith. Nor, of course, is Abraham a modern self-expressive individual, as Kierkegaard himself is. Yet the implicit point is that for a religious culture truly to honour Abraham as an ideal model of true faith, it must surely be open to the possibility of such conscientious 'suspensions' *in general;* not only in the context of legendary antiquity, but equally in the modern context.

Kierkegaard himself invokes this possibility in his own case, as an exemplar of modern self-expressive nonconformity. But then again, Rose urges, let us be quite clear: this does not make him a wholesale antinomian. What he is invoking is the possibility that the traditional authority of *Sittlichkeit* be, from time to time, exceptionally 'suspended'. This is not, by any means, to say that it should be relaxed in all contexts. Where the ethical is *properly* 'suspended', there the highest moral truth emerges. For Kierkegaard, however, everything depends upon our recognizing how very exceptional an occurrence, in principle, this actually is.

And therefore Rose protests against the way in which the contrast between Kierkegaard and Kafka has sometimes been represented, as though Kierkegaard's greater faith somehow made his moral nonconformity *easier*. She quotes Maurice Blanchot as an example of this:

> Kafka's story and the story of Kierkegaard's engagement have been compared, [Blanchot writes], by Kafka himself among others. But the conflict is different. Kierkegaard can renounce Regine; he can renounce the ethical level. Access to the religious level is not thereby compromised; rather it is made possible. But Kafka, if he abandons the earthly happiness of a normal life, also abandons the steadiness of a just life. He makes himself an outlaw, deprives himself of the ground and the foundation he needs in order to be and, in a way, deprives the law of this ground.[25]

When Blanchot speaks of Kierkegaard 'renouncing the ethical level', this sounds as though he regards Kierkegaard as a positively antinomian advocate of self-expressive nonconformity, constrained only by the requirements of conscientious authenticity. In fact, though, Kierkegaard does not 'renounce' the ethical level; he does not just dismiss the authority of *Sittlichkeit*. On the contrary, he develops an understanding of the ethical transfigured by the possibility of its exceptional 'suspension'; a 'suspension' only made possible, however, by a truly exceptional intensity of faith.

The true 'single individual', for Kierkegaard, is the 'knight of faith'; he speaks of *Sittlichkeit* as the 'universal'. But, in his own words:

> Anyone who believes that it is fairly easy to be the single individual can always be sure that he is not a knight of faith, for fly-by-nights and itinerant geniuses are not men of faith. On the contrary, this knight knows that it is glorious to belong to the universal. He knows that it is beautiful and beneficial to be the

single individual who translates himself in to the universal, the one who, so to speak, personally produces a trim, clean and, as far as possible, faultless edition of himself, readable by all.[26]

Kierkegaard's faith spares him Kafka's sheer despair, yet hope is not the same as ease. Blanchot implicitly appears to confuse the one with the other. Antinomianism, as a lowering of the bar, makes the negotiation of moral consensus as easy as possible. Is this not a form of complacency? (It is a complacent simple acceptance of life at the level of what Hegel, in the *Phenomenology*, calls the 'spiritual animal kingdom'.[27]) Once again, however, Kierkegaard's ambition is on the contrary that which he expresses under the pseudonym of 'Johannes Climacus': always 'to make difficulties everywhere'.[28] He is not merely a Christian advocate of self-expressive nonconformity. Far rather, he is a peace-negotiator, seeking to reconcile the demands of true, nonconformist self-expression, at their most intense, with the claims of traditional Christian *Sittlichkeit*, also at their most intense. And so he occupies the 'broken middle'.

His final prophetic attack upon Christendom is also the outcome of a 'teleological suspension of the ethical'. For it is certainly not ethical behaviour, in any conventional sense, for a Christian believer so to try and undermine the prime actual agency of Christian *Sittlichkeit*, the institutional church. Indeed, Kierkegaard was precisely calling for a corporate testimony to the 'teleological suspension of the ethical': not just for people to leave one particular, corrupted form of church life in order to participate in another, better form instead; but, provisionally, for them to abandon church life altogether, until the institution repents. And yet, the *provisional nature* of this proposed gesture still clearly distances it from any mere antinomianism. The whole purpose of the 'teleological suspension of the ethical' here is to help make possible an eventual full restoration of the ethical with renewed authority. There is no such prophetic fire in Kafka's thinking, his despair precludes it. Kafka is trapped on the edge of Jewish *Sittlichkeit*, half in, half out. Kierkegaard advocates a prophetic strategy of stepping right outside of Christian *Sittlichkeit* in order, hopefully, then to step right back in again. He is, at all events, not trapped. But the sort of hope which drives prophecy nevertheless really is quite different in kind from that which makes life, in any sense, easier.

Kierkegaard/Freud

Kierkegaard may be said to be a true peace-negotiator between the demands of true, nonconformist self-expression and the claims of traditional Christian *Sittlichkeit*, just because he is the utmost opposite to the sort of false prophet who cries '"Peace, peace", when there is no peace' (Jeremiah 6.14; 8.11). He does not deny the difficulty here. On the contrary, he relentlessly insists upon it. And, moreover, he does this on two quite distinct levels. First, in the person of 'Johannes de Silentio' he addresses the religious challenge of self-expressive nonconformity at its most exceptionally intense. But then one year later, in 1844, under the pseudonym 'Vigilius Haufniensis', author of *The Concept of Anxiety* (or *Dread*), he also goes on to analyse the problems of spiritual individuation at their most universal.

It is in this latter context that Rose juxtaposes his thought, especially, to Freud's. Indeed, she evidently admires Freud as a thinker the whole thrust of whose thought, like that of Kierkegaard's, is to promote the cause of the most thoughtful individuality; yet who, again like Kierkegaard, is very much a rebuilder, not a mere antinomian would-be destroyer of *Sittlichkeit*. For, notwithstanding Freud's complete lack of religious faith, he is no 'nihilist', the way Rose uses that term in *Dialectic of Nihilism*.[29] So Freud does not simply set out, as 'nihilist' thinkers do, to debunk all forms of institutionalized moral authority as such. On the contrary, the Freudian project is an attempt to construct a whole *new* form of institutionalized moral authority, that of the psychoanalyst: a 'scientific' rather than religious form of authority. Such authority is

distinguished from other forms above all in the way it systematically works, so far as possible, to release those who submit to it from
neurotic dependence upon it – but otherwise it is in direct continuity from the authority of the Christian priest-confessor. To be
sure, one may doubt whether anything like this new secular form of
authority could ever even remotely rival the older church form as a
bonding principle for large-scale catholic *Sittlichkeit*. Nevertheless,
psychoanalysis – torn as it is between the guidance of authoritative
'scientific' dogma, as a secular mode of *Sittlichkeit*, and the imperative of non-directive listening openness to the self-expressive individual – also in its own way assigns its practitioners to the 'broken
middle'. And this is the basic point of analogy, which Rose for her
part wants to open up, with Kierkegaard.

In particular, she contrasts the evolving Freudian notion of
'anxiety' with the Kierkegaardian notion. It is not that Freud any-
where refers to Kierkegaard; his doctrine emerges quite independ-
ently. But – Rose argues – in its later form, as developed from the
mid-1920s, it does at least begin to converge on the teaching of
Kierkegaard's 'Vigilius Haufniensis'. Thus, in *The Broken Middle*
she is concerned with what happens to Freud's thinking in the
period initiated, in 1923, by his book *The Ego and the Id*.[30]

For her, Kierkegaard and Freud basically belong together as two
thinkers who have both sought, each in his own systematic fashion,
to analyse the 'anxiety of beginning' in terms of the 'beginning of
anxiety'. By 'anxiety of beginning' she means all the stress involved
in free-spirited dissent from prevailing social norms – the conscientious dissent of the moral explorer, seeking to strike out on his or
her own distinctive path – insofar as that dissent allows itself, where
necessary, to become confrontational. 'Anxiety of beginning' is a
necessary concomitant to the true philosophic peacemaker's
dedication to the 'broken middle', inasmuch as true peacemaking
is the very opposite of crying 'peace, peace' where there is no peace.
It is what flows from self-expressive nonconformists' *willingly
embraced* loss of innocence, as they break free from the mere

inertia of moral tradition and honestly open themselves up to the reproaches of its defenders; the necessary price of their free-spiritedness.

But, as analysts of the 'beginning of anxiety', both Kierkegaard and Freud alike trace this stress, the 'anxiety of beginning', back to its origins – in that it is the exceptional accentuation of a universal defining feature of properly human existence. The 'beginning of anxiety' is Rose's formula for that universal defining feature, as such.

In Freud's earlier work, prior to 1923, he actually uses the term 'anxiety' in a much more restricted sense. Here it refers only to the stress resultant from failures of repression: all the various ways in which one may continue to be troubled by the after-effects of traumatic memory and socially unacceptable desires even after one has erased them from one's consciousness. And therapy, in this context, is narrowly envisaged as a bid to liberate individuals from the impediments signalled by such anxiety. *The Ego and the Id*, however, represents the advent of an altogether more comprehensive sense of therapeutic ambition. For from now on Freud thinks of therapy not only as a matter of consciously facing up to and 'working through' repressed traumas and illicit impulses. But he also sees it as a loosening up of neurotic moralism. Whereas, in other words, his primary therapeutic concern hitherto was with the problematic *return of the repressed*, now it is, just as much, with the problem of an over-zealous, self-punitive *will to repress*.

Following on from *The Ego and the Id*, Freud wrote two major essays on 'anxiety'. The first, 'Inhibitions, Symptoms and Anxiety', appeared in 1925; the second, 'Anxiety and Instinctual Life', in 1932.[31] In these works 'anxiety' is the general discomfort of the ego, as it is hemmed in by its three severe 'masters': the outside world, the 'id' and the 'super-ego'. The outside world exercises its 'mastery' through memories of trauma, beginning with the original trauma of birth itself.[32] The id, comprising all that derives from repressed but not eliminated libido, makes the ego anxious with its submerged unruliness. But the super-ego is the anxiety-generating voice of internalized repressive authority. Thus, to the extent that anxiety is the ego's unease in relation to the super-ego, Freud now argues, against the limitations of his earlier theory, that

> It was not the repression that created the anxiety; the anxiety was there earlier; it was the anxiety that made the repression.[33]

This *primordial* anxiety actually begins as a consequence of our mixed feelings, in early childhood, about our parents. As we learn both to identify with our parents and yet also to fear them, we are made anxious by the tension between that identification and that fear.[34] All going well, this tension becomes the nucleus of a healthy conscience. But it may equally generate the despotic 'master'-aspect of what Hegel calls the 'unhappy consciousness', namely, a condition of self-imposed inner servitude in which nonconformist self-expression is more or less crushed. The 'super-ego' is, in effect, Freud's term for the essential co-inherence of both these two quite opposite possibilities, to some extent in all of us.

In Rose's terms, Kierkegaard and Freud are akin as two thinkers systematically concerned to develop strategies for coping with the 'anxiety of beginning', that is, providing for the most truly authoritative legitimation, and effective nurturing, of free-spirited self-expression. Or, again as Rose puts it, 'Reflection in both authorships is dedicated to releasing for risk.'[35] It is just that Freud, as a latter-day Epicurean, medicalizes the problem. In other words, he opts to renounce any sort of moral, as distinct from medical, judgement; the better to minimize any potential for manipulation intruding into the process.

At the end of 'Inhibitions, Symptoms and Anxiety', on the other hand, Freud draws up a list of what he now sees as the chief potential resistances, in the mind of the patient, for psychoanalytic therapy to overcome.[36] First, here, he cites three forms of ego-resistance:

1 *'Knowledge resistance'*, the hindrance to self-knowledge simply intrinsic to the process of repression, itself.

2 *'Transference resistance'*, the tendency for the patient addicted to submissive irresponsibility merely to transfer onto the analyst the sort of authority which that addiction craves.

3 *'The gain from illness'*, the attractions of self-pity and the protection which illness may afford against other people's moral claims.

Then comes

4 *'Id-resistance'*, which is the 'compulsion to repeat', or sheer inertia of established habit.

But the list culminates in:

5 *'Super-ego resistance'*.

And this – for him, as he says, 'the last to be discovered' – is also, he acknowledges, potentially the most intractable of all. For it is the resistance of those who, in their heart of hearts, do not really want to be well, because they do not feel that they *deserve* to be; whose neurosis is a form of compulsive self-abasement. Faced with such compulsion, Freud concedes, 'there is often no counteracting force of a similar order of strength which the treatment can oppose to it'.[37] Especially where the patient is a devout believer in God, the analyst is up against their implicit understanding of God's will; so that, he actually remarks, in extreme cases no real progress could ever be possible unless the analyst were somehow, against all the proper self-restrictive rules of analysis, to adopt the role of 'prophet, saviour and redeemer'![38]

But, in a certain sense, Kierkegaard's path to faith may surely be seen as addressing just this problem, which a purely medicalized approach cannot tackle. For, by contrast to Freud, he of course has no fear of invoking the authority of one who is a 'prophet, saviour and redeemer'. On the contrary, the way he uses the term, 'anxiety' becomes a name, precisely, for that basic problem – explored through, but preceding, sin – for which the only ultimate solution is true faith.

At one level, what Kierkegaard's 'Vigilius Haufniensis' is analysing in *The Concept of Anxiety* is identical with what Freud also calls 'anxiety'. Both authorships use the term to designate the stress that, from the beginning, necessarily accompanies the impulse to free self-expressive individuation. Only, the Kierke-gaardian account differs from the Freudian by virtue of its much bolder practical orientation towards confronting what Freud calls 'super-ego resistance'. Thus, such resistance is a sheer moralized, and 'faith'-associated, repression of self-expressive nonconform-ity. For 'Vigilius Haufniensis', however, true faith is the authentic sublation of anxiety – in that it is just as much a positive achieve-ment of self-expressive nonconformity as sin itself. Whereas sin is self-expressive nonconformity defying *Sittlichkeit* unjustly, faith is self-expressive nonconformity breaking through the limitations of existing *Sittlichkeit* justly. That is to say: in genuine love, looking for an ever greater openness towards the Other.

Anxiety, according to this understanding, is in short the consti-tutive stress of the life of the spirit, on its way to faith as the final vindication of true individuality. And what therefore especially interests 'Vigilius Haufniensis' is the interaction between anxiety and the actual guilt of having sinned. So he begins his account by separating the two phenomena: looking at the form of anxiety which precedes guilt. In poetic terms, this is the anxiety of Adam and Eve before the Fall. Of course, the pre-lapsarian innocence of Adam and Eve is not the 'innocence' of *wanting to be* recognized as innocent; it is not protested innocence, the wilful turning away of fallen humanity from the knowledge of good and evil. It is real innocence, sheer ignorance of good and evil – the condition of moral infancy. Yet even at this level, the point is, anxiety is already stirring. 'In observing children', he remarks, 'one will discover this anxiety . . . as a seeking for the adventurous, the monstrous, and the enigmatic.'[39] What is anxiety? Kierkegaard's answer is, it is the ambiguous stirring of an impulse to '*leap*': to leap out of the purely natural, collective existence of the human race as a whole, into the spiritual existence of a self-expressive individual. It is the condition of wanting to make that 'qualitative leap', but also not wanting to, held back both by fears and loyalties, hovering on the brink; a 'sympathetic antipathy and an antipathetic sympathy'.[40] Or again,

> Anxiety may be compared with dizziness. He whose eye happens to look down into the yawning abyss becomes dizzy. But what is the reason for this? It is just as much in his own eye as in the abyss, for suppose he had not looked down. Hence anxiety is the dizziness of freedom.[41]

It belongs to our awareness of what we can do, our ability, if we choose, to leap – down into the abyss.

We leap downwards. And 'in that very moment everything is changed, and freedom, when it again rises, sees that it is guilty'.[42] The first qualitative leap is inevitably down, away from heaven, into sin. People sometimes talk of 'simple faith', and it is true that faith does not, of itself, require any degree of intellectual articulacy, but, in existential terms, Kierkegaard's whole project is to insist upon the impossibility of simple faith. One cannot leap straight from innocence to the truth of true faith, the leap of faith can only come much later. First, one must be thoroughly initiated, like Adam and Eve, into the knowledge of good and evil; which is, at the same time, the knowledge of one's own guilt.

However, there are two sorts of acknowledged guilt. One is the guilt that belongs to what Freud calls 'super-ego resistance'. 'Vigilius Haufniensis' for his part calls this 'the demonic'; which he also describes as 'inclosing reserve', or 'unfreedom that wants to close itself off'. The other sort is that which, in Rose's terms, belongs to the 'broken middle'; the very opposite to closed-offness.[43] Everything, for Kierkegaard, depends upon our confronting the pathos of the former with the truth of the latter, *pitched at an even greater intensity of pathos*. And 'Vigilius Haufniensis' further contrasts three basic different types of ethical culture, from that point of view.[44] He criticizes pagan culture, generally, for its basic inability to articulate the pathos of true guilt. For in pagan culture, lacking as it does any very vivid imagery of divine moral judgement, anxiety comes to expression not so much as a relationship to guilt, but rather as a relationship to impersonal fate, instead. The culture of ancient Hebrew religion – which he anachronistically calls 'Judaism' – represents a partial opening to what is required. But, he suggests, the problem here is that the practice of ritual sacrifice serves merely to alleviate the anxious pathos of guilt and repentance in neurotic fashion. Only with the abandonment of ritual sacrifice does a culture begin to emerge which is really capable of doing what is required. This, for him, is above all the historic achievement of Christianity – although, as Rose remarks, the same might just as well be said of rabbinic Judaism.[45] Or indeed, let us add, of Islam.

The special truth-potential of this whole family of religious cultures begins with their unique capacity to articulate the pathos of guilt and repentance. But, again, this capacity, considered in itself, is an absolutely ambiguous phenomenon. The false guilt of 'the demonic' may after all, in its more veiled forms, be just as devout, just as orthodox, just as sincere as the authentic repentance of faith. Yet, at its more or less hidden heart, it nevertheless remains essentially an expression of *despair*.

Kierkegaard, in fact, wrote two books on psychology: not only *The Concept of Anxiety* but also, under the pseudonym 'Anti-Climacus', *The Sickness Unto Death*, which is a study of 'despair', in its relationship to faith. In this work he is, effectively, filling out the earlier account, given by 'Vigilius Haufniensis', of 'the demonic'. Be it noted: this is 'despair' as defined from the perspective of faith, 'despair' as an orientation of *will*, away from faith. It need not necessarily imply a desperate *mood* – even if, from the perspective of faith, it ought to! In terms of mood, the 'despairing' one may well be quite cheerful. But right at the core of the argument in *The Sickness Unto Death* is a basic distinction between 'the two forms of conscious despair':

1 the 'despair' of 'in despair not wanting to be oneself', and
2 'the despair of wanting in despair to be oneself'.[46]

These are, one might say, precisely the two primary ways of wilfully opting out of the 'broken middle' between the demands of nonconformist self-expression and the claims of *Sittlichkeit*; both of them, in the end, options for 'despair' in preference to 'brokenness'. Thus, the 'despair' of 'not wanting to be oneself', which is the potentially devout form of 'despair', is none other than a wilful sheer repudiation of the demands of nonconformist self-expression. But the 'despair of wanting in despair to be oneself' is just a wilful sheer repudiation of the claims of *Sittlichkeit*. The true leap of faith, for Kierkegaard, is the leap out of 'despair', in both these forms. To put it in Rose's terms: it is none other than a God-inspired leap into the 'broken middle'.

Nothing, it might seem, could be further removed than this from Freud's resolute irreligiousness. And yet, Rose argues, look again at Freud's particular critical focus on the sort of self-punitive 'paternalistic' religion most directly informing 'super-ego resistance' to psychoanalytic therapy. 'It is this critique', she remarks, 'which, *prima facie*, might seem most at odds with a "religious" authorship, that most coincides with it.'[47] It would indeed be irredeemably at odds with any authorship that simply sought to vindicate religion as such. But the real difference between the two thinkers on this score is not that Kierkegaard is in any sense more indulgent than Freud towards 'paternalistic' religion. It is just that, whereas Freud is driven to confess the ultimate inability of psychoanalysis to overcome the more religiously entrenched forms of 'super-ego resistance', Kierkegaard by contrast has a serious strategy for confronting such religion on its own imaginative and theoretical terms.

In the end, the strategy that Rose primarily wants to endorse is Kierkegaard's. Only, it would seem, she is concerned that many secular-minded people will immediately be deterred – by secularist prejudice – from approaching such a profoundly religious thinker with the seriousness he deserves. And so she compares him with Freud, as a way of at any rate trying to open up access to his thought even for the most militant of secularists.

❧

Again, the ultimate complementarity that Rose sees between Kierkegaard and Hegel – notwithstanding all the sound and fury of Kierkegaard's own critique of Hegel – is essentially that, whereas Kierkegaard is a thinker of the 'broken middle' in pre-political or existential terms, Hegel is a thinker of the 'broken middle' in political terms. To be sure, Hegel's politically centred thought reaches back into the pre-political and existential, just as Kierkegaard also has his (somewhat reactionary) political views. But the whole difference between them derives from a basic difference of emphasis in this regard. Kierkegaard is primarily torn between traditional Christian ethics and modern self-expressive nonconformity, as two alternative ways of thinking about personal vocation; Hegel is primarily torn between traditional Christian politics and modern secular humanism, as two alternative ways of thinking about institutional justice.

In the Introduction to *The Broken Middle* Rose remarks that the argument here 'develops' the argument previously opened up by her in *Hegel contra Sociology* and *Dialectic of Nihilism*.[48] These two works, taken together, might be described as an attempted extension of Hegelian grand narrative to history after Hegel. Thus, they seek to account for the prevailing rejection of Hegelianism by subsequent philosophers, as Hegel himself might have done, were he alive today.

As a thinker of the 'broken middle', Hegel has a basically ambivalent response to what I am calling 'secular humanism'. He rejects the sort of secular humanism that attempts to build a broad moral and political consensus on the basis of the sheer negation of *Sittlichkeit*; that is to say, by simply devaluing everything that contributes to the differentiation of neighbouring communities shaped by different religious and ethnic-cultural traditions. Yet that does not mean he rejects the typical secular humanist interest in the promotion of universal human rights, as such. This interest is what, in the *Philosophy of Right*, he calls the 'principle of subjectivity'; set over against what he calls the 'substantive unity' of effective *Sittlichkeit*. In the *Philosophy of Right* as a whole he is intent on vindicating what he thinks is the unprecedented truth-potential inherent in the liberal modern state. 'The principle of modern states', he argues, 'has prodigious strength and depth because it allows the principle of subjectivity to progress to its culmination . . . and yet at the same time brings it back to the substantive unity and so maintains this unity in the principle of subjectivity itself'.[49] Precisely this, indeed, is the political telos of Hegelian grand narrative: a culture in which the demands of the 'principle of subjectivity' are maximally incorporated into the most lively and authoritative possible traditions of *Sittlichkeit*. In relation to Christian theology, above all, Hegelian grand narrative is an attempt to argue that the revelation of gospel truth is a very long-term process. For gospel truth has in fact always been an implicit symbolic affirmation of the 'principle of subjectivity', as a basis for *Sittlichkeit*. But this implicit truth is only made fully explicit – 'absolute knowing' is only fully attained – to the extent that its ideal political out-working is fully revealed. And that, as Hegel saw it, was only just beginning to happen in his own day.

Pure secular humanism, on the other hand, is an all too impatiently modern expression of the 'principle of subjectivity'. So it tends to become as much of an obstacle to the ideal as the merely conservative Christianity that it loves to attack.

Hegel welcomed the 'principle of subjectivity' at work in everything tending to liberalize the political life of his day.[50] Nowadays this principle has of course become far bolder. It is what inspires the whole array of contemporary campaigns against torture, censorship, racism, sexism and homophobia. Presuming he remained consistent, Hegel, were he alive today, would surely have wanted to affirm all these, as clear out-workings of the inner truth of the gospel. But, meanwhile, pure secular humanism has also become much more firmly entrenched than ever it was in his day, right at the heart of global academic culture. The most notable manifestation of this is in the flourishing of 'sociology' – hence the anachronistic title of *Hegel contra Sociology*. Thus, classic 'sociology' is framed as a general study of all the various phenomena with which *Sittlichkeit* is critically concerned, systematically however excluding any of the sort of value judgements which belong to, and express, a form of *Sittlichkeit*. It is, in short, secular humanism unscientifically smuggled into – and, it would seem, made a necessary part of – the basic principles of social science.

In fact, as Rose points out, the early development of sociology emerges out of quite a clearly circumscribed particular philosophic milieu: the world of later nineteenth- and early twentieth-century German 'neo-Kantianism'. The commonly observed divergence of systematic approach between the two primary schools of early sociology, those of Weber and Durkheim, corresponds to the philosophic divergence between the 'Heidelberg' and 'Marburg' schools of neo-Kantianism. In the opening chapter of *Hegel contra Sociology* she briefly traces these historic connections, and then goes on to sketch the history of what she calls 'neo-Kantian Marxism': a broad category, for her embracing the work of Simmel, Lukács, Adorno, Habermas and Althusser. Then, in the rest of the book, she looks at Hegel's critique of this whole type of thinking in its earliest form, as represented by Kant himself – and more especially, in fact, by that most significant of the early Kantians, *Fichte*.

Rejecting everything bound up with strong moral loyalties to the past, and yet intent on providing a foundation for large-scale solidarity-building, secular humanist philosophy, generally, may be said to face the systematic challenge of having to develop a sort of ethico-religious Esperanto. Hegel actually addressed this general species of thinking in several quite different versions, not only the doctrine of Kant and Fichte, but also Enlightenment deism, and (a much more serious alternative than deism) Spinozism. However, it was above all Kant and Fichte who dominated the philosophical world within which his own thought originally emerged.

And one of the most original features of Rose's reading of Hegel is her particular focus on his relationship to Fichte – whom she quite rightly, I think, regards as a somewhat sinister figure.[51] Let us retrace this reading.

Fichte is an important thinker for Hegel – and therefore also for Rose – in the first instance, because of the way in which he systematically strips Kantian ethico-religious Esperanto of Kant's own metaphysical agnosticism.

We have already noted Hegel's deep mistrust of agnosticism, as a stance that in his view merely serves to cut proper theological conversation short. Kant, of course, distinguishes sharply between two realms of reality, the 'phenomenal' realm which is the world as we experience and know it, and the 'noumenal' realm which is the world of the 'thing-in-itself', prior to, and quite independent of, our knowing, but therefore also absolutely unknowable. The supposed activity of God, Kant insists, can only belong to the noumenal realm. But, against Kant, it is often argued that the very notion of the thing-in-itself, and hence of the noumenal realm, is incoherent. For, as Rose puts it,

> If the thing-in-itself is unknowable, how can it be called a 'thing'?
> If it is unknowable, how can its relation to appearances, which

are knowable, be specified? The relation cannot be *causal*, because we could then subsume it under the concept of cause, a category of the understanding, and it would be knowable.[52]

A 'cause', after all, is a relationship between phenomena. The fact is that we simply have no language to speak of the quite different relationship of phenomena to noumena. And Fichte, therefore, opts to abandon this whole aspect of Kant's doctrine. Indeed, he sees Kant's talk of 'not knowing', essentially, as a loss of nerve. For (he argues) it allows the adherents of superstitious or even downright depraved notions of God to evade critique, simply by presenting their ideas as tenets of 'faith', a direct intuition of the noumenal, as opposed to knowledge. He observes how conservative Christian theologians, faced with the critical threat of Kant, typically just retreat into epistemological modesty, as if that were all that was required. And then they feel quite free to carry on as before.[53] So, against Kant, he wants to insist that the enlightened philosopher really does *know* the falsehood of conservative theology, no matter how carefully it may be veiled in such modesty. He frames his philosophy as a systematic account of this knowing; he calls it a *Wissenschaftslehre*, a 'doctrine of knowledge', in just that sense.

Christian faith becomes a basis for *Sittlichkeit* inasmuch as it lays claim to the authority of an historic divine revelation. Fichte's first published work was his *Attempt at a Critique of all Revelation* of 1792. In this book he rejects the very possibility of historic divine revelation as a basis for *Sittlichkeit*, just as Kant does.[54] He exalts 'religion', against 'theology' in general. And by 'religion' he means, precisely, the content of Kantian ethico-religious Esperanto, 'religion within the limits of reason alone' as Kant himself called it.[55] This essay first appeared without the name of the author being given, and was widely supposed to be an anonymous work of Kant's. When the true authorship became known, it made Fichte an instant philosophic celebrity, whereupon, thanks not least to the warm support of Goethe, he was appointed a professor at the University of Jena. And it was during his Jena period, 1794–9, that he began his move beyond Kant, to develop the *Wissenschaftslehre*. Like Fichte, the later neo-Kantians also made the same move, of abandoning Kant's distinction between phenomena and noumena. Indeed, Rose suggests, they are therefore perhaps more accurately described not as 'Kantians', but rather as 'Fichteans'. So, for instance, she speaks of the 'latent Fichteanism' of classical sociology.[56]

Then, though, came a change of public mood, a general resurgence of cultural conservatism, and Fichte's career at Jena was cut short by controversy. He lost his job there, driven out by enemies who accused him of 'atheism'. (Never emollient, he had also taken to delivering Sunday morning public lectures, as a gesture of defiance against the Jena clergy.) He indignantly protested that he was not an 'atheist'. But what positive idea did he have of the divine?

On the one hand, Fichte worships the transcendent authority of the categorical imperative: the imperative, in Kant's formulation, to 'act only on that maxim through which you can at the same time will that it should become a universal law'. In other words, he affirms the abstract sacredness of sheer moral consistency as such. On the other hand, he identifies divine inspiration with the outworking – discernible to some extent within all human life – of what, in his Jena writings, he calls the 'absolute', 'pure' or 'transcendental' ego. In his later writings he adopts other terminology for this sacred principle; there he calls it, variously, 'the infinite Will', 'Life' or 'Being'. The later terminology has the advantage of being more distanced from anthropomorphic, mythic notions of God. However, the earlier formulations more directly capture the core polemical thrust of the Fichtean vision. For he is thinking about the character-development of any finite ego: how this unfolds as an interplay between active and passive-reactive impulses. And by the 'absolute ego' he means the energy at work in all of the former. That is: the 'absolute', in the sense of the purely active – not passive-reactive – impulses to ego formation. The 'absolute ego' includes all the energy of human life, insofar as it remains (as Fichte would see it) untainted by any passive-reactive accommodation to the world – or, therefore, by any peace-negotiative compromise with other people.

Thus, Fichte represents the most decisive possible repudiation of the 'broken middle', precisely generalized as the first principle of ethics. In the end, he values just two things: strict altruistic moral *rationality* as defined by the categorical imperative, and moral *spontaneity*, pure self-identification with the 'absolute ego'. He is concerned, above all, to disentangle the fresh inspiration of the 'absolute ego' from all the various limitations it undergoes, resulting in general from our passive reactions to the given natural and cultural environment in which we find ourselves. Therefore, true wisdom, for him, springs from a twofold basic refusal either, in a spirit of mere fatalism, merely to submit to the influence of one's natural environment, or, out of gratitude, to accept any aspect of one's given cultural tradition as having real authority over one. By the 'absolute ego' he means, in both regards, the latent sheer rebel within each one of us. The sole authority he is prepared to recognize as authentically divine is the summons of the utopian future, towards which the sheer infinite negativity of the 'absolute ego' presses, with absolute impatience, ever onwards.

Here, then we have secular humanism at its most revolutionary. Fichte repudiates the brokenness of the 'broken middle' for the sublime innocence of one who has cut himself altogether free from the religion and politics of the past. A man always very conscious of his plebeian origins – he owed his education, as a child, entirely to the generosity of a local nobleman who had happened to spot his intelligence – he was driven, as a result, by a furious *ressentiment* against every sort of privileged establishment. As a young man he welcomed the French Revolution with fiery enthusiasm, and wrote polemical tracts in praise of it. He himself directly linked the abstract radicalism of his metaphysics to this political impulse: it was, he once wrote, 'while I was doing a work on the Revolution [that] the first signs, the first hints of my system welled up inside me'.[57] On the other hand he emphatically rejected Napoleonic imperialism as a terrible betrayal of the Revolution, and in the period of the Napoleonic Wars he turned to German nationalism, to be a new vehicle for his revolutionary passions. He was also a pioneering socialist thinker. But his nationalism and his socialism were always framed by a ferocious belief in philosopher-rule. Fichte was anything but a liberal democrat. Like Marx after him, he looked forward to an eventual withering away of the state – made possible by a decisive refashioning of human nature by the enlightened governance of Fichtean philosopher-rulers, such that there would no longer be any need for coercion. In the meantime, though, so as to effect the necessary transformation in human nature, the state as a whole, he argued, must be converted into a systematic pedagogic enterprise, backed up by the very sternest discipline. The Fichtean philosopher is one who has learnt to break free from the 'dogmatism' of old habits and old loyalties simply by virtue of an inner theoretical self-identification with the 'absolute ego'. Other people, however, lacking the philosopher's capacity for inner transformation by theory, must be liberated from 'dogmatism' by force, instead. In his political writings Fichte looks a bit like an early precursor of Maoism. He invokes the authority of Kant, to argue for a permanent frenzy of cultural revolution.

Of course, Kant's own form of secular humanism is far milder.[58] However, this political mildness of Kant's is bound up with his very dubious dogmatic agnosticism. Hegel, by contrast, stands for quite a different sort of liberal alternative to the stark logical coherence of the Fichtean vision, precisely because of the much deeper rootedness of his liberalism in secularized Christian *Sittlichkeit*. And Rose, for her part, places especial emphasis on Hegel's early critique of Fichte, as the germ out of which his mature thinking, generally, then grows.

Thus, when in 1801 Hegel arrived in Jena to take up the humble role of *Privatdozent* at the university, it was not much more than a year and a half since Fichte's dramatic dismissal. Hitherto, he had largely been in sympathy with Fichte's original counterposing of 'religion' to 'theology'; now however, along with his two friends, the poet Hölderlin and the young philosopher-prodigy Schelling, he began to develop an, at least implicitly, much more 'theological', as well as metaphysical, critique of Fichte. Rose traces the trajectory of this critique through his essays on 'Natural Law', the 'System of *Sittlichkeit*', 'The Difference between Fichte's and Schelling's System of Philosophy' and 'Faith and Knowledge', and on into his two great works, the *Phenomenology* and the *Logic*.

Whereas in the *Phenomenology* Hegel is developing not only an un-Fichtean philosophical point of view, but also a quite un-Fichtean basic conception of what philosophy might include, in the *Logic* he goes back, as it were, to tackle Fichte on Fichte's own territory of pure metaphysics. So the *Logic*, like Fichte's *Wissenschaftslehre*, serves to frame a systematic programme for thinking, in general, understood as a pursuit of truth-as-correctness. But, as I have said, the *Phenomenology* differs in that it traces the path of Spirit towards a perfectly articulate sacralization of truth-as-Honesty instead.[59] Again, a proposition judged by the criteria of truth-as-correctness may be either true or false, simply in itself. The criteria of truth-as-Honesty, by contrast, compel one to consider the conversational context. For at this level one and the same proposition may sometimes be true and at other times false, entirely depending on who is talking to whom, and how. What I am calling 'Honesty' is the truth not of propositions considered abstractly in themselves, but of whole conversations insofar as they bring fresh insight. Or it is the truth of whole lives, insofar as they are lived 'in the truth', ideally opened up towards others. Fichte's idea of Truth combines two elements: the supposed metaphysical truth-as-correctness of the *Wissenschaftslehre* – expressive of a consistent irreverence towards 'nature' and tradition – plus a blazing, moralistic sincerity. Yet, such sincerity is not yet necessarily Honest, in the sense that Honesty is what comes to its ideal articulation in 'absolute knowing'. For I repeat, 'absolute knowing', as analysed in the *Phenomenology*, essentially involves a maximum *open-mindedness*. That, after all, is what the *Phenomenology* studies: it is primarily a systematic survey of attitudinal obstacles, as such, to an ideal reciprocity of communication, on every different level of consciousness. But how open-minded, really, is Fichtean sincerity?

The *Phenomenology* is an exposition of the open-conversational ideal of 'absolute knowing'; the *Logic*, on the other hand, is an exposition of the 'absolute *idea*'. By 'absolute knowing' Hegel means the truth-ideal that is properly shared between philosophy and theology. But the 'absolute idea', by contrast, is the truth of pure metaphysics *as opposed to theology*. Abstracted from any phenomenological consideration of conversational context, Hegel's celebration of the 'absolute idea' is on the same level as Fichte's celebration of the 'absolute ego', and is in that sense a much more direct counter-thrust to it. Fichte's *Wissenschaftslehre*, as distinct from his more 'popular' writing, is a pioneering new form of metaphysics, in that it effectively *brackets* all questions of theology. Here we have metaphysics re-emergent after the Kantian negation of traditional metaphysics. And, unlike traditional pre-Kantian metaphysics, it is not about the God of revealed religion, the God of *Sittlichkeit* and theology. It scarcely speaks of 'God' at all. So Fichte seeks to step back from any theory either positively or negatively locked into the presuppositions of a particular form of *Sittlichkeit*. He sets out to specify the proper logical criteria for assessing intellectual and moral practice in the most purely trans-theological sort of terms.[60] This, in itself, surely *is* a great liberation of metaphysical Reason, and Hegel in the *Logic* does the same. In sharp contrast to theology, which deals with the self-revelation of God in history, the *Logic*, he remarks, regarded from a theistic point of view, is 'the exposition of God as he is in his eternal essence before the creation of nature and a finite mind'.[61] Certainly, for any believer in God, it has to do with God, inasmuch as God is Truth, and all pursuit of truth is therefore a drawing closer to God. Yet what appears here is God, so to speak, only implicitly made manifest. That is to say, it is God outside the proper domain of theological explicitness, 'before the creation' of that domain. The *Logic* just does not impinge upon theology, as a study of God at work in *Sittlichkeit*, in any way. Nor does it by any means *require* to be regarded from a theistic point of view. There is nothing in its core argument that a non-theist, as such, would find impossible to accept.

To this extent the *Logic* and the *Wissenschaftslehre* are doing the same thing: both, alike, systematically separate metaphysics from theology. But Hegel only, in fact, moves onto Fichte's territory the better to clarify his absolute rejection of Fichte's polemical stance, along with all that is akin to it. Thus, both the *Logic* and the *Wissenschaftslehre* are systematically trans-theological celebratory accounts of the pursuit of truth-as-correctness, in general. But the basis for the celebration is quite different in each case. Hegel celebrates the labour of theoretical reflection purely and simply for its own sake, as an opening up towards the intrinsic complexity of experience. Hence the systematic structure of the *Logic*, which surveys the key vocabulary of trans-theological metaphysics, term by term, arranged in sequence of ever more complex intrinsic meaning, ascending towards the supreme complexity of the 'absolute idea'. The elementary moral of the book lies in this structure: 'the more thinking', it simply says, 'the better'. Fichte's argument however differs in that he celebrates the labour of theoretical reflection, fundamentally, as a contribution to something else. He is *not* just saying, 'the more thinking the better'. But he is saying, 'we need to think through the overthrow of "dogmatism"'; which, for him, by definition includes all traditional *Sittlichkeit* as such. The whole point of Fichte's (dogmatically anti-'dogmatic'!) doctrine of the 'absolute ego' – quite unlike Hegel's doctrine of the 'absolute idea' – is thus to close down the scope for theology. They agree about the need to separate metaphysics from theology; but, in sharp contrast to Hegel, who then seeks to refound theology on the quite different basis set out in the *Phenomenology*, Fichte for his part simply wants to abolish it.

The radical one-sidedness of Fichte's thought actually emerges both in the way he understands the ultimate origin of all meaning and in the way he understands the ultimate goal of all interpretation. 'Our task' – he writes at the beginning of his key treatise, *Foundations of the Entire Science of Knowledge* (1794) – 'is to *discover* the primordial, absolutely unconditioned first principle of all human knowledge'. In the first instance, this means our conceptualizing the origination of all meaning as a creative 'Act' (*Tathandlung*, Fichte's own coinage, literally 'fact-act'): an 'Act'

> which does not and cannot appear among the empirical states of our consciousness, but rather lies at the basis of all consciousness and alone makes it possible.[62]

The creative agent from whose 'Act' all the true meaningfulness of things derives, according to Fichte, is the 'absolute ego'. What makes the world meaningful – he argues, in other words – is just the seething rebelliousness of this primordial principle, in all its perfectly unconditioned original spontaneity; in Hegelian terms, outside all *Sittlichkeit*. The 'absolute ego' is not 'God' in any conventional sense. But it is, Fichte thinks, what the symbol of the divine Creator properly represents – fundamentally subverting everything conventional as such. The treatise as a whole is a wondrously elaborate, or verbose, purely abstract analysis of the 'Act' by which the 'absolute ego' may be said to enter into reality by making things meaningful, and to give things meaning through the process of realizing itself. Or, in Fichte's own terminology, it traces the dialectical interplay between the '*self-positing*' of the 'absolute ego' – emerging into human consciousness, progressing towards self-knowledge – and the 'absolute ego's' concomitant interpretative '*positing*' of the 'not-self'. That is, the process by which the whole world of nature and cultural tradition is supposedly given its true meaning, or reality – essentially, as a set of constraints to be battled against and overcome. Fichte here sets out to show the all-encompassing necessary interdependence of these two processes: creativity as inventiveness (self-positing), and creativity as constant rebellion (against every limitation imposed by the not-self). Although the *Wissenschaftslehre*, as such, is not a doctrine about God, Fichte protests he is no atheist. The Fichtean 'scientific' notion of the 'absolute ego' and its creative 'Act' need not altogether rule out more popular talk of creation by 'God', and Fichte himself in his later writings also indulges in more popular, religious-Esperanto rhetoric, invoking the supposed will of God. But what this doctrine, most emphatically, does preclude is any attribution of authority to an actual heritage of theological *Sittlichkeit*. Indeed, as I have said, that is really the chief practical point of the doctrine. This primordial 'Act' of 'self-positing', attributed to the 'absolute ego', is, to all intents and purposes, nothing other than the very boldest possible back-projection of the self-assertive, self-defining disdain felt by the Fichtean philosophical elite towards traditional, popular religion. While it does not negate all God-talk, it absolutely does negate theology, in the sense that theology is what exceeds religious Esperanto, to incorporate the philosopher into a larger catholic community. The *Wissenschaftslehre* begins, in effect, by elevating that prejudice to the status of supreme fount of all meaning. So it represents a spirit of defiant adolescent arrogance, systematically moralized and sacralized. Such is its radicalism.

For Hegel, on the other hand, the primordial 'Act', from which all true meaning flows, is the self-unfolding of the 'absolute idea': an unlimited opening up towards the actual complexity of experience; and therefore an unlimited opening up towards all manner of peace-negotiative conversation. The key difference between the two doctrines already emerges here, in these opposing definitions of true meaningfulness. Hegel, right from the outset, seeks metaphysically to hold open the sort of conversation, between philosophers and non-philosophers, which only religious *Sittlichkeit* makes possible. Whereas Fichte, right from the outset, seeks to close it down, and replace it with the dismissive simplicities of his religious Esperanto.

And then, in both cases alike, the primordial 'Act' is the inauguration of an infinite task for thinking; it points towards an infinitely demanding goal. Only, as Hegel insists, the infinity of the 'absolute idea' is in fact a completely opposite sort of infinity to that of the 'absolute ego'. The former represents an infinite peace-negotiative patience with conflicting theoretical claims; so it takes shape as the infinite enrichment of a certain criss-crossing pattern. But the latter, in its character as an endless sheer repudiation of authoritative tradition, is a line disappearing off into the distance, running away. At any rate in that regard, the infinity of the 'absolute ego' is not an infinity of enrichment, but just an infinity of extension. Judged from the point of view of the 'absolute idea', it actually begins to look like the summons to a labour of Sisyphus, a panicky nightmare. In Hegel's own phrase, it is a 'bad infinite'.

What – one might therefore wonder – makes a doctrine infused with this type of spirit historically possible? In the *Phenomenology* Hegel discusses the doctrine of Kant and Fichte, essentially, as a *symptom*. Or, rather, he alludes to it; he speaks of their secular humanism as the 'moral view of the world'.[63] And he sets it in a highly impressionistic historical narrative. Rose cites Lukács, who once described Fichte as the 'supreme representative of bourgeois thought'. In this judgement, she remarks, Lukács is very close to Hegel.[64] Moreover, she herself also concurs with the judgement. So, for Hegel, Fichte is the most radical of all apologists for 'bourgeois' culture, the spiritual home of secular humanism, understood as the culmination of a process that begins in the culture of pagan Rome. Loosely contrasting Ancient Greece and Ancient Rome, Hegel sees the former as a world of warm *Sittlichkeit*, the latter as a world in which *Sittlichkeit* had to a large extent cooled. Thus, in his portrayal, the Ancient Greek *polis* appears as the paradigm of a whole political community bonded by strong emotional ties of mutual loyalty, in which there is minimal need for coercion, and human dignity is largely identified with free participation in public life. But Ancient Rome appears as the paradigm of the opposite: a world governed by ruthless coercion, where the cause of human dignity is identified, above all, with the defence of private property rights. And 'bourgeois' culture, then, is the heir to Ancient Rome, not only holding fast to the culture-specific presuppositions of Roman law as if they were the very law of Nature itself, but also reinforcing them with the specific cultural legacy of the Enlightenment. Until, at length, this legacy generates the murderous frenzy of the French Revolution and all that follows, both politically and intellectually; that whole series of destructive blows against *Sittlichkeit* in Christian form.

The most distinctive essential truth of the Christian gospel, on the other hand – Hegel thinks – lies in the deep meaning of the incarnation, faith's perception of God apparent in the figure of a representative human individual, understood as a symbolic revelation of the infinite intrinsic value of all human individuality. Beyond the merely cerebral inner freedom of 'stoicism', and the merely playful inner freedom of 'scepticism', true Christian faith, interpreted this way, is in his view precisely the most radical challenge to all kinds of inner despotism. And so it is the ideal proper basis for the 'principle of subjectivity'; that is, the actual political championing of the rights of the human individual, as such, in every form. Again, let us recall his great endorsement of political modernity:

> The principle of modern states has prodigious strength and depth because it allows the principle of subjectivity to progress to its culmination . . . and yet at the same time brings it back to the substantive unity [incorporates it into a living tradition of *Sittlichkeit*], and so maintains this unity in the principle of subjectivity itself.[65]

Here is the political ideal now in fact made possible, as never before, by the evolution in potential Christian self-understanding which Hegel discerns and advocates; it is a wishful programmatic invocation of what would happen, if only the resultant true Christianity were to gain serious power. But, apart from the obstinate persistence of more primitive forms of Christian theology, the other great obstacle to this happening is that 'bourgeois' culture, in general, is all too *irreligiously* individualistic.

In the *Phenomenology* militant irreligious individualism appears in a number of sometimes overlapping popular variations.[66] One type is a crude hedonism. Another is the sentimental 'law of the heart', moral nonconformity with a strong admixture of self-dramatization. Yet another is an expression of puritanical self-righteousness: the 'knight of virtue' who rejects any organized expression of *Sittlichkeit* out of sheer exaggerated intolerance for the inevitable elements of worldliness which are always liable to get mixed up in it. To be sure, Kant and Fichte are not endorsing any of these attitudes. But to what extent is their 'moral view of the world' a truly *effective* alternative to them? That is the question.

Hegel has an, at first sight, rather curious way of speaking about the life of a whole moral culture negatively defined by its simple lack of a strong *Sittlichkeit*. He calls it an approximation to the '*spiritual animal kingdom*'.[67] The 'spiritual animal kingdom' is human life considered simply in its resemblance to the life of other animals; in this fictional 'kingdom', therefore, individuals are characterized not at all by their cultural, historic loyalties, but solely by their natural temperaments and innate abilities. Nor is there any truly authoritative criterion, of the kind supplied by *Sittlichkeit*, for objective judgement of people's actions, whether in terms of their purposes, their choice of means, or the actual results. The one and only widely accepted universal requirement here is that people should be free to do whatever they themselves determine is their own 'thing' (*die Sache selbst*). 'Judge not, that you be not judged', said Jesus. But this, itself, is a judgement. It is a rejection, in Hegel's terminology, of the 'hard-heart'. That is, the mentality of those who adopt an extremely judgemental attitude towards others, basically, as a form of pre-emptive self-defence against their criticisms.[68] The 'spiritual animal kingdom', on the other hand, is a world in which there is no practical capacity for truly serious moral judgement of any kind. Not even for the judgement that rejects the judgemental stance of the 'hard-heart'. Whereas the 'hard-heart' aggressively protests its innocence, the gentler inhabitants of the 'spiritual animal kingdom' enjoy something not unlike the 'animal' innocence of Adam and Eve before the Fall. Each pursues their own 'thing', but, whatever it may be, it is never in reality anything much more serious than a hobby – it cannot be, because by definition this is a world without the proper means of making life more serious. Of course, Kant and Fichte for their part are committed to the very utmost moral seriousness! Only, for Hegel, again the question is: does their brand of pure secular humanism have the real *imaginative/emotional power* needed actually to lift people – not just philosophers like themselves, but people in general – out of the latent 'spiritual animal kingdom' pervasively underlying bourgeois modernity? He contends that it does not. In the end, the trouble with secular humanism is that it fails to rehumanize the dehumanized inhabitants of the 'spiritual animal kingdom'. Nothing else can do the job, on any large scale, as well as true, well-rooted religion can.

'Hegel's battle with Fichte', Rose remarks in summary, 'was fought on two fronts'. First 'it was fought against Fichte's positing reflection (*setzen*) because positing was indeterminate and could not recognise real determinations'. In other words, it was a struggle against Fichte's metaphysical notion of wisdom as a self-identification with the self-positing of the 'absolute ego' – inasmuch as this represents a glorified mere prejudice against everything which determines the actual givenness of who we really are, as historically situated individuals. And then the battle was also fought 'against Fichte's theory of (natural) law (*Gesetz*), for Fichte gave *legality* [in the sense of secular governmental ideology], not morality [in the sense of *Sittlichkeit*], the prime task of welding together the [enlightened] ego and [social] non-ego, the general will and the [actual] community of rational beings, [the true] concept [of justice] and [the everyday, common sense guidance of] intuition'.[69]

The Fichtean utopia is supposed to be brought about by the revolutionary action of a state apparatus which is set over against civil society as a legal mechanism, *in no way morally integrated with it*. Indeed, the whole point of Fichte's argument is that the state ought *not* to be morally integrated with what it has to transform. Integration with civil society, for Fichte, can only mean counter-revolutionary corruption, selling out to the enemy. But Hegel takes the opposite view. What Fichte demands here is just what Hegel deplores in the progression from pagan Rome to modern bourgeois culture as a whole; Hegel sees Fichte's proto-Maoist dream as the ultimate culmination of that trajectory, and he shudders at the prospect. Fichte is the 'supreme representative of bourgeois thought' in the sense that the bourgeoisie are the would-be, or actual, ruling class of a world in which traditional bonds of *Sittlichkeit* have largely lost their authority, and have been replaced, as a basis for civilized life, by contracts and coercion alone. He is the 'supreme' representative of such thinking by virtue of his sheer systematic extremism. And, in his extremism, he is also the great bourgeois-intellectual forerunner of totalitarian ideology. For what else is totalitarian ideology if not bourgeois thought (in this sense) masquerading as the revolutionary cause of the nation, or of the proletariat, and infused with a tremendous impatience for spectacular effects?

Rejecting any such revolutionary aspirations, the Hegelian ideal is, on the contrary, a renewed form of religious faith, capable precisely of reintegrating modern civil society, at its most free-spirited, with the state. 'In general', he argues, religion and the foundation of the state is one and the same thing; they are identical in and for themselves.[70]

As Rose remarks, this is intended neither as a straightforward description of any actual historical reality, nor as a simple prescription, according to the usual common-sense understanding of the key terms, 'religion' and 'state'. Rather, it is what Hegel calls a 'speculative proposition'.

'Speculative' for Hegel (as indeed for Fichte before him) is a word with the most positive connotations. A 'speculative proposition' is one the whole purpose of which is to call into question the meaning of its key terms, bring them into a dance together, refresh them, and energize them. It is the opening up of a certain force field of ideas, or a certain sort of 'middle' in that sense. But in bourgeois modernity this particular 'middle' – between 'religion' and the 'foundation of the state' – is 'broken'. Rose puts it very starkly:

> The identity of religion and the state is the fundamental speculative proposition of Hegel's thought, or, and this is to say the same thing, the *speculative experience of the lack of identity* between religion and the state is the basic object of Hegel's exposition.[71]

The 'speculative proposition' defines Hegel's peace-negotiative project, the 'middle' to which he is committed; the 'speculative experience' is his resultant exposure to the 'brokenness' of that 'middle'. Hegelian wisdom, at any rate as Rose understands and affirms it, is none other than the experience of that exposure at its most intense, the anguish of 'the speculative Good Friday'.

With regard to Hegel's own personal appropriation of this 'speculative experience', Rose (following Emil Fackenheim) focuses especially on the closing passage of his 1821 manuscript version of the Berlin *Lectures on the Philosophy of Religion*.[72] Again, in this passage Hegel compares the contemporary bourgeois world to pagan Rome. And, again, he deplores the influence of hard-line Enlightenment secularism. But he also criticizes modern theological apologists for Christian faith, such as his colleague Friedrich Schleiermacher, who in effect depoliticize the gospel by presenting it essentially as a matter of *private* religious 'feeling'. For how can this serve as the 'foundation of the state'? And he attacks the clergy. He complains of sermons that are nothing but a dry account of biblical and church history as such, lacking any real connection with the present-day sufferings and problems of the community. Also, of church teaching on ethics which is all 'harshness, objective commands', that is to say, establishment pomposity. And of forms of piety in which Christian faith is reduced to the merest sentimental complacency:

> Where the gospel is not preached to the poor, who are the ones closest to infinite anguish; where the teaching of love in infinite anguish is abandoned in favour of enjoyment, love without anguish; where the gospel is preached in a naturalistic way – there the salt has lost its savour [Matthew 5.13].[73]

The Lutheran laity – he declares – is being betrayed by their church. And so now it becomes the vocation of philosophy, as a haven apart, to try and rescue Christian truth from its official guardians.

> Religion must take refuge in philosophy . . . But philosophy . . . is also partial: it forms an isolated order of priests – a sanctuary – who are untroubled about how it goes with the world, who need not mix with it, and whose work is to preserve this possession of truth. How things turn out in the world is not our affair.[74]

To judge from this, it might indeed seem that having measured out the 'broken middle' between 'religion' and the 'foundation of the state', in the end, Hegel finds it all too much to cope with. He himself calls it a 'discordant note' on which to conclude.[75]

Yet it is only a momentary lapse. The fact is that 1821 was a year of rather bleak immediate political prospects for a political liberal like him. The Prussian government was growing more and more reactionary, and twitchy; a number of his close associates were under police investigation, on suspicion of being subversives. That moment having passed, in later versions of these *Lectures* (those dating from 1824, 1827 and 1831) the 'discordant note' has been removed.[76] Not that he has become any less critical of contemporary church life. Only, he no longer permits himself *any* flinching – not even this kind of purely rhetorical flinching – from the 'middle' he has mapped.

⤳❋⤶

And then – in addition to the basic sort of challenge to traditional *Sittlichkeit* primarily represented, for Rose, by Kant and Fichte – there is also the challenge of what she calls '*nihilism*'.

The difference between these two directly corresponds to the distinction I have suggested between the critical impulses of 'secular humanism' and 'self-expressive nonconformity'. For just as Kant and Fichte represent the impulse of 'secular humanism' at its most intransigent, so, likewise, 'nihilism', in Rose's sense of the term, represents the impulse of 'self-expressive nonconformity' allowed absolute dominance over everything else.

Thus, both Kantianism/Fichteanism and 'nihilism' are premised on a wholesale repudiation of traditional religious loyalties. But the simple difference is that whereas Kant and Fichte justify this with an invocation of self-denying love for all humanity, immediately understood in political terms as a project for overcoming traditional religious divisions between people, 'nihilism' by contrast begins, far rather, from an originally pre-political affirmation of creative, nonconformist self-expression as such. That is to say: it is definable as a species of thinking that sets out, systematically and absolutely, to dissolve everything in one's ordinary, pre-political sense of 'self' that has, on the contrary, been *im*pressed upon one from outside. And it differs from 'secular humanism' in that this includes not only the given-ness of traditional religious identities but also, just as much, the given-ness of traditionally understood humanist ideals.

Nietzsche once boastfully described himself as 'the first perfect nihilist of Europe who, however, has even now lived through the whole of nihilism, to the end, leaving it behind, outside himself'.[77] In *Dialectic of Nihilism* Rose adopts the term from Nietzsche. And she approves of Nietzsche's aspiration, at any rate, to point beyond his own 'nihilistic' repudiation of Christianity – rather as the early Christian Church itself went beyond its 'nihilistic' repudiation of Classical paganism, and managed to found a whole new alternative form of *Sittlichkeit*, to replace the old one. But the evidence seems to suggest that, in Nietzsche's case, it is a futile aspiration. For even where the Christian Church is most of all in decline, this is not because it is losing out to any new alternative form of *Sittlichkeit*, as Classical paganism did. What is in decline here is not just Christianity, but rather *Sittlichkeit* itself. The Jacobins, the Communists, the Fascists and the Nazis all failed in their bids to replace the Church; the crass violence of these movements reflects their fundamental incapacity; and, unlike them, Nietzsche lacks even the rudiments of an organizational strategy for the purpose. Still, for Rose, it nevertheless does count in his favour that he was so discontented within the limitations of his 'nihilism', and so keen to 'leave it behind' in this way. The thinkers that she really wants to attack are Nietzsche's – in her view, altogether more complacent – intellectual heirs.

Her main targets are, in fact, first *Heidegger*, and then the French: *Deleuze, Derrida* and *Foucault*. Is the attack fair? She certainly shows no sympathy for any of the French trio. But let us, at any rate, note the I think rather interesting critical move she makes in relation particularly to Heidegger – as she sets his critique of metaphysics into the context (which he, in his constant preoccupation with things Greek or German, never considers) of ancient Hebrew thought.

Nietzsche dreams of being a moral legislator, on the grandest possible scale; the Nietzschean notion of 'nihilism' belongs to a grand narrative, an account of history which is intended, however implausibly in this case, to serve, somehow, as inspiration for a popular movement of revolutionary *Sittlichkeit*-founding hope. And, unlike the later French trio, but like Nietzsche, Heidegger is also very much a grand-narrative thinker. It is just that, following his traumatic disillusionment with (mainstream) Nazism, he develops a distinctly less hopeful, and to that extent more straight-forwardly 'nihilist', form of grand narrative than Nietzsche's.

Heidegger has two primary terms for the truth of what I am calling 'self-expressive nonconformity', belonging to different periods in his career. At first, in *Being and Time*, he speaks of it as *Eigentlichkeit*, 'authenticity'. But in his later writing he calls it *Gelassenheit*, usually translated 'releasement'. This shift in termi-nology is a direct result of his brief period as a Nazi revolutionary activist, immediately following Hitler's seizure of power in 1933; by contrast to *Eigentlichkeit*, the notion of *Gelassenheit*, which he develops afterwards, has a strong flavour of radical withdrawal from political activism of any kind. Yet Heideggerian *Gelassenheit* is still a form of self-expressive nonconformity, it still means a proper owning of what is most distinctively one's own. The stem *eigen*, meaning 'own', which was there in *Eigentlichkeit*, recurs in that key term of his later thought, *das Ereignis*, meaning 'the Event', the revelatory advent of *Gelassenheit*. (*Ereignis* is the ordinary German word for 'event', but Heidegger seeks to invest it with hitherto unheard-of significance by focusing on the element of *eigen* within it: 'the Event' in which revealed truth is truly 'owned'.) In Heidegger's trans-metaphysical thinking, what 'the Event' reveals is the truth of 'Being'. But then his grand narrative is none other than a history of humanity's progressive *forgetfulness* of that truth. All the established popular religious traditions of the modern world, without exception, are essentially seen as aggravating symptoms of such forgetfulness. And so this grand narrative is, not least, a systematic undermining of their authority.

At the same time, though, Heidegger also criticizes purely metaphysical philosophy for its spiritual superficiality. As a designation for the 'God' of pure metaphysics he adopts the Latin technical term, *causa sui*, the 'self-caused'. And he complains,

> Man can neither pray nor sacrifice to this god. Before the *causa sui*, man can neither fall to his knees in awe nor can he play music and dance before this god.
>
> The god-less thinking which must abandon the god of philosophy, god as *causa sui*, is thus perhaps closer to the divine God . . .[78]

There is of course a very widespread and, research indicates, steadily growing tendency these days for people to identify themselves as 'spiritual' but not 'religious'. By which they mean that they reject all forms of organized religious belonging, and have no interest in any sort of metaphysically framed doctrinal orthodoxy, but see these as mere obstacles to a proper communion with what is truly sacred. This is not how Heidegger himself expresses it. But it is nevertheless exactly what he stands for. He, basically, represents the current consumerist fashion for 'post-religious spirituality', at its most sophisticated. (Or, one might perhaps say, at its most mystified.) Rose calls it 'magical nihilism'.[79]

And yet – what else is such 'spirituality', after all, if not just another spurious bid for innocence?

The 'spiritual' person who rejects 'religion' no longer has any very troubling relationship with the religious past; is able simply to denounce past injustices, committed in the name of religion, secure in a sense of not being in any way involved or answerable for them. Heidegger's claim is to have adopted the most *thoughtful* of all possible stances, a stance of maximum openness to the provocation of whatever may prove most thought-provoking. It is certainly a thought-provoking claim to make. But Rose wants to make a direct counter-claim.

As it happens, Heidegger's remarks, cited above, about the 'god of philosophy' and the 'divine God' come in the course of a lecture, delivered in 1957, on Hegel's *Logic*. In this lecture he claims to have gone decisively beyond Hegel by virtue of the unprecedented 'step back' he has accomplished: 'the step back', as he puts it, 'out of metaphysics into its essential nature'.[80] But what exactly is meant by 'metaphysics' here? It seems that we need to distinguish between two quite different levels of meaning which are systematically mixed together in the Heideggerian usage of the term. In what one might call sense (a), 'metaphysics' may be defined as

> any sort of thinking about the purposes of thinking in general insofar as it focuses not on the demands of existential truth, that is truth-as-Honesty, but is concerned, *instead*, exclusively with questions of truth-as-correctness.

This is how I have been using the term, above. And for much of the time it is also what Heidegger means. But, as noted above, the fact is, Hegel in the *Phenomenology* is already 'stepping back' from metaphysics in this sense. In just the same way that the Heideggerian notions of 'authenticity' and 'releasement' are essentially interpretations of truth-as-Honesty, so too is the Hegelian notion of 'absolute knowing'. And therefore, if Hegel is, despite this, still to be declared a thinker trapped within the limitations of 'metaphysics', then it can only be in quite a different sense (b), where the category of 'metaphysics' has in effect been expanded to include

> absolutely every form of philosophy that does not fit Heidegger's own 'magical nihilist' agenda!

What is Heidegger's 'step back'? It is a step back, not only out of metaphysics in sense (a), but *also*, (b) precisely, out of the 'broken middle'; a step back into an option for illusory innocence.

Although, to be sure, Heidegger's 'step back' does not signify anything as simple as a straightforward return to an earlier stage of the Western intellectual tradition, it does, he thinks, make possible a renewed connection with the at least somewhat *pre-*'metaphysical' thought of the very earliest Greek philosophers. Rose, however, seeks to bring Heidegger into connection with what is after all an even older source of Western tradition. For where he speaks of the 'divine God', as opposed to the metaphysically conceived 'god of philosophy', this, in itself, might surely also be taken as a description of *Yahweh*, the God of ancient Israel. And so why does he not even begin to consider that other tradition? Here, she suggests, we actually come up against the very essence of his nihilism. 'Heidegger', she remarks,

> seems to give us *Yahweh* without *Torah*: the event [*Ereignis*] seems to include advent and redemption, presence and owning, but not the giving of the law on Mount Sinai, and its repeated disowning.[81]

'*Yahweh* without *Torah*': Heidegger invokes the 'divine God' beyond all metaphysics, but has no real commitment to anything like the tough peace-negotiative work of *halacha*, the detailed legislative exegesis and development of what is said to have been initiated on Mount Sinai, within a living tradition of *Sittlichkeit*.

Why not? The true *Yahweh*, the *Yahweh* of *Torah* and prophecy from Amos onwards, is radically distinguished from all other ancient gods, first and foremost, by the sheer relentless fury with which he forbids his people any illusion either of corporate innocence, or of individual non-involvement in corporate sin. As for the actual implementation of sacred tradition, it is forever negotiable. But the *non-negotiable core truth* of the Sinaitic, and post-

Sinaitic, revelation of *Yahweh* is just this elementary turning away from the desire to be accounted innocent, as distinct from the quite different desire to be just. And that, in the final analysis, is what it seems Heidegger – along with all those others who today exalt 'spirituality' over 'religion' – cannot accept.

Against Heidegger, Rose wants to insist that the true 'divine God' can only be that God who, most of all, forbids us any illusion of innocence. Beyond all differences of metaphysical 'correctness', in other words, the God of the very deepest thoughtfulness is actually one whom Heidegger as a nihilist cannot recognize, any more than Kant or Fichte and their militant secular humanist followers can: the God of the 'broken middle'.

5

Against Modern 'Gnosticism'

❧

I have already referred to Rose's discussion of what she calls the 'anxiety of beginning', in relation to Kierkegaard and Freud. But she also develops that concept in other contexts. Indeed, she regards the willing endurance of such anxiety as the prime philosophic virtue; the 'beginning' in question here is none other than a beginning properly to occupy the 'broken middle'. Thus, this is the dissident courage that essentially distinguishes the true mediating peacemaker, installed in that 'middle'.

To be truly opened up to – and by – the 'anxiety of beginning' is, on the one hand, to value dissident free-spiritedness very much *for its own sake*, as a challenging of clichés. Not every free-spirited dissident does this. Rose cites especially Kierkegaard's verdict on Luther, in this regard. The way Kierkegaard sees it, Luther was a free-spirited dissident who however, in the end, simply sought to replace one form of oppressive *Sittlichkeit* with another, just as rigidly insistent on the imposition of its own orthodoxy.

> Instead of 'arousing restlessness' and making spiritual life 'more strenuous', Luther makes it soothing and reassuring. Transfiguration of anguish, which occurred in Luther's own case after twenty years of fear and trembling, is universalised by Protestantism so that it is made available for all – without any 'one' undergoing the intensity of Luther's testing.[1]

Rose agrees with Kierkegaard. In his intolerance of dissent, Luther, as she puts it, 'explicitly abolishes anxiety of beginning'.[2] And so Lutheranism – even Lutheranism! – tends to become an ethos of easy warm consensus; part of what Kierkegaard calls 'Christendom'. That is, it becomes an all too immediately peaceable piety, leaving nothing to be negotiated, no real way in for the Holy Spirit.

But there is, on the other hand, no true exposure to the anxiety of beginning, either, if the free-spirited self-expressive individual remains *disengaged* from the actual inner struggles of organized ethical (*sittlich*) community. Already well before her own incorporation, by baptism, into the Church Rose is convinced, in principle, of the need for intellectuals to be fully incorporated into such community; and to frame their thought in terms of that belonging, with all its inevitable stresses. One is not yet properly exposed to the true 'equivocation of the middle', as she understands it, if one's only real loyalty is to a narrow affinity group, or to a loose communion of like-minded friends and allies. For this is much too sheltered, much too innocent-seeming a posture.

And neither is it only the radical disengagement of 'nihilism' that she repudiates. What she wants to affirm really is the very fullest free-spirited engagement with the difficulties of *sittlich* belonging. So it is not enough, for her, just to affirm a theoretic appreciation of the spiritual truth at the heart of biblical tradition, while remaining, as it were, at a safe distance from the actual mess of existing religious life. But to be opened up to – and by – the 'anxiety of beginning' is to be plunged straight in.

She is therefore very critical, also, of those in the modern world whom she calls '*Gnostics*'; devout folk who want to preserve their innocent detachment from any ecclesiastical, or rabbinic, institution.

'Gnosticism', in the broad sense she intends here, might perhaps be defined as the, nowadays, increasingly widespread attitude of those who profess to be 'spiritual' people without being 'religious'; and yet who nevertheless still want to use elements of biblical tradition in their 'spirituality'. 'Non-religious spirituality', in the modern context, might then be said to come in two basic forms: either Neo-Pagan, as exemplified by Heidegger, or else 'Gnostic'.[3]

Original, ancient Gnosticism was a form of Christian spirituality more or less disengaged from the *sittlich*, institutional-religious community of the Catholic Church. It was a Christianity of small affinity groups, each gathered around their own guru; a free-spirited ethos, certainly, but a form of free-spiritedness made easy by disengagement. The Gnostics revelled in their claim to be a spiritual elite movement. They wanted nothing to do with the unenlightened herd, held together by the hierarchic religious discipline of Catholicism. The only people they really wanted, at all seriously, to talk with were each other. Theirs was a loose community of self-expressive nonconformists, parasitically using the religious language of Catholic *Sittlichkeit*, yet forever abstracting that language from its original *sittlich* context, so as to weave it into elaborate new myths. And modern 'Gnostics' are those who *mutatis mutandis* do likewise.

Looking for the most formidable representatives of this very widespread, but diffuse mode of thought, in *The Broken Middle* Rose finds two in particular: *Thomas Mann* and *René Girard*. In fact, I think her critique of Girard is somewhat unfair – but even in this case the argument is interesting, if only as testimony to the positive principle she is attempting to affirm against him.

Mann and Girard are both thinkers who have taken biblical themes and sought to infuse them with fresh imaginative life; Mann especially in his humorous epic *Joseph and His Brothers*. Yet both have done so without any direct involvement in the political struggles of ecclesiastical *Sittlichkeit*. It is just this omission that Rose wants to criticize. She sees it, in both cases, as a wilful

'Gnostic' holding-back from the theological 'broken middle'. And moreover in the 'Prelude' of Mann's great novel (or rather the two Preludes) we actually find a direct reworking of ancient Gnostic myth, which provides further justification for her terminology.[4]

Ironically informing the whole light-hearted entertainment of *Joseph and His Brothers* there is, in fact, quite a serious theological argument: a 'theology of irony', as Erich Heller has called it.[5] The Joseph of this narrative is a character richly endowed with self-expressive individuality. As an outsider, exiled from his people, he matures into a sharp-eyed ironical observer of Egyptian *Sittlichkeit*, even as he flourishes in relation to it. The hero's ironical understanding of the world around him reflects that of the narrator, as a modern outsider, as it were sojourning in antiquity. Joseph triumphs because he encounters a Pharaoh with a matching passion for self-expressive individuality – Mann implausibly identifies the Pharaoh of the Bible story with the weird figure of Akhenaton, who may very well be represented in such terms. And we, the readers, are naturally drawn to rejoice in this triumph. Taken as a whole, *Joseph and His Brothers* is thus nothing other than a vast celebration of ironic outsider-wisdom. But, by the same token, it is also an outstandingly ambitious implicit glorification of the novel as art form. For, of all art forms, the novel is surely the one with the greatest capacity to articulate this particular species of wisdom. No other form is so well adapted to show the ironic disjunction between actual reality and people's perceptions of it. In *Joseph and His Brothers* Mann takes the art form of the novel and converts it into a vehicle for sacred history; by so doing, he symbolically affirms the sacred potential of the novel as art form, in general.

Joseph and His Brothers is, in that sense, a sacramental novel. And the reworked Gnostic myth in the Prelude is a condensed encapsulation of the theological ideal it embodies. The traditional elements in this myth are in fact common to a number of different ancient doctrines.[6] It is set in the time before the creation of the natural world and mortal life; it purports to explain those acts of God. So, alongside God, at the outset of the 'romance', there exist only the angels and various types of unformed matter. Not content with this state of affairs, God first decides to create a new being, a creature in his own image, the original archetype of the human soul, a luminous giant called Adam Qadmon. The natural world has not yet been created; Adam Qadmon is created first. But then two things go wrong. On the one hand, the angel Shemmael refuses to obey God's order that all the angels should bow down in reverence before Adam Qadmon. In his irredeemable pride Shemmael becomes a principle of sheer evil. And then, on the other hand, Adam Qadmon is also corrupted – albeit, unlike Shemmael, in his case not irredeemably. He is seduced by the charm of his own reflection, as mirrored in matter. The creation of the natural world is an initial response, by God, to this primordial fall of Adam Qadmon; which the subsequent fall of the human Adam only repeats. God creates the world so as to indulge Adam Qadmon's fallen appetite for natural beauty. Adam Qadmon is now the Soul of the World, imprisoned in human souls. And so – next – God also sends a 'second emissary', the Spirit, to struggle, within the world, for the Soul's release. In the original Gnostic doctrine this struggle was understood to be the summons to fierce asceticism, as the Spirit intransigently confronts the fallenness of the Soul. But here we come to Mann's own modernization of the story: according to his version, the original fall of Adam Qadmon had in reality been part of God's plan all along. And the Spirit, therefore, is not sent as, in Mann's phrase, a 'principle of death'; just to cancel Adam Qadmon's aesthetic engagement with the world. Rather, the Spirit comes to complete the process which that engagement has begun. The angels may take the view that Adam Qadmon has been catastrophically corrupted, but then the angels always were hostile to Adam Qadmon – Shemmael's rebellion was only the most extreme manifestation of the hostility they all felt. To regard the Spirit as being, properly, an absolute *enemy* to the Soul's constitutive love for the beauty of nature and historic tradition is, in short, to mistake the angels' stern point of view for God's. True wisdom, on the contrary, consists in an ultimate reconciliation between the austere reforming impulse of the Spirit and the more indulgent, or conservative, impulse of the Soul. The apparent conflict between the two needs to be transcended. Implicitly, the message is: let the antagonism of the two principles be softened into a gentle dialectic of amused, and amusing, irony! Wherever Soul and Spirit appear to be at war, let irony go to work on both sides, to mollify their mutual resistance. And, supremely – let ironic novels be written, like this one.

So Mann transforms the myth, rejecting the radical asceticism usually associated with Gnosticism. Yet, why does he adopt the format of a Gnostic myth in the first place? The ancient Gnostics preferred to develop an understanding of salvation in terms of cosmic myth, not earthly history, above all so as to signal their disdain for the historically grounded loyalties of popular *Sittlichkeit*. They thought of their own affinity-group community as heavenly, rather than historical, in the way that institutions are historical. And in this regard it seems that Mann remains very much at one with them.

Hence, he sticks closely to the ancient Gnostic understanding of God's historic relationship to his chosen people.[7] The original reason, he tells us, for the creation of the two Adams – both Adam Qadmon and the father of mortal humanity – is that God is on a quest for self-knowledge. God wants, experimentally, to observe the life of creatures made in his own image. And his option for a particular form of *Sittlichkeit*, that of Israel, belongs to this process of experimentation. But it is also, partly, the malicious work of Shemmael – who tempts God to try the experiment. In fact, it is a mistake. This option for *Sittlichkeit* merely leads to pointless humiliation for God, when – to Shemmael's delight – the chosen people are historically humiliated. So, in all too typical Gnostic fashion, Mann presents his gospel of salvation-by-art, essentially, as a fundamental alternative to the 'error' of popular *Sittlichkeit*.

Ultimately, in criticizing Mann, Rose is aiming at all that great multitude of modern intellectuals who, in their disenchantment with institutionalized religion, have more or less decided to replace it, as an education for the moral imagination, with the reading of serious novels, the watching of serious plays or films.[8]

The basic problem with this substitution is surely that, unlike institutionalized religion, the reading of novels and the watching of plays and films can never create a community in which intellectuals are properly thrown together with non-intellectuals. In other words, it can never create a truly catholic ethos. To try and build a moral community on the basis of novels, plays and films is immediately to confine its membership to those who have the necessary education, and aptitude, to appreciate those novels, plays and films. In giving up on institutionalized religion one is not just rejecting a certain set of doctrines. One is closing down a whole space for serious conversation, with regard to the very deepest aspects of life, between people of every different social class.

But, again, the point is that in order to hold that space open intellectuals have truly got to *inhabit* it. They must, to the very fullest possible extent, belong to it; look out at the world from inside it. It is not enough just to use religious ideas as items of rhetoric, without such belonging. If Rose were simply concerned to criticize the substitution of novels, plays and films for the practice of institutionalized religion, then she might well have focused on a completely secular-minded thinker like Richard Rorty.[9] But she fixes on Mann instead, because to her he represents this other possibility. She sees him as masking his actual disengagement from the strategic problematics of catholic religious community-building, by a Gnostic show of Christian rhetoric.

And then she also attacks René Girard in the same terms. She writes of Mann and Girard as if they were both exponents of one and the same standpoint, only in two different styles: Mann in 'the facetious style', Girard – since, as a literary critic originally, he is judgemental by profession – in 'the severe style'. How does Girard qualify for this criticism?

He is among the most original, and truly thought-provoking, of twentieth-century commentators on Christianity, with a quite fresh take on the essential truth of the Christian gospel. And yet it is true, he never writes as a catholic theologian. That is to say, his ostensible approach is never (to adopt the old Anselmian phrase) one of 'faith seeking understanding'. He does not write formally, and explicitly, from within the catholic community of faith. But rather he adopts various different secular standpoints. Thus, the trajectory of Girard's thought begins in literary criticism, with a study of how novelists, in particular, have understood, and portrayed, the elementary dynamics of 'mimetic desire': the way we *learn* what to desire, by imitating the desire of others, and the resulting conflicts, especially where we enter into direct rivalry with those we imitate. Then he becomes a speculative anthropologist, constructing a sort of meta-myth about the origins of civilization, in terms of its strategy for putting back together what mimetic rivalry tears apart. He traces these origins, hypothetically, back to the primal murder of a human scapegoat; the community-unifying effect of which is, he suggests, commemorated in dreamlike fashion by primitive sacrificial rites and their accompanying myths. Finally, he enters the domain of comparative religion, analysing what he sees as the persistent apologia for the 'scapegoat mechanism' at the heart of all non-biblical mythology; and emphasizing the uniqueness of the Bible as, by contrast, the first and only body of ancient literature to give a voice to the unjustly persecuted. He strongly affirms the wisdom of this tradition, culminating as it does in the Christian perception of God incarnate in the figure of a crucified victim.[10] Nevertheless, his scholarly persona throughout is that of a detached, secular observer.

Rose takes this to imply a positive rejection of catholic theology. Despite Girard's affirmation of gospel wisdom, she sees in the persistently non-theological form of his thinking a positive 'Gnostic' disdain for theology grounded in a primary allegiance to Christian *Sittlichkeit*, the catholic faith of the Church as such. So she criticizes Girard for having, like Mann, merely 'abolished' – rather than, like Kierkegaard, 'suspended' – the 'ethical', in the sense of *Sittlichkeit*. 'In both cases', she remarks, 'the feast is spoiled.'[11] Spoiled – because the guest list is too restricted, including only the ironical or scholarly elite.

Dissociated as it is from any practical ecclesiology – or, for that matter, any close engagement with issues of political realism in the secular context – it is certainly the case that Girard's understanding of the dialectics of actual Christian discipleship in the contemporary world does seem somewhat abstract. There is no doubt a degree of justice in Rose's complaint that, in this sense, he oversimplifies the elementary opposition he is analysing, between the violence of the 'scapegoat mechanism' and the love that is to overcome it. When the ancient Gnostics repudiated Catholic institutional religion as being infested with a spirit of violence, this was closely bound up with their palpable desire to think of *themselves*, on the contrary, as a band of innocents. The result in their case is a very abstract, mythic doctrine. And in this particular regard Girard's doctrine is little better.

Only, consider, on the other hand, *James Alison*'s reading of him.[12]

Alison writes, quite unequivocally, as a Girardian Roman Catholic theologian. He deploys Girard's theory in the strategic context of an intra-ecclesial polemic against ecclesiastical homophobia, understood as a prime example of the 'scapegoat mechanism' at work, and hence as an elementary betrayal of the gospel.

This is a thoroughly concrete application. Granted, it is not one that Girard anticipates. However, there can be no denying that his theory lends itself to such Catholic usage, just as well as it does to a 'Gnostic' one. Indeed, Girard has not demurred from Alison's interpretation. To read Alison is, thus, immediately to see the arbitrariness of Rose's alternative reading, and its essential unfairness.

Rose is clearly unfair to Girard – and yet, even so, I think there is an interesting point of principle that still emerges here. The point is this: Rose criticizes Girard as a thinker who, despite all his appreciation of religion, always remains in the role of secular scholar. *But then so does she herself.* The Gnostic 'Girard' whom she attacks may perhaps be something of a fiction. But, as a representative figure, he stands for the intrinsic limitations of any secular-scholarly approach to religion, also including hers. In criticizing Girard, she is saying that this sort of thinking-from-the-outside about religion, which she herself practises, can never be self-sufficient. In the end, its proper function is always to serve as prolegomenon to another, very different sort of thinking; one far more directly conceived as a contribution to one's own religious community, and therefore caught up into its internal struggles.

Beyond even the most profound secular thinking-from-the-outside about religion – in other words – is the sort of thinking that springs right from the very middle of the religious community's existential brokenness.

6

The Threefold Moral of the Disaster

❦

Let us go back to the philosophic lessons of the Nazi Holocaust, and of twentieth-century genocidal totalitarianism in all its other forms, as well. And let us now consider these in relation to a form of thinking truly open to the 'brokenness' of the 'broken middle'.

There are, I think, three basic modes of possible philosophic response to such horrors. They may be seen as highlighting the need

1 for a spirit of sheer *universal neighbourliness*, beyond all divisiveness of propaganda ideology, such as totalitarianism pushes to its ultimate extreme;
2 for practices of *creative solidarity*, in resistance to the lust for exploitative domination which lies at the heart of totalitarian ambition; and/or
3 for an ethos of *well-institutionalized pluralism*, the most decisive possible antithesis to totalitarian coercive impatience.

By 'neighbourliness' I mean morality as a matter of the purely trans-political relationships of individual to individual. (As in Luke 10.29–37, Jesus' parable of the Good Samaritan, his answer to the question, 'Who is my neighbour?') And by 'solidarity' I mean political strategy for co-operation between the like-minded. But, by contrast, what I am calling an ethos of 'well-institutionalized pluralism' is a background political consensus, a large-scale form of *Sittlichkeit*, enshrined in laws and framing every sort of morally significant conversation; not only between the closely like-minded, but also between all manner of quite different people. Rose is, above all, concerned with this third response.

In the context of European culture the key agencies for the large-scale promotion of *Sittlichkeit*, generally, are of course the Christian churches. But in order to promote the particular species of *Sittlichkeit* in question here, the churches have got to be systematically opened up towards the 'broken middle'. Sects, which simply flee the middle of their environing culture, are clearly not going to contribute to the cause of well-institutionalized pluralism. And neither can larger religious organizations do the necessary job if they, themselves, are coercively impatient with the actual brokenness of the middle. That is: if they seek forcibly to suppress internal debate, and impose a rigid party line on their adherents, over against the rest of the world.

Rose admires Hegel as a thinker who, in the most resolutely systematic fashion, places himself in the 'broken middle' between the proper moral claims of the Church and the proper moral claims of the liberal, secular state. She applauds the way he develops a grand narrative designed to mediate between the two, by showing how the former have, in principle, evolved towards a vindication of the latter. And she admires Kierkegaard as a thinker who, notwithstanding all his differences from Hegel, likewise systematically places himself, as a mediator, in the 'broken middle' between traditional Christian ethics and the partly justified challenge of the 'aesthetic', or truly self-expressive, individual as such. She affirms the way he struggles to open up the institutional Church to that challenge. For both of these are major philosophic contributions to the development of a Christian *Sittlichkeit* ideally opened up to the imperatives of a well-institutionalized pluralism.

In her critique especially of *Emmanuel Levinas* and *Simone Weil*, however, she is dealing with thinkers for whom the prime philosophic lesson of the horror is simply to underline the need for universal neighbourliness, in the trans-political sense. She takes issue with the essential one-sidedness, as she sees it, of this approach.

And, at the same time, she is no less critical of *Hannah Arendt*, as representing an equally one-sided philosophical emphasis on the requirements of creative solidarity between a free-spirited few, alone.

Her basic aim, once again, with regard to each of these major figures, is to try and resituate their various insights into an altogether more open conversational context than that which they, for their part, seem to allow.

~✦~

One of the essays in Rose's book *Judaism and Modernity* is entitled 'Angry Angels: Simone Weil and Emmanuel Levinas'.[1] Here she considers the anger that so bitterly divides the two 'angels' in question, as it relates to the anger that unites them.

Two French-speaking Jews; two great religious thinkers; contemporaries – Weil was born in 1909, Levinas in 1906; both are naturally preoccupied by the moral lessons of the Nazi horror. But whereas Levinas belongs to, and represents the world of rabbinic Judaism, Weil, coming from an altogether secularized background, very emphatically does not.

'Universal neighbourliness' is my phrase. But this is also just what Weil seeks to advocate – in her case, to the exclusion of any actual belonging to a *sittlich* community. She came to identify the inner truth of the Christian gospel with the most radical articulation of universal neighbourliness, and so to affirm it. But, for that very reason, she nevertheless resolved not to be baptized. In early 1942 (shortly before her eventual escape from Vichy France), she wrote a series of letters to her friend, the priest, Father Perrin, setting out the rationale of that resolution:

> What frightens me [she declares] is the Church as a social structure. Not only on account of its blemishes, but from the very fact that it is something social. It is not that I am of a very individualistic temperament. I am afraid for the opposite reason. I am aware of very strong gregarious tendencies in myself. My natural disposition is to be very easily influenced – and above all by anything collective. I know that if at this moment I had before me a group of twenty young Germans singing Nazi songs in chorus, a part of my soul would instantly become Nazi. That is a very great weakness, but that is how I am . . .
>
> I am afraid of the church patriotism which exists in Catholic circles.[2]

Weil is afraid of this 'patriotism' as something tending to set limits on the proper universality of universal neighbourliness. What is the philosophic lesson of the totalitarian nightmare, for her? Totalitarianism, as she sees it, is just the most extreme political expression of the spirit that also comes to expression in 'church patriotism'. Observing it, she thinks, ought to bring home to us the urgent need to mistrust this 'social' – as opposed to neighbourly – impulse, in all its multifarious forms. Everything, she wants to insist, simply depends upon our not confusing the true 'absolute' good with any lesser set of goods bound up with one's belonging to a particular 'social' group.

At the same time, in her 1943 study *The Need for Roots*, she analyses the new socio-economic factors militating against good neighbourliness in the modern world, that have made totalitarianism possible. To be truly 'rooted' in the sense Weil intends here is to participate in a neighbourhood that is truly a neighbourhood. Her basic diagnosis is that totalitarianism thrives by recruiting people who are spiritually uprooted, and who crave a 'social' belonging by way of artificial substitute for such participation. *The Need for Roots* is a sustained polemic against capitalism in its moral character as an uprooting energy. Above all, it is an attack on the existing educational system, inasmuch as this is essentially designed to serve the needs of capitalist enterprise, and so fails to provide the necessary moral and imaginative resources to envisage and sustain true neighbourhoods.

Then, in a whole series of writings, she seeks to open up the question, why the Christian Church, especially, has not been more effective in upholding the demands of universal neighbourliness, against totalitarianism. Weil attributes the problem to the distortion of the Christian gospel, in the actual practice of church life, by two primordial influences: the rival, but also, she thinks, twin heritages of 'Rome' and 'Israel'. By 'Rome' she means the pagan Roman glorification of coercive force, as carried forward into the Church's historic use of coercion to impose religious orthodoxy. And when she speaks of 'Israel' what she chiefly has in mind is the literature of what one might call the Yahweh alone-ist movement: the dominant portrayal of God in the pre-exilic parts of Hebrew scripture, as the literature of those who sought to abolish the worship, in Israel, of any other god alongside Yahweh. After the Babylonian exile, she thinks, Hebrew religion was somewhat redeemed by having been exposed to foreign influences. But she completely rejects the Yahweh alone-ist picture of God as a fundamentally jealous, angry and punitive figure. Indeed, she repudiates the whole idea, basic to Yahweh alone-ist thought, of God intervening in, and controlling, history, from the outside. And, as an advocate of universal neighbourliness, she has no time for any notion of God privileging a particular chosen people.

Simone Weil died in August 1943. Her religious writings were posthumously published, in successive instalments, from 1947 onwards. And in 1952 Emmanuel Levinas published a critique of her work, from his Jewish religious point of view, in an article entitled 'Simone Weil Against the Bible'.[3]

Weil's argument is not in fact conceived as an attack on rabbinic Judaism at all – she knows nothing of rabbinic Judaism. It is an attack on what she sees as the corruption of official Roman Catholicism. She is not in the full classic sense a Gnostic, that is, not in the sense that Gnosticism is essentially sectarian, for she is far too much of an isolated individualist to be at home in any sect. But she is nevertheless reviving an ancient Gnostic form of argument, interpreting Christian revelation as a sheer antithesis to the Old Testament. No doubt, at one level, it is all rather silly. She is clearly determined always to think the worst of ancient Hebrew religion, and at the same time always to think the best of all other ancient cultures, by contrast. Her approach is by no means conducive to a balanced understanding of Hebrew scripture. Rather, she is simply constructing a caricature. Yet, this caricature is overlaid upon what is otherwise a profoundly original, and searching, meditation on the ideal philosophic preconditions for the promotion of universal neighbourliness.

Levinas responds to the caricature with perhaps justifiable sarcasm. By way of response to the underlying argument however, he adumbrates, as Rose puts it, 'three strategies of confontation'.[4]

In the first place, he points to the actual practice of rabbinic Judaism, over the two millennia of its existence in exile. After all, this does seem to stand in quite a strikingly paradoxical relationship to the harshness of its founding scriptures. As he puts it:

The extermination of the Canaanite peoples during the conquest of the Promised Land is the most indigestible passage of all the indigestible passages in the Bible. The texts vainly insist on the evil committed by the Canaanites; it is vain to insist on the very idea of perverted and irreparable civilisations, contaminating those who pardon them, which have to disappear in order for a new humanity to begin – Simone Weil is revolted by such cruelty. The extraordinary thing is that we are with her in this. The extraordinary thing is that the Jewish consciousness, formed precisely through contact with this harsh morality, with its obligations and sanctions, has learned to have an absolute horror of blood, while the [Christian] doctrine of non-violence has not stemmed the natural course towards violence displayed by a whole world over the last two thousand years. The harsh law of the Old Testament is perhaps not a doctrine based on kindness, but what does this matter, if it is a school of kindness?[5]

This was written before the modern state of Israel had become a regional military superpower. Clearly the 'kindness' of traditional Judaism was largely a product of its political powerlessness. But at any rate it shows that 'cruel' texts need not always inspire cruel practice. On the contrary, in the powerless communities of the Jewish diaspora these 'cruel' texts simply functioned as metaphors for the need to maintain Jewish cultural separateness – in effect, serving to keep Jews set apart from the actual cruelty practised by the dominant Gentile cultures of their world.[6]

Second, Levinas suggests that the harshness of Hebrew scripture needs to be understood as God's wake-up call, a necessarily brutal one, calibrated to the sheer moral insensitivity of ordinary sensual humanity. The chosenness of the chosen people lies above all in their unique exposure to this brutal call. The notion of a chosen people is not necessarily – as Weil seems to assume it must be – an assertion of patriotic arrogance. On the contrary:

The fact that God was known to all the peoples of the earth and, in a certain sense, better served by them than by the Jews, is proclaimed not by Simone Weil but by the prophet Malachi, the most 'nationalist' of the prophets – in a certain sense. For God is both universal and yet not universal. His universality is not accomplished so long as it is recognised only by thought and is not fulfilled by the acts of men. It remains abstract, then.[7]

The reference here is to Malachi 1.11–12:

For from the rising of the sun to its setting my name is great among the nations, and in every place incense is offered to my name, and a pure offering; for my name is great among nations, says the Lord of hosts. But you [the Jerusalem priesthood] profane it . . .

The actual meaning of Malachi's text is disputed: is this late prophet merely referring to the worship of Yahweh by Jews in the diaspora? Or does he in fact regard all forms of worship, even of other gods, as being, at least to some extent, implicitly directed towards the one true God? Levinas supposes the latter. In which case, of course, pagan worship is, from the prophet's point of view, deficient in understanding. And yet, the point is, it may nevertheless be more acceptable to God than the better-informed worship of the chosen people – for the simple reason that so much more is required of them than of other people. Malachi is only talking about the performance of priestly ritual. But when Amos, centuries earlier, represents Yahweh declaring to his chosen people,

You only have I known
    of all the families of the earth;
  therefore I will punish you
    for all your iniquities (Amos 3.2)

the context shows that this refers to his people's whole moral life. Clearly, such a notion of chosenness is no mere assertion of patriotic arrogance. And, in general, the harshness of Hebrew scripture is designed to press home God's brutally infinite demand, not just for a correct, 'abstract' profession of faith, but also for corresponding action.

Totalitarian propaganda denounced the Jews as 'rootless cosmopolitans'. Weil speaks of the 'need for roots' in quite a different sense. Levinas, using the term in yet another way – and so talking at complete cross purposes to her – celebrates the 'rootlessness' of traditional Judaism, as a condition of being torn loose from the comfortable moral inertia of paganism, as such:

> It is on the arid soil of the desert, where nothing is fixed, that the true spirit descended into a text in order to be universally fulfilled.[8]

One of the prime lessons of the totalitarian nightmare, he suggests, is precisely that we should learn to mistrust the pagan attachment to 'roots' – as limiting the proper universality of universal neighbourliness.

And then, third, he attacks her particular understanding of divine love. Weil is filled with a passionate rage for justice, just as the ancient Hebrew prophets often were. But, unlike them, she does not understand her rage as the inspiration of an interventionist God. On the contrary, she identifies true attention to God with a counter-balancing serene acceptance of 'necessity', *amor fati*. This is what she sees in the story of Christ's passion: God submitting, in exemplary love, to the dictates of creaturely necessity. Levinas just cannot accept this. As he puts it,

> God's supernatural love, in Simone Weil's Christianity, if it goes beyond a compassion for creatures' misery, can signify only love of evil itself. God loved evil; this is perhaps – we say it with infinite respect – the most fearful vision of this Christianity and the whole metaphysics of Passion. But our respect is mingled with a strong sense of dread. Our path lies elsewhere.[9]

Thus, he, in effect, wants to reconnect, as directly as any sophisticated modern philosopher can, with the sheer, untrammelled prophetic rage of the book of Amos. That is to say, he simply wants to lift that rage, Amos's infinite demand for justice, out of its original prophetic form – bound up with threats of corporate punishment – so as to reproduce it in modern philosophical terms. And he repudiates Weil's Stoic *amor fati* as, in the end, a mere mystificatory inhibition of this.

But, notwithstanding these three 'strategies of confrontation', duly noted, Rose's real interest is in what at the deepest level these two great thinkers nevertheless have in common. She does not, in fact, adjudicate between them. Rather, she seeks to criticize both of them, on the same grounds, alike. For both, after all, are equally focused on the ethical demands of universal neighbourliness – to the unfortunate *exclusion* of the sorts of insight that Hegel stands for, or the sorts of insight that Kierkegaard stands for.

It is that exclusion – explicit in the case of Levinas, but also clearly implicit in Weil's argument – which Rose sets out to criticize here.

As a prophetic philosopher, Levinas is preoccupied with *uncovering* the primordial, he would say, true 'ethical' impulse, more or less concealed within, and by, the usual deliberations of *Sittlichkeit*. Again, this is the impulse of universal neighbourliness, at its purest and most demanding. It is the impulse that for example, at the time of the Nazi genocide, led some Gentiles to take Jews in, hide them or help them escape – even sometimes Jews who were pretty much strangers to them. That is to say, an impulse of conscience still operative even when quite contrary to social pressure; even in situations of great danger, such that no one in the rescuers' own community would have blamed them for opting otherwise. The usual deliberations of *Sittlichkeit*, as Levinas sees them, are a constant interaction between this impulse and all sorts of arguments essentially designed to limit it, and supply justifications for ignoring it. His writing on 'ethics', then, takes shape as a systematic rhetorical evocation of the covered-up imperatives already inherent in the simple mute 'proximity' of the Other, before any such argument comes into play. Or perhaps one should say that it is an 'anti-rhetorical' evocation of those imperatives – inasmuch as all conventional moral rhetoric is implicated in the cover-up. It is a

117

meditation on one's encountering the 'face' of the Other, as an 'infinite' claim upon one, quite independent from any knowledge of their personal identity. Or on what it means to respond to the sheer 'saying', as opposed to the 'said', of what the Other has to say. In other words: to abandon all self-protective judgement of the Other – what they have said, what has been said about them – and simply to open up to them. Thus, in this elaborate, ruminative anti-rhetoric, the 'said' terrifyingly subverts itself. It has no other purpose than to gesture towards the 'saying', so to speak, behind everything ever said – as that towards which we are called, quite defencelessly, to open up.[10]

Both Weil and Levinas are thinkers who identify the highest wisdom with the most decisive possible liberation from the desire to feel innocent, just as Rose also does. But they proceed in quite a different way from her. Thus, again, what Rose wants to affirm is the non-innocence of the, forever, skilfully compromising philosophic mediator, situated in the 'broken middle' between the incompatible moral claims of opposing parties. And, hence, her primary concern is with the clash of competing *assertions of right*. Namely: the asserted rights of *sittlich*, especially religious, communities and their members, as such, *versus*

1 the asserted rights of the secular state and its citizens, as such; and

2 the asserted rights of the self-expressive nonconformist, as such.

(The first being the core topic of Hegel's thought; and the second, of Kierkegaard's.) Weil and Levinas, however, are not concerned with either of these conflicts. Indeed, they are both of them deeply mistrustful of any assertions of right – because such assertions are, in essence, stakes providing a basis for moral negotiation, and they are not negotiative thinkers at all. For Weil, no less than for Levinas, the ideal is, far rather, the non-innocence of the ultra-conscientious individual, simply resulting from the most intense, stripped bare, awareness of infinite moral *obligation*. As she, in particular, puts it in the opening sentence of *The Need for Roots*:

> The notion of obligation precedes that of rights, which remains subordinate and relative to it.[11]

She presents this as if it were a statement of objective fact, but it would surely be more accurate to say that she is describing her chosen point of view; deriving from a fundamental indifference to the virtues of the good philosophic peace negotiator. Neither of these two 'angry angels' wants to negotiate at all. They only want to be ever more intransigent, in their witness to universal neighbourliness.

Hegel's grand narrative is essentially a framework for peace-making negotiation between the proper rights of *sittlich*, especially religious, communities and the proper rights of the secular state. So it traces the progress of the divine/human Spirit, through world history, towards an ultimately convergent recognition of both species of right; a goal only perceptible, Hegel thinks, for the first time in his own day. It is a history of emergent freedom, in the sense that true 'freedom' is precisely the successful assertion of one's proper rights. But Levinas, for his purposes, rejects this notion of freedom. If 'freedom' is a name for the moral aspect of the highest wisdom, then – he argues – it is not to be understood as any sort of self-assertion, not even the most justified. Rather, it is something with which one is 'invested', by fulfilling one's obligations to the Other.[12] The 'rights' that truly matter are always the rights of the Other – paradoxically, this is an argument tending to devalue the Other's own actual assertion of their rights. Levinas, therefore, has no interest in the philosophic skills, or virtues, ideally required for peace-making mediation between such assertions. And, in consequence, he repudiates Hegel's whole project.[13]

So too Kierkegaard's distinction between the three 'stages on life's way' – the 'aesthetic', the 'ethical' and the 'religious', in the higher sense he gives to that word – provides a framework for mediation between competing assertions of right. The first, 'aesthetic' stage is where the rights of the self-expressive individual are given priority; the second, 'ethical' stage is where the rights of *sittlich* community are allowed to prevail. In *Concluding Unscientific Postscript* Kierkegaard also distinguishes between 'religiousness A', the religion of the 'ethical' stage at its very best, or the most impassioned 'ethical' sincerity, and 'religiousness B', true third-stage religion. What differentiates them is just that 'religiousness B' transcends the conflict between the first two stages in such a way as to reconcile both their legitimate claims. In Rose's terms, this is the religion of the 'broken middle', where the virtues of the good philosophic mediator are recognized as sacred. Kierkegaard ultimately seeks to bear prophetic testimony against forms of first-stage 'aesthetic' thinking, or forms of second-stage 'ethical' thinking, that remain locked fast into mutual opposition. Yet, as a mediator, before condemning them he is nevertheless scrupulous in letting them have their say. Indeed, he adopts pseudonyms that allow him to speak, as eloquently as he can, on behalf of each. Levinas, however, rejects what he sees as Kierkegaard's alternate *collusion* with both.[14] Thus, on the one hand, he complains that Kierkegaard's thinking has been infected by a tendency towards 'violence'. He associates Kierkegaard here with Nietzsche – he is thinking of everything in Kierkegaard's work that affirms the swagger of the free-spirited self-expressive nonconformist. And, on the other hand, he thinks that Kierkegaard has succumbed to the typical assumption of ideologized philosophy, that 'the ethical means the general': general rules for cohesive *Sittlichkeit*. This he regards as a sheer error: mistakenly valuing *sittlich* cohesion for its own sake, and so obscuring its proper transparency to universal neighbourliness, the sheer *particularity* of relationships face to face. Unlike Kierkegaard – in short – he does not want to undertake any sort of negotiation between the opposing viewpoints of pure self-expressive nonconformity and closed *Sittlichkeit*. Rather, it seems that he wants to break off conversation with the protagonists of both these viewpoints alike, and just talk about the infinite demands of universal neighbourliness, *instead*.

But why should the one sort of project be in competition with the other? Surely, they are complementary enterprises. At all events, a culture properly immunized against totalitarianism would not only be one that celebrated universal neighbourliness, as such. It would also be one with the strongest possible institutions, structures of law both secular and religious, designed to promote the moral principles that totalitarianism destroys. The strength of such institutions derives from people's positive loyalty towards them, a consensual loyalty overriding all sorts of other moral conflict. And so it depends on people not being alienated from them. Both Hegel and Kierkegaard, in their very different ways, are interested in the *Sittlichkeit*, the ethos, of Christian institutions, how that ethos sometimes becomes alienating, and how it needs to be reconceived, in order to minimize alienation. They are up-holders of an ideal Christian *Sittlichkeit*, capable of supporting robust institutions, one that is truly open, therefore, in its negotiating response to criticism from the alienated.

By contrast, universal neighbourliness is a quality of face-to-face relationships, unmediated by *sittlich*, institutional loyalties. But why should thinking about relationships at that level exclude one from *also*, just as seriously, thinking about the problems of *Sittlichkeit*, and how to negotiate its reform, in the sorts of way that Hegel and Kierkegaard do?

In *The Broken Middle* Rose focuses on the basic 'diremption' to be found at the heart of Levinas's thought. Namely: the diremption between his advocacy of 'ethics', in the sense of universal neigh-bourliness, and his devout acceptance of *halacha*, traditional strategy for the actual organization of Jewish *Sittlichkeit*.[15] This diremption is by no means a problem in itself, for her. On the con-trary, the wisdom of the 'broken middle' is essentially an ideal thinking through of such diremptions. But the problem she sees is just that, in this particular case, the diremption is *not* thought through. Thus, Levinas does not set himself to develop any historical understanding of *halacha*, as it has evolved in the context of Jewish life as a whole. Nor does he systematically compare the various different possible understandings of its authority, as set over against the values of the secular world. In general, he has a great deal to say about 'ethics', but, even as an interpreter of Talmudic texts, very little about *halacha*. With regard to *halacha*, he provides nothing like what Hegel provides – or what Kierkegaard provides – with regard to the Christian gospel.

And, as for Weil – in a sense she offers a still more radical testimony to the universality of universal neighbourliness than Levinas, in that, with her option against baptism, she remains resolutely outside any form of actual *sittlich* community. Indeed, she identifies intellectual integrity, in the most straightforward way, with not fitting in. Rose, however, responds to that whole attitude of hers with a wry comment. She cites a remark of the Catholic writer Gustav Thibon, who in 1941 had helped Weil evade the registration of Jews in Marseilles by giving her a job on his farm in the Ardèche. Meeting Weil for the first time, Thibon tells us, he was struck by her strange, weary intensity.

> Nor will I dwell on the way she was outfitted and her incredible baggage – she had a superb ignorance not only as to the canons of elegance but extending to the most elementary practices that enable a person to pass unnoticed.[16]

Rose fixes on Thibon's observation, and adds, 'I would argue that this inability to remain unnoticed may have been her spiritual, her *supernatural* failing.'[17]

Quirkily, she contrasts Weil in this respect with Agatha Christie's fictional creation, Miss Marple: a type of the most sharp-eyed intelligence, masked by the most inconspicuous appearance of elderly ordinariness. For, after all, the virtues of the good peace negotiator as such are virtues of self-effacement. And she also refers, in the same context, to Kierkegaard, on the self-effacing 'incognito' of the true 'knight of faith'. In *Fear and Trembling* Kierkegaard imagines meeting such a 'knight', and somehow being acquainted with his true identity:

> Here he is. Acquaintance made, I am introduced to him. The moment I set eyes on him I instantly push him from me, I myself leap backwards, I clasp my hands and say half aloud, 'Good Lord, is this the man? Is it really he? Why, he looks like a tax-collector!' However, it is the man after all.[18]

The good peace negotiator is a self-effacing individual, in the sense of being a good listener first, more than being a good talker. Someone quiet enough to be a good, honest listener – this is what Kierkegaard means by the 'knight of faith'. And in satirizing his startled self here, Kierkegaard is satirizing all philosophers, in that their whole profession is to be good talkers. Weil, too, was a brilliant talker. But, unlike Kierkegaard, she does not satirize that gift of hers. As Thibon remembered her, 'she went on arguing *ad infinitum* in an inexorably monotonous voice and I emerged from these endless discussions literally worn out'.[19] To be sure, she affirms Christian faith as, in a sense, an ideal of self-annihilation. Only, in her case, self-annihilation did not include self-effacement. On the contrary, it remained to the tragic end of her life a quite unreservedly flamboyant performance.

Again, in *Love's Work*, Rose writes of herself, 'I like to pass un-noticed, which is why I hope I am not deprived of old age. I aspire to Miss Marple's persona.'[20] And when, unlike Weil, she chose in the end to ask for baptism, this clearly expressed a fundamentally different understanding of faith from Weil's; above all, because she agrees with Kierkegaard in seeing faith as a pathway towards the self-effacing virtue of the good listener and mediator. Weil declined baptism, so as to underline her freedom of flamboyant prophetic utterance. Rose evidently came to the opposite decision because she understood baptism, in principle, as entry into a community of good, honest listening, the special gift of the 'knight of faith'.

∽✲∾

To both Levinas and Weil the great philosophic lesson of the totalitarian nightmare is that philosophers need – ever more urgently and imaginatively – to champion the pre-political principle of sheer universal neighbourliness. Hannah Arendt, on the other hand, draws quite a different philosophic (or anti-philosophic) lesson from the same experience.

Rose is a warm admirer, especially, of Arendt's first great book, *The Origins of Totalitarianism*.[21] But she is much more critical of the broader argument that Arendt goes on to develop in *The Human Condition*, and subsequently.[22] Because, again, she thinks that this is all too one-sided.

Thus, in *The Human Condition*, which was first published in 1958, Arendt steps back from the immediacy of the nightmare to explore the general lesson she sees there. Namely: that philosophers need, as never before, to celebrate the sort of *political spontaneity*, as such, that totalitarianism suppresses.

Arendt speaks of this spontaneity, here, as the ethos of pure 'action'; which she fundamentally contrasts, first, with the ethos of 'labour', and then with that of 'work'. These are, in essence, three different ways of evaluating 'creative solidarity'. Like 'universal neighbourliness', 'creative solidarity' is my phrase – I have chosen these two phrases, precisely, to balance one another, and so to point up the elementary contrast between Arendt's approach and that of Levinas or Weil. By 'creative solidarity' I mean any sort of fresh campaigning alliance, springing up as it were from below, so as to challenge the natural inertia of the established order. So the ethos of pure 'action', in the first place, might be defined as an affirmation of *self-propagating* creative solidarity, simply for its own sake.

Totalitarian movements are just the most extreme example of creative solidarity that is *not* self-propagating: when they come to power, they are quite ruthless in suppressing creative solidarity of any other sort, apart from their own, anything that might be a rival to theirs. Thus they represent the most extreme failure to appreciate such solidarity for its own sake. To put it in Arendt's terms: as opposed to the ethos of pure 'action', they appeal to the ethos of 'labour', or to that of 'work'. The ethos of 'labour' is the thinking of those who value creative solidarity only in so far as it promises to bring its adherents greater material wealth, in the sense of consumer goods. And the ethos of 'work' is the thinking of those who value it only in so far as it promises to bring its adherents a share in the glory of monumental achievements, great empires, or prestigious works of art. Totalitarian propaganda is – all of it – a mixture of these two species of promise. But it is not only totalitarian thinking that is tainted by the corresponding mentalities. The mentality of the '*animal laborans*', underlying the ethos of 'labour', and the mentality of '*homo faber*', underlying the ethos of 'work', pervade the whole culture of modern mass democracy, even at its least totalitarian. In this sense, Arendt wants to go well beyond conventional accounts of what has gone wrong; accounts still confined by those mentalities. She wants to argue that everything depends upon our learning, on the contrary, to value the actual enterprise of creative solidarity *in itself.* That is to say: for what, when valued in that way, it potentially has to teach us, the virtues that it then leads its practitioners to develop.

She develops this argument with much reference to Ancient Greece. *The Human Condition* is, not least, a polemic against the classical tradition of philosophy, in so far as this exalts the virtues of the contemplative life to the point of devaluing the characteristic virtues of true political creativity. Plato clearly does this, turning against the ultra-activism of Athenian citizenship. The Platonist devaluing of active citizenship was then reinforced, in the Christian world, by the spirit of monastic other-worldliness. It remains – Arendt complains – the all too automatic assumption of philosophy generally. But the result, she thinks, is that philosophers in general have failed to be sufficiently alert to the potential danger of nascent totalitarian movements; since the destructiveness of these movements is first visited upon the domain of the political activist, rather than upon that of the purely contemplative thinker. For her, the great philosophic lesson of the totalitarian nightmare is that philosophers need to unlearn the ancient, over-generalized philosophic prejudice against political activism. They need to start thinking with far greater urgency, precisely, about the fundamental contrast between the ethos of pure 'action' and the mentalities of the 'animal laborans' and 'homo faber'.

And so far, so good: Rose evidently has no interest in defending Platonism against this critique. Only – as with Levinas and Weil – she is concerned with what Arendt's approach appears to exclude in another way.

For Arendt celebrates creative solidarity in just two forms. On the one hand she celebrates the sort that comes to fullest expression, evanescently, in revolutionary crises: political creativity at its most intense, spontaneous and exhilarating. This is the theme of her book *On Revolution*.[23] On the other hand she affirms, in particular, Lessing's celebration of political friendship: the friendship of informal affinity groups, dramatically counterposed to other, more institutionalized cultural loyalties in Lessing's great play, *Nathan the Wise*.[24]

But that is all. Again, Rose is primarily concerned with 'the question of law': the question, namely, of how to maintain long-term durable institutions that do not rely on close like-mindedness among their stakeholders, but rather on a spirit of respectful negotiation between people who may otherwise be very differently minded from one another. Arendt, by contrast – celebrating revolution and friendship – impatiently turns her back on the inevitable, compromising messiness of such institutions. Yet, if we are talking about the philosophic lessons of the totalitarian nightmare – how can we afford this sort of impatience? Of course, Levinas and Weil are right that totalitarianism is the extreme form of what emerges where the spirit of universal neighbourliness is eclipsed; and so, too, of course Arendt is right that it is the extreme form of what emerges where the spirit of creative solidarity is forcibly repressed. However, totalitarianism is *also* the extreme form of what emerges where institutions designed to enable cultural pluralism collapse, to be replaced by mere violence. All three factors surely need serious consideration, alike. Good institutions are needed as a bulwark against totalitarianism – a good civil service, a good judiciary, above all perhaps good, well established religious institutions – defusing the tensions, between rival groups and individuals, on which totalitarianism feeds. Once again, what Rose finds missing in Arendt is what she sees pre-eminently exemplified by Hegel, inasmuch as Hegel sets out to try and define the proper ethos of the Christian state, as a set of mediating institutions. So, for Hegel, these institutions need to be as stable and coherent as possible, while nevertheless, to the fullest possible extent, remaining open to dissent, and protective of minorities; with that in view, he considers how they are, self-critically, to understand themselves in historic terms. And, again, Kierkegaard is the other model, as he sets out to define the proper ethos of the Christian Church, in particular, as a large-scale institution meant to be as responsive as possible to the workings of individual conscience. Fundamentally at stake in his thinking, therefore, is how the institutional Church is self-critically to understand itself in terms of its preaching and prayer life. The trouble is, there is none of this in Arendt's thought. She cannot engage with such questions – *because her thinking remains essentially unframed by any sort of institutional belonging.* Rose sees this as a major weakness.

Arendt's tacit resistance to institutional belonging emerges, above all, in her idiosyncratic usage of the general concept, 'society', as opposed to the *ideal* 'public realm'. Thus, in the first place, by the ideal 'public realm' she means what appears at its most vibrant in a revolutionary crisis; or, more generally, the whole space constituted by political friendships as such. And, as a contrast term, 'society', for her, simply designates every other mode of human interaction, so that it therefore includes everything structured by stable, law-governed institutions as such.

But, at the same time, it also has other connotations. In Arendt's usage, it is, as Rose puts it, a 'hybrid' concept.[25] Above all, it gets caught up into a sort of secularized Augustinianism: Arendt's secular reworking of St Augustine's classic contrast between the heavenly 'City of God' and the earthly 'City of Man'. Arendt's first book, her doctoral dissertation (written under the supervision of Karl Jaspers, and still very much under the influence of Martin Heidegger) was in fact a philosophical study of Augustine.[26] Her biographer, Elizabeth Young-Bruehl, might indeed seem only to be stating the obvious when she remarks that there is a hiatus in Arendt's philosophic development, and that her later thinking, as chiefly developed in *The Human Condition*, 'was [by contrast to this early work] rooted not in any Christian philosophy, but in Greek and Roman thought'.[27] Rose, however, disputes this.[28] After all, she argues, there is a crucial sense in which Arendt remains an Augustinian thinker even here. For the point is that, right at the heart of Augustine's argument in *The City of God*, he develops a polarized contrast between two basic species of culture, differentiated by opposing orientations of will: on the one hand, the 'Heavenly City', which includes every form of human organization in so far as it derives from, and expresses, an authentic love for God, 'even to the contempt of self'; on the other hand, the 'Earthly City', which includes every form of human organization in so far as it derives from, and expresses, the opposite. The 'Earthly City' is thus what springs from the exploitative lust for domination (*libido dominandi*) or from the associated love of this-worldly glory.[29]

Augustine's whole argument is an extended exploration of that primary contrast. And in *The Human Condition*, Rose suggests, Arendt is actually doing something quite similar. The terminology has been secularized, but the underlying pattern is nevertheless analogous. 'Society' is, largely, her term for what Augustine calls the 'Earthly City', or 'City of Man'. So, again, it is the domain of exploitative domination; and, hence, of conformist 'behaviour' among the dominated, as opposed to 'action'. It is what totalitarianism tends to universalize. In this sense, the term has become entirely derogatory.

Augustine shows no interest in the question of how the 'Earthly City', as such, ought to be organized. He is only interested in denouncing it. And Arendt's attitude to what she calls 'society' is the same: she shows no interest in the question of how 'society', as such, ought to be organized. Or, to put it in Rose's terminology – Arendt shows no interest in the 'question of law'. For her, the question of law is effectively closed down. It is hidden away behind her rhetoric of sheer contempt for all things merely 'social', quite regardless of how 'society' is organized. She remains an 'Augustinian' thinker, above all, in her adherence to this Augustinian mode of closure.

The chief lesson Arendt draws from the totalitarian nightmare is that we need, ever more radically, to appreciate what totalitarianism most immediately suppresses: the necessary space for political spontaneity. There is just one short text in which she begins to open up another possible response. In her essay 'On Authority' she considers the inclination of totalitarian regimes also to try and suppress traditions of 'authority' in the classical sense of *auctoritas*.[30] That is to say, 'authority' understood not as an outcome of successful coercion, but on the contrary as an alternative to coercion, in the bonding together of society; ideally minimizing the need for coercion. This is, above all, the authority of traditional, non-revolutionary religious *Sittlichkeit*. Augustine, one might say – like all the early Christian fathers – is both a cultural-revolutionary thinker, in relation to paganism, and an advocate of new, Christian traditions of *auctoritas*. And whereas *The Human Condition* is Arendt's secularized reworking of Augustinianism in the former aspect, 'On Authority' is at any rate a nod towards the continuing relevance of the latter.

Yet, unfortunately, it is no more than a nod. Arendt remains a resolutely non-religious thinker. She acknowledges the anti-totalitarian potential of traditional religious loyalties here, but only from the outside. Her indiscriminate contempt for 'society' keeps her on the outside: with regard to the corruptions of religious 'society' she continues, all too briskly, to preserve her innocence, untainted by any direct association. And therefore she can only discuss *auctoritas* in the abstract. What Rose calls the 'question of law' might indeed be defined, precisely, as the calling into question, and theoretical re-legitimation, of specific, concrete structures of *auctoritas*. Thus, it is the question of how the *auctoritas* of one's own particular religious tradition – a tradition considered *from within* – interacts with the requirements of legal coercion. Arendt's essay is a repudiation of any over-generalized 'liberal' repudiation of *auctoritas*, inasmuch as naive liberalism, in that sense, is knocking away a major sort of bulwark against totalitarianism. But this repudiation of naive liberalism is still not a full opening up of the question of law. For it remains, from Rose's point of view, far too disengaged.

༄༅

In *The Broken Middle* Rose discusses Arendt in close conjunction with two other figures, both of whom had also been important for Arendt herself: *Rahel Varnhagen* and *Rosa Luxemburg*. Varnhagen, Luxemburg and Arendt – here we have three thoroughly secular-minded Jewish intellectual women, each from a very different historic background. For Rose, in this text, they are three *alter egos*, by contrast to whom she sets out to define her own distinctive way.

Rahel Varnhagen is usually remembered by this, her eventual married name, but she first became known in the world as Rahel Levin, hostess to the most distinguished intellectual salon in Berlin during the period up to 1806. Afterwards the Napoleonic Wars changed everything; the newly prevalent mood of German nationalism tended to be antisemitic, and the Jewish-hosted salon became a thing of the past. Following a series of love affairs, with Gentile men, beautifully chronicled in her letters, she ended up being baptized and marrying Karl August Varnhagen, who, after her death, published those letters in the form of an epistolary novel. He was a friend of Hegel's. (Unfortunately – somewhat to Hegel's discredit, perhaps – it has to be said that Rahel herself never felt Hegel took *her* at all seriously.) Arendt wrote a biography of Rahel Varnhagen.[31] Indeed, she once described Rahel as 'my closest friend, even though she has been dead for some one hundred years'.[32] It is a curiously abstract biography – no doubt because a good deal of it is in fact implicit autobiography, by projection. The central theme of the book is Varnhagen's struggle with her Jewish identity; her wavering between the role of 'parvenu', in flight from that identity, and 'pariah', defiantly affirming it.

As for Rosa Luxemburg: Arendt's mother, in Königsberg, had been a firm supporter of the hard-line tendency in the German Social Democratic Party that Luxemburg represented, and had idolized her. Arendt's husband, Heinrich Blücher, had participated in the 1919 Spartacist Uprising in Berlin that Luxemburg led. In Part Two of *The Origins of Totalitarianism* Arendt largely draws on Luxemburg's pioneering theoretical analysis of modern imperialism; in *On Revolution* she approves of her characteristically open and supportive response to the phenomenon of revolutionary workers' councils. And she wrote a notable essay, reviewing J. P. Nettl's great biography of Luxemburg, which is warmly celebratory in tone.[33]

Rose, for her part, draws Varnhagen, Luxemburg and Arendt together with particular reference to three key elements in chapter

6 of Hegel's *Phenomenology of Spirit*, the chapter in which he is most directly discussing what she calls the 'broken middle', as such. She associates them with Hegel's discussion, there, of three particular general attitudes, or mentalities. It is a startling and I think rather brilliant interpretative move. In fact, it seems to me that her suggestions here represent quite a significant improvement on the actual Hegelian argument.

Thus, one of the forms of Spirit discussed in this chapter of the *Phenomenology* is the 'beautiful soul'. In addressing this figure, Hegel evidently has a whole collection of contemporary German novels in mind: most notably Goethe's *Wilhelm Meister's Apprenticeship* and *The Sorrows of Young Werther*, Jacobi's *Woldemar*, Novalis's *Heinrich von Öfterdingen*, Hölderlin's *Hyperion*, Schlegel's *Lucinde*. All of these novels may be said to illustrate, and more or less celebrate, the type. The 'beautiful soul' is one who practises a cult of the most high-minded, and most ostentatious, conscientious sincerity – veering towards a sort of moral narcissism. This renders it impossible for such a one ever truly to belong to a *sittlich* community, or even the narrowest sort of sect. They feel too compromised by being associated with other people who, in any way, have different moral priorities from their own; it feels to them like a taint on their own inner purity. Although they yearn for a community of others like themselves, their moralized egocentricity tends to mean that they are forever frustrated. And so, as Rose puts it:

> 'The beautiful soul' repulses the world and retreats from it. She can give neither her knowledge nor her love away; and the sect she flirts with but fails to found or join returns her to a solipsism which wastes away the body and which is impotent in the world – unable to educate or form others. She is a *beautiful* not a holy soul (as Schiller wanted her to be called) because she does not sanctify life, however reduced, but both denies it and sublimates the denial into an ethereal ethos without form or contact.[34]

The allusions here are especially to the section of *Wilhelm Meister's Apprenticeship* entitled 'Confessions of a Beautiful Soul': the central character of this text, withdrawing from the world of aristocratic society, 'flirts with' the possibility of joining the sectarian Herrnhut community of the Moravian Brethren, but then does not. She is also frustrated in her desire to supervise the education of her dead sister's children. And in the end she 'wastes away'. Rose gives priority to this particular text, above all, because of its great importance to Rahel Varnhagen, who was one of the main instigators of the 'Goethe cult' of her day.

Let us be clear, Rose insists: 'Rahel Levin/Varnhagen was not a "beautiful soul".'[35] Yet Thomas Carlyle, in an essay of 1838, called her one.[36] The sensibility at work in her letters is one essentially shaped by the literature of soul-beauty. Her secularity and her Jewishness, together, rendered her just as incapable as any 'beautiful soul' of effective participation in *sittlich* community. She yearned, just as much as any 'beautiful soul', for a true spiritual community of friends – no doubt this yearning was a major factor in making her such a good salon hostess. And after 1806 she was just as frustrated in this yearning as any 'beautiful soul' would be. Only, the point is, she was not a 'beautiful soul' in the way that Hegel describes the type. She was not a 'beautiful soul' because she did not lapse either into complacency or into self-indulgent despair; essential characteristics of the condition in his portrayal. But, rather, in the most admirable fashion she held fast to the 'struggle' of her life precisely as a struggle, a constant discontented wrestling with her fate.

Closely related to the 'beautiful soul', in Hegel's text, is another type, also illustrated by the same literature: the 'hard-heart of hypocritical judgement'. In Rose's words,

> While the beautiful soul withdraws herself from the world by repulsing it and retreating from it, the hard-heart remains in the world but survives by retreating from and repulsing the other in

judgement – judgement of hypocrisy – the self-conscious dispar-
ity between declaring universal duty yet living particular inner
being, which is itself hypocritical in appealing to its own law and
also failing to act – making duty a mere matter of words.[37]

The 'hard-heart' resembles the 'beautiful soul' in his or her reluctance to 'act', where 'action' means taking real risks – being
exposed to the hostile judgement of others – out of a truly conscientious moral motivation. Such a person is 'hypocritical' inasmuch
as their rhetoric of duty is chiefly deployed for the purpose of
denouncing the supposed 'hypocrisy' of others. What differentiates them from the 'beautiful soul' is just that they do not with-
draw from the world of political struggle.[38] The 'beautiful soul' is
unfitted for political struggle by her fundamentally self-defensive
reluctance to judge or be judged. 'Do not judge me', she says,
'simply accept my claim that I am following the dictates of my conscience, and in return I promise I will not judge you, if you assure
me you are doing the same.' But the 'hard-heart' is altogether more
aggressive. Thus, self-defence here becomes pre-emptive attack: 'If
you disagree with me, it is because your motives are corrupt. And
therefore any critical judgement you may make of me is worthless.'
    In the same way that Rahel Varnhagen was not a 'beautiful soul',
the sheer courage of Rosa Luxemburg clearly renders her far more
than just an exemplar of the 'hard-heart' mentality, as Hegel
describes it. For unlike the essentially hypocritical 'hard-heart' of
Hegel's description, she did 'act'. And yet – at the same time – she
was a Marxist. She was no hypocrite, but she did wholeheartedly
adopt the typical Marxist style of polemic: 'If you disagree with me,
it is because your motives are corrupt. You have been enslaved by
your own class interests, or by the class interests of your patrons.
Therefore your arguments deserve nothing but scorn.' Might one
not call such an attitude 'hard-hearted', even when it is not hypocritical? Luxemburg surely represents Marxism at its moral best;
nevertheless, the question remains, even in her case.

'This judgement', Rose continues, 'exalted into a culture, would eliminate barbarism – of evil, of hypocrisy, of "banality" of evil . . .'[39] That last phrase, 'banality of evil', immediately indicates that we are back here to considering Arendt, alluding as it does to the famous sub-title to Arendt's book on the trial of Adolf Eichmann.[40] '"Judgement" here becomes a "pure culture".'[41] Rose wants to criticize Arendt for her affinities to what Hegel calls 'pure culture', an earlier figure in his argument than the 'beautiful soul' or the 'hard-heart', but still related to them.

In his account of 'pure culture' Hegel alludes especially to Diderot's dialogue, *Rameau's Nephew*, which had first appeared in a German translation by Goethe in 1805, just at the time the *Phenomenology* was taking shape in his mind. The dialogue features two speakers. One is a representative *philosophe*, representing the standard attitudes of his class; the other is Young Rameau, the nephew of the great composer, himself also a musician, but a failure in life, a sponger, bohemian and buffoon. Young Rameau however is also a very witty man. And he confounds his interlocutor with his rollicking contempt for all norms of respectability. He represents a hyper-civilized universal disgust. Nothing any longer seems natural to him – this, basically, is what Hegel means by 'pure culture'. Thus, to put it in Augustinian terms: Young Rameau is a man who sees the 'Earthly City' for what it is, and therefore despises it, but who has no access to the 'Heavenly City', since *its* virtues also seem quite unappetizing to him, and he completely lacks any taste for its supposed rewards. 'From pole to pole', he declares, 'all I can see is tyrants and slaves.'[42] Everywhere, under the polite surface of life, he discerns the *libido dominandi* at work, and role-playing pretence, flattery, servility of every kind in response; manipulation by rulers interacting with manipulation of the rulers. He himself is torn in two: the hanger-on who is bound to be pleasantly amusing to his patrons, and the sharp-eyed disgusted observer – he is both equally, but they are opposites. And this is intolerable to him. The only relief he can find is in not taking anything seriously. So he has come to identify wisdom, in effect, with his own cultivation of a sardonic mocking wit.

Just as judgemental as the 'hard-heart', the devotee of 'pure culture' nevertheless opts not, barbarically, to *rage*, as the 'hard-heart' does, against the damage done to 'nature', and 'natural rights'; but, instead, to live life as an ironic game.

Now, there is of course an obvious basic difference between Arendt and Diderot's hero: unlike him, she does have a taste for something like the 'Heavenly City' – even if it is in a quite unreligious form. Alongside her disdain for the 'social' is her celebration of the ethos of ancient Athens, and its partial, albeit fleeting recovery, she thinks, in the élan of modern revolutionary upheavals. (Indeed, other twentieth-century philosophers are much closer in spirit to Young Rameau. Alexandre Kojève is one example, Jean Baudrillard is another.) But in associating Arendt with the notion of 'pure culture', what Rose chiefly has in mind is Arendt's idealization of *Lessing*.

Thus, Lessing served the cause of Enlightenment in mid-eighteenth-century Germany as a great theological provocateur, repeatedly teasing the orthodox conservatives, as it were, with guerrilla polemics, little sallies here and there. Arendt praises him as a 'completely political person', one for whom the claims of political friendship, she suggests, decisively outranked those of 'truth', in the sense that institutional religion understands 'truth'; an anti-philosophical, witty reveller in the sheer pluralism of 'opinion'. Going beyond any actual statements of Lessing himself, the Arendtian ideal, as set out in her essay on him,

> affirms the 'infinity of opinions', so that 'going astray with Plato' is taken to mean opting for the charm of Plato's person in preference to whatever truth is chanced upon by his opponents.

But, Rose remarks,

This interpretation reduces the difficulty of truth to opinion, and the play of opinion to fancying persons.[43]

She is highly sceptical about the ideal, attributed by Arendt to Lessing, of 'friendship without intimacy, but also without truth'. Arendt's 'Lessing' shrugs his shoulders. With playful contempt, he simply concedes the word 'truth' to religious bigotry. He prefers this to the hard work of properly negotiating with the bigots, or disputing their pretensions to represent orthodox tradition.[44] But Rose by contrast greatly prefers Kierkegaard's rather different praise of Lessing in Book 2 of *Concluding Unscientific Postscript*. (That is, the portrayal of Lessing by 'Johannes Climacus', Kierkegaard's pseudonym here.) For Kierkegaard's interpretation seems to her, simply, more challenging:

> Unlike Arendt, Climacus' 'Lessing' serves truth not infinite opinion; he displays not [just] respect for the finite difference of the other, but concern for the inner agon of the other – for the anxiety of beginning; not cool and sceptical in face of the 'inhumanity' of truth, but 'mingling jest and earnest' in face of the equivocation of the ethical.[45]

Far more than Arendt – but like Kierkegaard – Rose in short wants to take seriously Lessing's claim, constant ironist as he was, nevertheless also to be a true Christian thinker.

Chapter 6 of the *Phenomenology*, which contains Hegel's discussion of these three types, the 'beautiful soul', the 'hard-heart' of hypocritical judgement, and 'pure culture', is the prelude to his discussion, in chapter 7, of comparative religion. The chapter begins with the disintegration of simple, primitive forms of *Sittlichkeit*, and then examines a whole series of resistances to what he would regard as proper reintegration. Such resistance may come to theoretical expression, at one level, in the ideologies of militant secularism or nihilism. At another level, infused with 'spirituality', it may appear in the phenomena of Gnosticism or Neo-Paganism. But

Hegel's concern, in this context, is not so much with theory as such. Rather, it is with pre-theoretic *attitudes of will*. What he is looking at are various forms of impatience: a series of very general mentalities fundamentally lacking the sort of peace-negotiative patience needed in order that one may, with real honesty, enter into, and contribute to, a properly reintegrating *sittlich* community.

To learn that sort of patience, the 'beautiful soul' must abandon her moralized self-obsession. The 'hard-heart', meanwhile, needs to break. She has got to forgive the sins of others, while at the same time confessing her own sins – for Hegel, the true *sittlich* community is first and foremost one with a rich capacity for ritually and politically enacting mutual forgiveness. And, for the same purpose, the devotee of 'pure culture' requires liberation from the all too easy pleasures of ironic, bohemian contempt.

Rose, however, is suggesting what I think is a real improvement on Hegel's original argument, inasmuch as Hegel has somewhat blurred the issues. Thus, the primary problem with the 'beautiful soul' is surely just the way in which she is permanently locked into the role of earnest solitary outsider. As I have said, in Hegel's portrayal this primary problem is compounded partly by gross complacency and partly by despair: at one point he describes a circle of 'beautiful souls' as an odious sort of mutual appreciation society, at another point he speaks of the 'beautiful soul' cracking up in madness, or succumbing to psycho-somatic illness.[46] He does so because that is what he finds in the novels he has been reading.[47] But the case of Rahel Varnhagen vividly illustrates the primary problem without any such compounded phenomena. So it serves to clarify the essential issue at stake. Varnhagen felt trapped in the role of outsider; a Jew outside the religious community of Jews, in a Gentile world growing more and more anti-semitic. And Rose invites us to agree with her: it was indeed a trap.

Likewise, the primary problem with the 'hard-heart' is surely just the way in which her aggressive hyper-sensitivity to other people's hypocrisy tends to inhibit genuine conversation. But Hegel, in his portrayal of this, has complicated matters by supposing that the 'hard-heart' is also a coward, always preferring moralistic talk to real, risky action.[48] In Marxism, generally, an aggressive hypersensitivity to other people's hypocrisy has been made into the guiding principle of a whole intellectual ethos. Yet Rosa Luxemburg represents the spirit of Marxism at its most courageous. Contemplating her work, we are thus confronted with the primary problem here, purely and simply in itself.

And, again, the primary problem with 'pure culture' surely lies in its devotees' sheer reluctance to engage religious bigotry in serious conversation, directly challenging the bigots' claim to be the true, authoritative representatives of authentic *sittlich* tradition. That they are reluctant to do this derives from their contempt. They are just too contemptuous of the bigots, as they are contemptuous of all mere social conformism, in whatever guise.

Hegel, in the *Phenomenology*, portrays such contempt at its most 'shameless', because most desperate. The reference to *Rameau's Nephew* is made clear by direct quotation; this is, as it happens, one of the very rare places in the *Phenomenology* where Hegel actually quotes another author.[49] And he sticks close to Diderot's picture, throughout. The basic issue illustrated by that example, however – in relation to engagement with traditions of *Sittlichkeit* – is surely not confined to the worldview of people like Young Rameau. As Rose argues, Hannah Arendt's image of 'Lessing' might very well be adduced as another, quite different example of the same. Arendt certainly represents the 'barbarism of pure culture' in a most formidable form. Her praise of 'Lessing' is directly set against the background of her pioneering analysis of the totalitarian nightmare. Yet, *even in this case* – Rose wants to argue – 'pure culture' remains 'barbaric'. That is to say, it fails adequately to confront the unequivocal barbarism revealed in the triumphs of totalitarianism. It fails inasmuch as a true resistance against that ultimate barbarism requires thinkers with a far greater *patience* than Arendt's 'Lessing' appears to have.

In fact, it requires thinkers far more like Kierkegaard's 'Lessing'. For what is wanted is, precisely, the most patient possible readiness to abide in the brokenness of the 'broken middle', as much inside a community of *Sittlichkeit* as outside. The crying need, in short, is for a strategy capable of investing the pre-requisites of freedom with durable *auctoritas*. And this can only be accomplished by thinkers absolutely within the sort of community that can confer durable *auctoritas* – who are, however, forever patiently struggling to renegotiate the terms of their belonging, to that end.

Against 'Holy Middles' in General

Rose is a Hegelian thinker, in that all of her work is ultimately oriented towards an evocation of 'absolute knowing'. And this is an intrinsically religious ideal, although not tied to any particular form of metaphysical correctness. For, again, 'absolute knowing' is just the 'knowing' that belongs to the most truly self-aware, sympathetic, and searching, conversational openness towards all and sundry. It is a religious ideal in the sense that religion is, first and foremost, an offer of intensified conversation. The basic Hegelian objection to irreligious secular humanism and nihilism is that the protagonists of these modes of thought, over-reacting to particular instances of corrupted religion, have closed down a whole species of conversation. The irreligious secular humanists and nihilists have colluded with the rigid religious dogmatists' attempt to identify religious faith with the dogmatists' own particular metaphysical beliefs. In rejecting which, the secular humanists and nihilists have therefore rejected religion in general – as if there were nothing more than *those* beliefs at stake.

And, by the same token, 'absolute knowing' is not a Gnostic sort of knowing. For Gnosticism – likewise, over-reacting to particular instances of corruption in more populist forms of religion – effectively restricts serious conversation to the elite affinity group of 'those who know', talking among themselves.

At the same time, too, the faith aspect of 'absolute knowing' clearly represents the most decisive possible opposite not only to Protestant bibliolatry, and to Catholic or Orthodox fanatical 'traditionalism', but also to any sort of mild-mannered religion-as-respectability. Thus, here we have faith, in the first place, absolutely liberated from any neurotic obsession with ideological checklists, or the rote-rehearsal of set polemical arguments – it allows no such reduction of conversation. And yet there is, equally, no shrinking back, in this faith, from harsh controversy. No such polite suppression of conversation, either. On the contrary: what 'absolute knowing' knows is none other than the true sacredness of that which, most profoundly, forever opens conversation up. Or one might also define it as an absolute readiness to face the full reality of the 'broken middle'.

But what, then, does this signify *for theology*, as such?

The 'broken middle' is existence torn between the justifiable authority claims of effective local *Sittlichkeit* and the justifiable counter-claims of a critical secularity. As a philosophical critic of theology, Rose basically sets out to call in question any rhetorical strategy, adopted by theologians, seeming, in whatever way, to *predetermine* the outcome of such conflicts.

Thus, in her view, good theology – just as much as good philosophy – is called upon to play the role of impartial referee here, not partisan advocate for one side or the other. The theologian, like the philosopher (one might say), is simply meant to be a partisan for Honesty, on both sides alike. She is against any approach to theology that, from the outset, is liable to narrow down the free play of conversation between them. That is to say: either, on the one hand, any abstract, general prejudice against the authority claims of *sittlich* tradition; or, on the other hand, any sort of abstract, general prejudice against the counter-claims of the secular. To the extent that theology is governed by either of these two opposite species of prejudice, she argues that it is a retreat from the actual reality of the 'broken middle'. It becomes instead, she suggests, essentially a substitution of seductive fantasies – she calls them fantasies of a *'holy middle'* – for that reality. She develops this twofold critique with reference both to early or mid-twentieth-century Jewish theology, and to contemporary Christian theology. Although the contexts are of course very different, the same principles apply in each case.

⌒⛥⌒

In *The Broken Middle*, and again in the lecture entitled 'Is there a Jewish Philosophy?' in *Judaism and Modernity*, the chief Jewish representatives of such oversimplification are Emmanuel Levinas and Leo Strauss. As Rose puts it: 'Strauss presents Judaism *contra* nature; Levinas, *contra* freedom.'[1] 'Nature', in this context, is a term for the supposed basis of *Sittlichkeit* as a sheer constraint on secular self-expressive nonconformity; what the upholders of a purely repressive religiousness like to appeal to. 'Freedom' designates the ideal of a militant self-expressive nonconformity, understood as an extension of Socratic doubt, at its most irreverent.

But, although Strauss advocates a strategic political alliance, so far as possible, between Socratic/Platonist philosophy and liberal Jewish theology – and Levinas has written a number of essays in the form of 'Talmudic readings' – neither is really a systematic theologian. If one wants to consider Jewish philosophic *theology*, the underlying point is surely better expressed in terms of the contrast between two other thinkers, whom Rose considers elsewhere in *Judaism and Modernity*. Namely: *Franz Rosenzweig* and *Hermann Cohen*. Levinas, after all, is lavish in his praise of Rosenzweig.[2] And Strauss wrote a perhaps slightly ironic, but nevertheless appreciative, 'Introductory Essay' to Cohen's great theological work, *Religion of Reason Out of the Sources of Judaism*.[3] The continuities are clear; the same basic critique also applies in their case.

The contrast between Cohen and Rosenzweig is, in fact, all the more striking because they are so close. Although Cohen was 44 years older, they were friends. Nevertheless, they also represent two diametrically opposite approaches to Jewish theology: Cohen, in effect, advocating an alliance between liberal Judaism and the forces of Enlightenment secularity in Gentile society, against Christianity; Rosenzweig, on the contrary, arguing for an alliance between Judaism and Christianity, as partners in biblical *Sittlichkeit*, against secularism. Rose rejects both approaches equally. Both in their opposing ways are classic examples of what she means by theology cleaving to a false 'holy middle', such as merely serves to obscure the true brokenness of the 'broken middle'.

Rosenzweig, like her, came from a thoroughly secularized milieu; also worked as a philosopher on the interpretation of Hegel; and, when he came to religious faith, wavered at first between Christianity and Judaism. But, unlike her, he rejected Hegel.[4] And he opted for the synagogue.

The crisis came for him in 1913: he was 27, and had more or less decided to be baptized. First, however, he decided he would sample the experience of Yom Kippur at a small synagogue in Berlin. And it proved to be an overwhelming experience. Caught up into the drama of the liturgy, then and there he realized that his true vocation was, as a modern philosopher, to try and re-appropriate the *Sittlichkeit* of his ancestors.

He began by enrolling on a course taught by Cohen at the Jewish Theological Seminary (*Lehranstalt für die Wissenschaft des Judentums*) in the city. Cohen had at that point just started to teach there, after retiring from a long career as Professor of Philosophy at the University of Marburg; where (with Paul Natorp) he had been a founder of the Marburg School of Neo-Kantianism. So, in his old age, he turned from pure philosophy to Jewish philosophical theology. Rosenzweig was filled with admiration for him: 'I had the surprise of my life', he wrote. 'I am used to professors of philosophy who are subtle, acute, lofty, profound, and whatever other attributes are used to praise a thinker – instead, I found something I

144

hadn't expected, a philosopher . . . The thing that, disenchanted with the present, I had long searched for only in the writings of the great dead – the strict scholarly spirit hovering over the deep of an inchoate, chaotically teeming reality, I now saw face to face in the living flesh.'[5] Cohen was, notoriously, a man of some vanity; but in Rosenzweig's view he had every right to be.[6]

Over the following years, during the First World War, Rosenzweig – conscripted into the German army and serving as an anti-aircraft gunner in the Balkans – started work on his masterpiece, *The Star of Redemption*. But a major impulse to that work came in 1918 when, on furlough, he visited Cohen, just a few months before the latter's death, and had the opportunity to read an early draft of the latter's *Religion of Reason*. He was never, however, an uncritical disciple of Cohen. And when at the beginning of the war Cohen delivered a lecture affirming his own brand of social-democratic – hence 'internationalist' – German nationalism, Rosenzweig protested. Indeed, he accused his teacher of 'betraying the messianic idea' by mixing it in this way with secular ideology.[7] (Cohen was at one with the majority of the German Social Democratic Party, against Rosa Luxemburg and her allies, in supporting the Kaiser's war effort.) The older man angrily repudiated the criticism, and then went on further to develop his patriotic standpoint in a lengthy article of 1915. Which, considered in historic retrospect, seems really rather poignant – as his whole argument was that there exists a special affinity between the true spirit of Judaism and the genius of German culture at its best.[8] The relationship between the two men quickly recovered. But, even so, the difference in outlook that came to the surface here was clearly fundamental.

Rose's essential objection to both Cohen and Rosenzweig is that, notwithstanding their differences, they each effectively identify Jewish truth with the corporate innocence that derives from a history of having been spared the temptations of power. The Judaism they seek to uphold is, strictly, the Judaism of exile. Neither of them therefore has any sympathy with Zionism. Cohen rejects it for the sake of a Jewish philosophic commitment to German patriotism; Rosenzweig, for the sake of an altogether depoliticized religious ideal. Either way, however, what is being celebrated is the virtue of an exile community. In other words: not so much virtue gained in the deliberate, free overcoming of temptation, but rather the virtue of an unchosen, violently imposed innocence.

According to Rosenzweig, among Cohen's papers, when he died, was a manuscript, now lost, on Kant's antisemitism. Such was his impassioned loyalty to Kant, he could not bring himself to publish it in his lifetime.[9] Yet, if Kant had only known a little more of true Judaism, Cohen wants to argue, he would no doubt have come to recognize, ever more vividly, just how close the special affinity is between the ideal of 'religion within the limits of reason alone', as he envisaged it, and Jewish tradition. For it is out of the latter that the actual possibility of our recognizing that ideal historically originates. And moreover no other historic tradition continues, in principle, to bear such unambiguous testimony to the ideal as Judaism does. In fact, Rose comments, Cohen's 'religion of reason' departs much more radically than he is willing to allow from Kant's 'religion within the limits of reason alone'.[10] Kant rejects any form of religious loyalty to a tradition framed by the authority of historic revelation. It is simple consistency in adherence to this principle – not prejudicial ignorance – that leads him to reject Judaism as he does; in just the same way that he also rejects Christianity. Cohen however wants, so far as possible, to exempt Judaism from Kant's critique – while at the same time holding fast to Kant's repudiation of Christianity, understood as a completely different sort of case.

Of course, Cohen acknowledges the historic role of Christianity both in helping spread biblical monotheism globally, and also in creating the cultural context out of which the German Enlightenment, Kant included, emerged.[11] But it is a grudging acknowledgement. He is much more interested in highlighting how Christianity, at the same time as spreading the truth of Jewish monotheism, has also, in his view, betrayed it. Thus, as he understands it, 'religion of reason' is monotheistic in form; but is also, in substance, a celebration of the sheer universality of the universal moral law, universal human rights, as that which is uniquely sacred. It can only gain its proper emotional power by being transmitted through national traditions. One's loyalty to such a particular tradition is, therefore, a necessary restriction on the universality of one's humanity. But the highest forms of national tradition – the liberal Jewish and the socialist German traditions – are, nevertheless, essentially openings towards the universal. Christianity is problematic, Cohen thinks, because it introduces another sort of loyalty, supplementary to, and in competition with, national loyalties, which is, by its very nature, highly divisive. Faith in Christ, loyalty to the Church, presents itself as a precondition for eternal bliss, which is supposedly denied to all outsiders, in a way quite unparalleled by Jewish faith.[12] St Paul's polemical affirmation of salvation by faith in Christ alone, Cohen argues, exalts faith in Christ to the status that properly belongs, on the contrary, to the universal moral law alone.[13] Indeed, Cohen has a very simple basic assessment of the Christian gospel: that it is essentially a spoiling of the beautiful poetic truth inherent in the 'Suffering Servant Songs' of Deutero-Isaiah. For the gospel takes the prophet's great affirmation of Jewish martyrdom, understood in principle as a suffering for the whole of humanity's sake, and, by applying it to Christ, understood as God incarnate, corrupts it into a mere ideology of spiritual imperialism – a bid to conquer and subdue, rather than affirm, humanity.[14]

There are various things to be said in response to this. (a) Cohen's critique would not apply to any form of Christian theology affirming the possibility of 'anonymous Christianity'; which immediately does away with the crude link he so deplores between salvation and actual membership of the Church. (b) It is a very abstract dismissal of Christianity. Cohen does not, for instance, engage at all with Hegelian understanding of Christology; nor does he engage with the Kierkegaardian understanding.[15] (c) As an interpretation of Judaism, Cohen's theology is purely apologetic. He develops no immanent critique of rabbinic Jewish tradition, to balance his critique of Christianity. Hence (d) there is no philosophic reading of Jewish history here equivalent to Hegel's philosophic reading of Christian history – as setting a context for criticism of the Church, in so far as it has failed to appropriate the historic opportunities of the present day, for a fresh and deeper understanding of gospel truth. And (e) neither is there anything equivalent to Kierkegaard's anguished prophetic critique of the Church. Certainly Kierkegaard seems much closer in spirit to classical Hebrew prophecy (above all, the prophecy of Amos!) than Cohen does.

From Rose's point of view, the great objection to Cohen's whole standpoint is that, as a result, he has effectively disqualified himself from the proper philosophic role of peace-making mediation – either between Jews and Christians, or between liberal, secularizing Jews and more orthodox Jews, simply intent on preserving a maximum intensity of Jewish *Sittlichkeit*. The trouble is that in both cases alike he is simply an advocate of one side against the other.

As for Rosenzweig, on the other hand: he, for his part, certainly puts himself in a much better position than Cohen to mediate between Judaism and Christianity – and between the different traditions of modern Judaism, in so far as these represent different degrees of separation from the Christian environment, as such. Only, the basic trouble here is, he does so in a way that conversely, in effect, disqualifies him from mediating between the upholders of biblical *Sittlichkeit* and the protagonists of post-Enlightenment secularism.

Indeed, Rosenzweig dedicates Part 3 of his classic work, *The Star of Redemption*, to setting out how he envisages the ideally complementary vocations of Judaism and Christianity. He expresses it in terms of a basic contrast between two relationships to 'History'. For its part, Christian faith – he argues – grows out of the commemoration of an historical event, understood as the launching of a grand historical project. The Church can, therefore, only connect with eternity indirectly, by way of that historical project: the quest for missionary growth. But, by contrast, Judaism is, uniquely, the existence of the 'eternal people', who relate to eternity much more directly. Inasmuch as the Jewish people's memories of God irrupting into history, and their hopes of a future messianic irruption, do not coalesce into anything like the Church's all-encompassing missionary project, they remain outside 'History', in the Christian sense. And this is, in its way, a great blessing. For the Christian project – necessary as it is – constantly tends to generate compromises with the pagan world, as the missionary community is tempted to adapt its gospel, so as to make it more attractive. But the Jewish people's existence 'outside History', by contrast, tends to keep them all the more focused on the two prime commandments: that we should love the Lord our God with all our heart, all our soul, all our mind, all our strength, and that we should love our neighbours as ourselves. It removes the more or less inevitable distractions arising from the Christian project.

Rosenzweig's argument is partly an apologia for Judaism addressed to philosophic Christians. And partly it is an advocacy of Jewish philosophic open-mindedness towards, at any rate, certain forms of Christianity. This, from Rose's point of view, is all well and good. Yet, note the limitations of this open-mindedness. In the first place, it certainly does not extend to Muslims. Christianity, in its impatience for missionary success, may be tempted, against its better nature, to become coercive; Islam, as Rosenzweig pictures it in Part 2 of *The Star of Redemption*, has no such better nature to betray. It is, he suggests, a form of religion radically corrupted by coerciveness from the outset. This does not seem to be a judgement based on any serious study of Muslim history. 'Islam', in this context, is quite an abstract concept; a sheer projection of prejudice. Anxious to build an alliance between Christians and Jews, Rosenzweig is simply interested in their uniting against a common enemy. So he constructs a bogeyman, and calls it 'Islam'.

And then, too, a core principle of Rosenzweig's theology is his implacable opposition to any association of religious symbolism with secular political hopes, or any alliance of religious people with secular political forces. Hence his rejection of Zionism, in particular – but it is not just Zionism. The same general principle is also what underlies his anti-Hegelianism. It is, in fact, a generalization of his original reaction against Hegel. Thus, when Rosenzweig speaks of the Jews as a people historically 'outside History', by 'History' he means the secular history of sovereign states, their wars and revolutions. As an exiled people, the Jews have developed a sense of salvation history completely detached from 'History', so defined. The Christian notion of salvation history, on the contrary, has been immersed in 'History'; but still, Rosenzweig thinks, everything depends on the two being kept conceptually quite distinct here. That is to say, they must not be mixed as Hegel above all mixes them. Hegel systematically secularizes Christian salvation history in the sense that, as he interprets it, the history of the revelation of the kingdom of God is none other than a religious envisioning of the history of progress towards the possibility of an ideal secular order: one that is supremely open to the free play of the free spirit. Rosenzweig will have none of this – because of the element of coercive violence inevitably involved in the establishment and maintenance of any secular political order. He wants religion kept, so far as possible, apart from all forms of coercion; not only that of 'holy war', but also that which belongs to secular law and order. And so, unlike Hegel, he completely rules himself out from acting as a philosophic mediator between the militant devotees of Jewish or Christian idealism and the defenders of secular 'political realism'. He rules himself out by putting himself, right from the outset, altogether on the side of the former.

Inasmuch as secular 'political realism' is surely a moral standpoint that, at least, merits being taken seriously, Rose deplores this purported move 'beyond' Hegel. In Hegelian terms, she argues that Rosenzweig's prescription for Christianity is really a mere advocacy for the 'beautiful soul'. Rosenzweig takes up what was originally Schelling's scheme of church history, distinguishing between three epochs: (a) the 'Petrine' epoch, which is the period culminating in the high Middle Ages; (b) the 'Pauline' epoch, the period inaugurated by the Reformation; and (c) the 'Johannine' epoch, the period beginning more or less in Schelling's own day, the early nineteenth century. This is understood to be a story of progress, as Christian hope is increasingly set free from strong this-worldly institutional loyalties; not only from the sort of loyalty demanded by the pre-Reformation Church – but then, also, from that demanded by the Protestant state. The ideal 'Johannine' church is supposed to be completely 'invisible'; with no institutional structure at all beyond a loose network of friendships, held together only by faith in the form of a certain pious, yearning hope. But, Rose remarks, 'the combination [here] of Piety, invisibility and hope delineates exactly the kind of integration with the world that Goethe . . . explored and deplored as "the beautiful soul" in Book VI of *Wilhelm Meister's Apprenticeship*. "The beautiful soul" expires from a surfeit of *unbounded* good will, for she can find no form, no middle, no world, to resist and reform her heavenly hopes.'[16]

Again, Hegel for his part sets out to undertake a systematic interrogation of history *at every level*, from the point of view of one looking for examples of Spirit at work, in the opening up of good, open conversation. In principle, therefore, the all-encompassing history of Spirit encompasses not only the world of 'History', in Rosenzweig's narrow sense of that word, but also, and just as much, the world of the people 'outside History'. It is true that Hegel, as a Christian, does not focus on the latter. As Rose sees it, though, a true Jewish move beyond Hegel would involve a systematic study of Spirit going about its conversation-opening work in the history of the Jewish diaspora, just as Hegel provides such a study of Classical Pagan and Christian history. In simply rejecting the Hegelian grand narrative, Rosenzweig, she argues, has still not managed, fully, to transcend the Christian-confessional limitations of Hegel's altogether Christian thought-world.[17]

In its political aspect the history of Spirit, as Hegel understands it, may be said to be the history of the institutionalization, through good law, of the preconditions for good public conversation of every kind. Yet, the point is, the 'law' in question here is not only the law of the state. One may equally well interrogate the history of Jewish community law from this point of view: asking to what extent it is well designed both to hold open a space for good conversation within the Jewish community, and also to open up at least an offer of good conversation with the surrounding world. Rosenzweig does not consider it theologically necessary to do this – he does not trace the *history* of Jewish responses to exile at all, any more than Cohen does. (Or than Levinas does, after him.) Instead, he draws a sharp distinction between historic religious 'law' and the trans-historic 'commandment' of love. And he argues that what is theologically significant is only what directly belongs to the 'commandment', not the 'law'. From Rose's point of view this distinction between 'commandment' and 'law' looks like a fundamental evasion of theology's proper task.

And neither does Rosenzweig go beyond Cohen to develop any very serious critique of actual rabbinic practice, comparable to Kierkegaard's prophetic assault, in the name of Christ, on 'Christendom'. He lists two sets of three 'dangers' each, one set attendant upon Christianity, the other upon Judaism.[18] In the case of Christianity, the 'dangers' are

- 'the spiritualization of God', or the excess of the 'Johannine' Church, in sheer withdrawal from the secular world;
- 'the humanization of God', or the excess of the 'Pauline' church, in sheer, inadequately critical celebration of the secular world's creativity; and
- 'the secularization of God', or the excess of the 'Petrine' church, where it seeks hegemonically to absorb the secular world.

And the corresponding Jewish 'dangers' are

- 'denial of the world', in comfortable, complete separation of the Jewish community;
- 'disdain of the world', in bitter resentment against Gentile persecutors;
- 'mortification of the world', in the elaboration of a merely neurotic legalism, to block the inertia of assimilation.

But he just lists these dangers, in the abstract. He does not tell stories about them, or wrestle with them. Therefore, in Rose's terms, he does not really break out of the 'holy middle' he has made for himself; he does not, after all, find himself in the 'broken middle'.

꧁❦꧂

The two contemporary Christian theologians Rose chiefly considers in *The Broken Middle* are *Mark C. Taylor* and *John Milbank*.[19] And, just as in the case of Cohen and Rosenzweig – or Strauss and Levinas – she understands Taylor and Milbank, also, as standing, in Janus-face fashion, for two opposing forms of prejudicial one-sidedness. For Taylor represents a singularly radical privileging of the secular, in its challenge to *sittlich* church tradition; Milbank, on the contrary, a no less radical rhetoric of hostility towards (what he calls) 'the secular' in general.

Taylor is a leading American thinker in the tradition stemming from the 'Death of God' movement of the later 1960s, most notably the work of Thomas J. J. Altizer. He was a friend of Jacques Derrida, and is comparable also to John Caputo, as advocate of a 'deconstructionist' approach to theology. In British terms, one might perhaps compare him above all to Don Cupitt. But he attracts Rose's interest more than any other figure from this milieu basically because of the way in which, like her, he too frames his thought as a project of bringing together Hegel with Kierkegaard. His first major book, *Journeys to Selfhood*, originally published in 1980, is entirely devoted to this project.[20] And the argument of *Journeys to Selfhood* persists as a major presence in his later thinking as well, alongside his subsequently emergent interest in Nietzsche and Heidegger, and their successors.[21]

Rose approves of the comprehensive way Taylor approaches the Hegel/Kierkegaard relationship. Yet, at the same time, she adumbrates a twofold critique of *Journeys to Selfhood*. In the first place, she questions the way Taylor 'presupposes and hypostatizes "selfhood" as a final goal'.[22] He adopts the concept for its neutral applicability to the subject matter of both Hegel's and Kierkegaard's thinking. Only, note the bias it imports. Thus: might not an equally neutral title for the book, for instance, have been '*Progressive Unfoldings of True Authority*'? Both Hegel and Kierkegaard, after all – each in their very different ways – are concerned, not least, to try and define the criteria by which to validate the proper authority claims of a reformed *Sittlichkeit*. Taylor, though, is just not interested in this aspect of their thinking. He is only interested in the ways they may both be said to attack the 'authoritarianism' of corrupted *Sittlichkeit*; the concern they both show to liberate the 'self' enslaved by such corruption. The phrase 'journeys to selfhood' immediately captures that first moment of negation in the thinking of each. It does not so immediately capture the subsequent negation of this negation, which is just as much a feature of both thinkers' intent; that is, their holding fast to the prospect of a reformed, no longer oppressive, but nevertheless re-energized *Sittlichkeit*. However, Taylor adopts the phrase because he wants to focus, exclusively, on the initial element of sheer anti-'authoritarianism' in the thought of both.

And then, second, she criticizes the way in which, as she puts it, Taylor 'attributes each and every position to "Hegel" or to "Kierkegaard" *simpliciter*, without negotiating phenomenology, system or pseudonym'.[23] This is perhaps overstated. But in a sense it is the same point repeated, from another angle. Thus, the 'Hegel' and 'Kierkegaard' of Taylor's account are thinkers who are simply working through their own experiences of *self*-liberation, from corrupt authoritarianism. Taylor just is not interested in the other aspect of their thought: the aspiration of both thinkers to attune themselves to the proper authority of *sittlich* tradition at its best, and moreover to *represent* that authority. Why, though, does Hegel write a *Phenomenology of Spirit*, rather than, more modestly, a spiritual autobiography? Why, in general, does he construct the sort of system he does? And why does Kierkegaard develop his peculiar strategy of pseudonymous authorship? Both thinkers, in the end, want to speak, not only on behalf of their own selves, but also on behalf of *sittlich* authority. They do not do so, however, as official, commissioned representatives; people who have straight-forwardly been given the right, by the institutions of *sittlich* tradition, to speak on its behalf. Rather, they are, both of them, acutely aware of their need as philosophers to *earn* that right, by hard conversational work. They are anxious, as Rose expresses it elsewhere in *The Broken Middle*, not merely to 'arrogate' the authority of spokespeople. And these are the elaborate ways in which they therefore attempt to earn what, in this regard, they aspire to. Taylor has no such ambition. Nor does he really seem to see it in either Hegel or Kierkegaard.

Indeed, the essential one-sidedness of Taylor's theological approach emerges all the more clearly in his work after *Journeys to Selfhood*. Rose focuses in particular on his book *Erring*, which begins with a fourfold bid, precisely, to liberate Christian tradition, as far as possible, from its traditional character as a system of *Sittlichkeit*. So he presents himself here, first of all, as a witness to the 'death of God' – the 'God' in question, it would seem, is quite simply the God of *Sittlichkeit*, as such. He also, now, proclaims what he calls the 'disappearance of the self'. The concept of true 'self'-hood at the heart of his earlier work has mutated into a concept of not-self-hood; but the difference is just a further escalation of rhetorical negativity towards any lingering identification of one's true 'self' with what a system of *Sittlichkeit*, as such, prescribes. Third, he confronts us with the 'end of history'. 'History', in this context, evidently means the historic content of any *sittlich* worldview. And, fourth, he offers his writing as a contribution to the 'closure of the book'. The 'closed book' for him is, first of all, Holy Scripture, in so far as it is understood as an authoritative basis for Christian *Sittlichkeit*; and then any other sort of text to the extent that it, too, seeks *sittlich* authority.

The resultant work is essentially good news for the 'beautiful soul'. In effect, it portrays the alienation of the 'beautiful soul', from any actual *sittlich* community, as a basic precondition for the very highest wisdom. Taylor's gospel is a message of consolation to the all too often despondent 'beautiful soul': a set of reasons for the 'beautiful soul' to be cheerful. In other words – it is the very purest modern 'Gnosticism'. It is not just that Taylor seeks to dissolve the authority of Christian *Sittlichkeit* at every level. His theology is, in fact, remarkable for its complete lack of apparent connection with *any* form of church life whatsoever, even the least demanding. In recent years he has become an internet entrepreneur; he co-founded the Global Education Network, a company dedicated to pioneer experimental use of the internet for purposes of higher education. The ultimate inspiration behind this enterprise seems to be something like a vision of virtual Gnostic community on a global scale. That is the sort of community Taylor believes in, far rather than any church.

And, again, it is not just that he repudiates any approach to theology attempting to appropriate *sittlich* authority for itself. But his writing is remarkable, generally, for its sheer, principled lightness of tone. It is often quite brilliantly witty, in its playful way. But in the end – lacking as it does the sharp-edgedness that comes from contested authority claims – the net result is, it comes across (to me at least) as little more than a sort of erudite *burble*. As the not dissimilar example of Jacques Derrida, especially, shows, such burble has the potential to fuel whole academic industries. It can become all-absorbing, to those who have acquired a taste for it. And yet, it is certainly odd in a commentator on Hegel and Kierkegaard. For there could scarcely be anything further removed in tone, than this, from the tremendous speculative intensity of Hegel's work; nor could anything less resemble Kierkegaard's critical ferocity!

Turning now to Milbank – he might well, at first sight, seem to differ from Taylor in every way. For here, in fact, we have a thinker who has been influenced by Rose. Specifically, he has taken up her critique of the classic sociological tradition, in *Hegel contra Sociology*. Milbank's breakthrough book, *Theology and Social Theory*, develops another version of this critique, on a truly epic scale. Thus, its argument begins with a thunder clap:

> Once, there was no 'secular'. And the secular was not latent, waiting to fill more space with the steam of the 'purely human', when the pressure of the sacred was relaxed. Instead there was the single community of Christendom, with its dual aspects of *sacerdotium* and *regnum*. The *saeculum*, in the medieval era, was not a space, a domain, but a time – the interval between fall and *eschaton* where coercive justice, private property and impaired natural reason must make shift to cope with the unredeemed effects of sinful humanity.
>
> The secular as a domain had to be instituted or *imagined*, both in theory and practice. This institution is not correctly grasped in merely negative terms as a desacralization . . .
>
> Received sociology altogether misses the positive institution of the secular, because it fully embraces the notion of humanism as the perennial destiny of the west.[24]

Not so, Milbank argues. But, instead, we need to see that 'positive institution' as the disastrous outcome of an entirely contingent (anti-)theological heresy, which classical sociology continues to

enshrine. And, he also argues, this is a heresy that the later developing traditions of postmodern nihilism then merely reinforce.

'Radical Orthodoxy', the whole movement of thought which
Theology and Social Theory was largely instrumental in launching,
represents a sort of revolutionary upheaval within academia,
spreading from Britain to America. Once upon a time, the more
turbulent university lecturers and students would naturally tend to
identify themselves as Marxists. That of course became less and less
of an attractive prospect as the realities of 'actually existing socialism' grew clearer, in the period up to 1989. But Radical Orthodoxy
now offers a 'Christian Socialist' alternative. The decline of old
fashioned religion-as-respectability, especially in British culture,
has helped set theology free, potentially, to fulfil this role. And
Radical Orthodoxy is a bid to seize that unprecedented opportunity. Its field of operations is very much the university, rather than
the institutional Church. It is largely a movement of lay theologians, and its thinking has not, on the whole, been developed with
the concerns and internal problems of the institutional Church
in mind at all. This is its basic difference from the other great
twentieth-century theological movements reasserting the fundamental claims of Christian *Sittlichkeit* – especially the Protestant
ones, the Dooyeweerdian or Barthian schools. Unlike them, the
theology of Radical Orthodoxy is not primarily oriented towards
the training of preachers, as such. The irritation with which liberal
clergy often respond to it is no doubt to some extent a symptom of
their clericalism. But Radical Orthodoxy is, in essence, an approach
to theology designed to outflank and bewilder the theologian's
more defensively secular-minded academic colleagues. The writings of its adherents tend to be quite ostentatiously scholarly,
difficult and polemical, to that strategic end.

This was by no means off-putting to Rose. Indeed, she was one of
the original publisher's readers for *Theology and Social Theory*.[25]
The text had grown, and mutated, into something rather different
from what had originally been commissioned; but, despite having

major reservations from the start, she recommended it enthusi-astically, recognizing its great importance straight away. She was both, at one and the same time, exasperated by Milbank's basic argument and also filled with admiration for the sheer prodigious ambition of the work; all the more exasperated, indeed, because of her unstinting admiration.

Radical Orthodoxy, in general, traces the 'positive institution of the secular', above all, back to the theology of Duns Scotus in the late thirteenth and early fourteenth centuries. What Scotus intro-duces – so the argument goes – is a disastrous new metaphysical understanding of what it means to know God. Hitherto, the whole Christian philosophic tradition, up to and notably including Thomas Aquinas, had agreed that to know God means the same as to know the inner rationality of all being; that is, the true, system-atic, natural and moral orderedness of all creatures, as this appears to human reason. And, conversely, it had always been agreed that to know the inner rationality of all being is, by analogy, to know the perfection of the Creator, in which all rationality participates. Faith and reason were thus essentially understood as being two aspects, the existential and the theoretical, of one and the same *sittlich* thinking. Scotus however, on the contrary, taught that to know God, in faith, is to encounter 'a' being, decisively set apart from all other beings – for the very reason that God uniquely transcends all grasp of reason. What is happening here? Scotus, in effect, sets faith over *against* reason, in a way that had never been done before: developing the supposed opposition in the form of a systematic philosophical argument. In other words, theology, as the intellec-tual discipline of faith, is here, for the first time in Christian intellectual history, starting systematically to come apart from philosophy, as the discipline of natural reason. Now, there are two possible motives for wanting to set theology and philosophy apart. Either (a) one wants to 'liberate' theology from the (originally pagan) traditions of philosophy, drawing it increasingly back to its other roots in prayer and the reading of the Bible, understood as being in some competition with philosophy. Or (b) one wants to 'liberate' philosophy from theology. Scotus's own motivation appears, in fact, to have been very much the former. He is a scholastic thinker seeking, in this way, to point beyond the sophisticated truth-claims of scholastic theology, towards the other, more primordial modes of theological truth. But the trouble is, the way he does so also serves the interests of those who are, on the contrary, eager to 'liberate' philosophy, in the sense of developing new approaches to moral and political thought unimpeded by the sorts of *sittlich* inhibition enshrined by theology. And over the following period, as theology and philosophy continued increasingly to split apart, the eventual upshot was the emergence of what Milbank calls 'secular reason'; which he regards not at all as a 'liberation', but far rather as a disastrous mere imaginative impoverishment of philosophy. Rose herself largely agrees with this. As a Hegelian critic both of hard-line secular humanism, as it culminates in the form of classic sociology, and also of postmodern nihilism, she likewise deplores the original Scotist splitting move. In *Dialectic of Nihilism* she specifically criticizes the twentieth-century appropriation, and adaptation, of 'Scotist' ontology both by Heidegger and by Deleuze.[26] In so doing, she already to some extent anticipates Milbank's later, more developed critique.[27]

She is altogether at one with Milbank in his reaffirmation of the old, originally Christian-Platonist, principle that to know God is to know the inner rationality of all being, and *vice versa*; only, the difference between them lies in her understanding of the actual *criteria* for such knowledge. For she accepts the criteria systematically analysed by Hegel in the *Phenomenology of Spirit*. But Milbank, on the other hand, along with Radical Orthodoxy as a whole, lacks this level of explicit theory. The chapter 'For and Against Hegel' in *Theology and Social Theory* unfortunately reproduces elements of the old prejudicial Hegel myth: in particular, that Hegel's encyclopaedic system is intended by him not just as an openly and freely evolving pedagogic strategy, but as a dogmatic, 'totalizing' closure to fundamental fresh insights. Nor does this chapter really get to grips with the true challenge of Hegel's Christology.[28] Its basic thrust is just that Hegel fails adequately to denounce 'modern politics and political economy' in the name of the gospel. 'There is, therefore, no true *Sittlichkeit* in Hegel's ethical and political theory', Milbank argues.[29] In Rose's terms, he simply does not value Hegel's fidelity to the 'broken middle'. He wants, from the outset, to be much more one-sided.

Against the secular humanist grand narratives of Enlightenment thinking, but also against the nihilist postmodern rejection of all grand narrative, Milbank advocates the boldest possible return to Christian grand narrative. However, it is not a return to Hegel. Rather, he develops a renewed, anti-Scotist 'Augustinianism'. He constructs a highly detailed grand narrative of theological, and hence wider cultural, decline, stemming from the time of Scotus; but also of potential theological recovery, in a 'post-modern' re-appropriation of the wisdom of Augustine above all. Thus, modern secular humanism and postmodern nihilism appear here as two great modes of ideological self-assertion on the part of what Augustine calls the 'Earthly City': the ethos essentially constituted by human fallenness, the lust for exploitative domination and its accompanying love of 'glory'. And they are therefore, according to Augustinian principle, to be combated by the most *intransigent* possible counter-imagining of the 'Heavenly City', the ethos constituted on the contrary by the pure love of God. That is: the very purest form of infinite, non-violent desire, as opposed to violent neediness, or addiction.

In terms of practical moral judgement, Milbank is in fact quite a cheerful product of originally 'secular' twentieth-century cultural developments. As a member of the Church of England, he approves for instance of the ordination of women to the priesthood, the actual pressure for which clearly originated from developments in the 'secular' world. Likewise, he takes a liberal line on the current struggles over sexual ethics in the Anglican Communion. He is, in general, politically progressive. These are not the attitudes of Augustine. But his Augustinianism is essentially a matter of rhetorical style. And Rose is mistrustful of it just because she senses that this immediate reduction of everything to the elementary struggle between the two 'cities', of God and man, merely serves, in the end, to mask and justify a basic reflex of recoil from the 'broken middle'.

Thus, a true Church of the 'broken middle' would be one that was essentially dedicated to conversational openness of every kind. Its worship would be a celebration of conversational openness, as the will of God; its whole prayer life would be a cultivation of the virtues that make for good open conversation. But Augustinianism is, at best, deeply ambiguous in this regard. The pure 'love of God' that constitutes the 'Heavenly City' signifies infinite non-violent desire. Yes, indeed – only, what does that mean in practice? The struggle between the two 'cities' *might* be interpreted as a struggle between the spirit of true conversational openness and all forms of conversation-distorting closure. More immediately, though, Augustine himself presents it as a struggle over the degree to which the Church is perceived as representing a distinctive *Sittlichkeit* all of its own, decisively set over against the prevailing values of the secular world. And the basic thrust of Augustinian rhetoric is just to intensify that sense of contrast. It does not necessarily impel its adherents to act as open-minded mediators between Christian *Sittlichkeit* and its thoughtful critics, in the 'broken middle' of that encounter. Rather, it is an advocacy of *sittlich* purity. So it is characterized by a strong bias against any concession to the critics; a constant inclination to denounce 'sell-outs'. In some circumstances this attitude is no doubt appropriate: the world of the apostolic Church is one example, where the Christian community's survival under persecution largely depended on a resolute determination never to give way. And the situation of the German churches in the Third Reich is certainly another very telling case in point. For here of course, the Augustinian impulse did, in actual fact, directly coincide with resistance to a tyranny that was intent on closing down all real public conversation. In other circumstances, however, the same general species of theology has functioned quite differently, with an altogether less friendly attitude towards conversational openness. As a matter of historical fact, where the Church has itself become a persecutory power Augustinian theology has continued to flourish among the persecutors, there being nothing in the Augustinian tradition, as such, to prevent it. Rose focuses, in *The Broken Middle*, on Milbank and Radical Orthodoxy, but the same basic objection applies to all forms of Augustinian theology. In the Protestant context, it is no less applicable to the Augustinianism of Dooyeweerd, or Barth, and their followers; and in the Catholic context, to such thinkers, whom Milbank especially admires, as von Balthasar, de Lubac, or Congar. These are arguably the finest theologians of the twentieth century, all of them profoundly civilized thinkers. And yet, the point remains. In their thinking, Augustinian habits of thought coincide with civilized instincts, the two are closely intertwined – but they are not identical. Hard-line Augustinianism certainly does look good in extreme circumstances like the German Church Struggle of the 1930s. Only, that is just because of the circumstances. Considered *in itself*, it is a form of theology that still falls well short of a true commitment to abiding in the 'broken middle'. In Rose's terms, it all too easily becomes the ideology of a certain sort of false 'holy middle': *sittlich* purity preferred to openness.

Augustine, intent on his advocacy of *sittlich* purity, speaks of two 'cities', the pure and the impure. Rose, for her part, writes an essay entitled 'Athens and Jerusalem: A Tale of Three Cities'; which, in fact, discusses four.[30] Briefly, these are

1 the 'city' of the true 'broken middle';
2 the 'city' of the false 'holy middle', in various *sittlich* or anti-*sittlich* kinds;
3 'the city in which we all live and with which we are too familiar',

made up of everything belonging to the banal thoughtlessness of everyday modern mass society; and

4 the 'city' of Auschwitz.

Again, ethical reflection today has to reckon with the terrible recognition that the third city harbours the latent possibility of the fourth. But Rose's question here is: what follows, in systematic prescriptive terms? All too often the solution to the problem is understood to lie in the second city – more or less explicitly set over against the first, as 'New Jerusalem' to 'Old Athens'. The particular thinker she refers to in this essay, by way of illustration, is Levinas. Other such arguments, however, are also advanced both by Augustinian theologians and by their polar opposite, 'Death of God' adversaries. The Augustinians want to interpret Auschwitz, perhaps above all, as an outcome of the decay of true Christian *Sittlichkeit*. Their 'Death of God' adversaries, on the contrary, are inclined to see it as a work of 'authoritarianism' in the abstract, clearly demonstrating the need to dissolve all authority of *Sittlichkeit*, not only that for which the Nazis yearned, but also that of traditional church life, at the same time. 'New Jerusalem' is a city with a wide variety of different would-be architects, proclaiming antithetical ideals. What, nevertheless, distinguishes all of them alike is essentially a certain sanctified distaste for mediation. That is what makes 'New Jerusalem' what it is. In all its variants, pro-*Sittlichkeit* or anti-*Sittlichkeit*, it is a city of embattled purists, forever crying: 'No surrender!' As if that was always the issue: a simple choice between hard-line resistance and surrender.

And notwithstanding all their differences, moreover, both Taylor and Milbank are also at one in portraying their ideal dream-'cities' as paradoxically 'nomadic' entities; a 'nomadic' modern individualism in Taylor's case, a 'nomadic *Sittlichkeit*' in Milbank's.[31] The suggestion appears to be that they remain uncorrupted by the sedimentary structures of settled life. As Rose puts it, 'There are no institutions – *dominium* – in either.'[32] Institutions are absent from these 'cities' in the sense that neither thinker seems to be much interested in the patient work of mediation – negotiating between all manner of competing interests, *sittlich* and secular – that institutions, in general, are designed to accomplish. Rose's ideal, by contrast, is not 'nomadic'. For it might be defined as a 'city' which, above all, knows how important it is to honour the mediating work of institutions: 'trade unions, local government, civil service, the learned professions: the arts, law, education, the universities, architecture and medicine'.[33] And one should certainly also add religious institutions to this list – to the extent that they recognize their catholic vocation, *as* institutions, to welcome internal pluralism. 'New Jerusalem', in all its forms, is a 'city' keen perhaps to honour supposedly homogeneous communities, or conscientious individuals, but not, it seems, institutions. Its protagonists believe in bearing witness; some, like Taylor, with a good deal of playfulness, others like Milbank more severely. But they are simply not interested in the somewhat divergent question of what it takes to be a good mediator, or institution-builder. In their vocabulary, the idea of an 'institution' does not appear to have any very exciting, or attractive, connotations. Rather, the rhetoric of 'nomadic' wisdom suggests a prejudicial association of settled institutions with banality, or oppression – almost as if, to these thinkers, institutions were, even where necessary, nothing more than a necessary evil.

There is no evidence of their having any real appreciation for institution building, as a creative art. That, as Rose sees it, is the basic problem.

8

Unwrapping the Gift

❦

In opting to be baptized on her deathbed, Gillian Rose was so to speak offering her philosophical work as a gift to the Church, for theological appropriation. And this has been my attempt to start unwrapping that gift. It seems to me a shame that her work has, in general, been so neglected since her death, and in particular that it has not received much more theological attention.[1]

Why has it, up to now, not sparked more debate in this context?

Well, in the first place, there is of course the obstacle of her style. I have tried to explain why her writing is so difficult; why, in a sense, I think it almost has to be, in order for her to accomplish the extraordinarily ambitious task she has set herself. Admittedly, there are not many people to whom one could recommend that they actually go and read her books; other than, perhaps, *Love's Work.* But then one might say the same about a good deal of the literature produced by Radical Orthodoxy, and it has by no means prevented that movement from flourishing. Why have there been no previous published books, attempting to get to grips with her thought from a theological point of view; and to try and rework it, so as to make it at least a little more accessible? I hope I have shown that she does in fact represent a very serious challenge to the prevailing intellectual fashions of the day. But then I wonder: maybe that is the real reason for this neglect? Does it merely go to show how stifling the grip of intellectual fashion is, both in the secular world and in the Church? I do not know. At all events, though, it is true: she has nothing to offer those theologians whose primary interest is in apologetics. And, at the same time, her approach is also fundamentally inimical to those others whose chief theological concern is with ecclesiastical border control, seeking to justify the always threatened, or actual, excommunication of their opponents.

In so far as 'liberal' theology is all about apologetics – that is, a project of aiming to make faith *easier* for secular folk – Rose is by no means a 'liberal'. She has not, herself, come to faith easily – on the contrary. And she is moreover, heart and soul, with Kierkegaard's 'Johannes Climacus': her whole philosophic ambition, in this regard, is 'to make everything more difficult'. Her systematic project aims, first and foremost, to uncover the proper difficulty of faith; not only in theory, but also in practice.

Yet, on the other hand, the implicit ecclesiological drive of her thought is surely all towards the ideal of the most all-inclusive Church. If our true meeting place with God's grace is in the 'broken middle', then we will certainly never be keen to excommunicate our opponents. For what else is excommunication if not a device for trying to protect the ecclesiastical middle from further breakage, by blocking out certain pressures on it? No doubt the Confessing Church in the Third Reich was justified in excommunicating the Nazi 'German Christian Movement', inasmuch as that movement threatened, otherwise, to take the Church over and forcibly extinguish all further public debate. But, again, this is not a model for many other situations.

The international Anglican Communion, today, actually presents quite a tragic scenario. Thus: charged with holding it all together is an Archbishop of Canterbury absolutely after Rose's own heart. Indeed Rowan Williams was a friend of hers; he knows her work well, and his own thinking is, at any rate, akin to hers. Yet the job is an impossible one. For all around him are people simply itching to declare themselves in 'impaired communion' with one another, and forever threatening each other with full excommunication. I am, myself, unequivocally on the side of the progressives in this dispute. Only – it is a question of what kind of Church one wants to belong to. Is it one that is a shelter against other people's folly? Or is it a Church that is fully opened up to the 'broken middle' of its environing culture, or cultures? The former puts its faith in excommunication; the latter, on the contrary, wants to include within itself every sort of moral standpoint that can be at all honestly, in the sense of open-mindedly, adopted. It understands the imperatives of the gospel not as demanding any suppression of internal theological conflict, but rather an ideal Honesty in the mediating of it. Tragically, this sort of true philosophic spirit is conspicuous by its rarity among the current leaders of the Communion.

꒰ঌ◈ʚ꒱

A year after her death, as noted above, the then Archbishop of Canterbury, George Carey, paid fulsome tribute to Rose in his Christmas sermon. Clearly, the story had captured his imagination. He was struck by the very idea of a major secular philosopher turning, right at the last, to God.

And yet, it makes me wonder: why, after all, should this seem *so* remarkable?

Indeed, what really is remarkable is how very few of the leading philosophers of the later nineteenth and twentieth centuries were also devout, orthodox Christians to whom their Christianity was philosophically significant. After Hegel and Kierkegaard, who else was there – of even remotely comparable stature?

Up to a certain point in the eighteenth century almost all European philosophers were also devout Christians, at least outwardly. The two scandalous exceptions were Machiavelli and (*mutatis mutandis* in a Jewish context) Spinoza. But these truly were regarded as scandalous. This is because it was taken for granted that to endanger the authority of religious faith, among the population at large, was to risk a total collapse of law and order. And that was still a widespread view at the end of the eighteenth century – witness for example Fichte's dismissal from the University of Jena, on a charge of teaching 'atheism'. Gradually thereafter, however, the old fear of irreligion lost its intellectual grip. And it is as though everything most creative in the world of philosophy from the mid-nineteenth century onwards was part of a great revelry in philosophy's new-found freedom, as a result.

I suspect that, in terms of generating truly original new modes of thought, the revelry is pretty much now spent; and that, looking back, the ferment of postmodern nihilism may well come to be recognized as having been its last great flurry. Confronted by the cultural traumas liable to arise in consequence of global warming and other ecological pressures – the difficulties of rebuilding after natural, or military, catastrophes, the shocks caused by abrupt, large movements of population, the struggles over dwindling resources – will not even the long-secularized intellectuals of the European tradition be driven to appreciate civilization's ever more urgent need for a certain sort of religious *Sittlichkeit*? No secular propaganda, after all, can do what religious liturgy potentially does, in cultivating, and organizing, compassion. Nor can any species of secular organization do what religious organizations can, in cultivating and organizing active international solidarity, right down to the most local level of community.

But if one identifies the call of God, precisely, in this way, with *the promotion and defence of civilization as such* – rather than with the self-assertion of a particular religious tradition, or sub-tradition – then what is needed is surely just the type of thinking that Rose advocates.

Every baptism is a sacramental enactment of conversion; either, in the case of infants, by anticipation, or else in celebratory retrospect. But what exactly had Gillian Rose been converted to? It would appear her being baptized came as something of a surprise to many of her more secular-minded friends. But there is no reason to suppose that it signified any recantation of her published philosophic views. These certainly leave no space for any form of faith supposed to be beyond the supervision of reason. And neither do they allow for any retreat from the 'broken middle', into the mere opinion-atedness of 'a' faith. (She nowhere lapses into that barbarous, new, secularist corruption of the English language, the usage of the word 'faith' as if it designated a type of entity that exists in the plural!) Rather, she represents faith at its most authentically philosophic. That is to say: faith understood, in essence, as a sheer *intensification* of true philosophic questioning. She was baptized in celebration of her faith in the God of the 'broken middle'. And, inasmuch as the 'broken middle' is the well-spring of restless creativity from which all true civilization, in the end, draws its life, this is faith, in the most direct way, dedicated to the cause of civilization as a whole.

Presented with an open choice between bequeathing her work, in the first instance, either to Judaism or to Christianity, her eventual option for Christian baptism simply reflects the obvious fact that, in principle, the lead role in showing forth the God of the 'broken middle' to European civilization *as a whole* must be played by the Church. She was held back from the decision, right to the end, by her sensitivity to the history of Christian antisemitism. But, against this background, her baptism is, not least, a gesture of hope for new relationships, of genuine mutual respect, between all three of the great Abrahamic traditions. It is not that she, by any means, repudiates rabbinic Judaism as such. On the contrary, what she would surely repudiate is any approach to theology that fails to rise above the immediate rivalry between Christians, Jews and Muslims.

As it happens, one of her favourite poets was the great

thirteenth-century Sufi Muslim mystic Jalāluddīn Rumi. In part because he is so very translatable, Rumi has of late become rather popular among English-speaking readers; Rose however discovered him more or less by chance.[2] And, as she delighted in the humour of Kierkegaard and the 'comedy of Hegel', she also, at once, warmed to the sometimes ribald humour, and the sublime comedy, of Rumi's work.

Here then, by way of conclusion, is a poem of Rumi's, one which I think quite beautifully celebrates the God of the 'broken middle':

'Subtle Degrees'

subtle degrees
of domination and servitude
are what you know as love

but love is different
it arrives complete
just there
like the moon in the window

like the sun
of neither east nor west
nor of anyplace

when that sun arrives
east and west arrive

desire only that
of which you have no hope
seek only that
of which you have no clue

love is the sea of not being
and there intellect drowns

this is not the Oxus River
or some little creek
this is the shoreless sea;
here swimming ends
always in drowning

a journey to the sea
is horses and fodder and contrivance

but at land's end
the footsteps vanish

you lift up your robe
so as not to wet the hem;
come! drown in this sea
a thousand times

the moon passes over
the ocean of nonbeing

droplets of spray tear loose
and fall back on the cresting waves

a million galaxies
are a little scum
on that shoreless sea[3]

Let us, very briefly, consider this poem: what, in actual reality, lies behind its comic hyperbole?

The poet is looking out of a window. He is looking out from the middle of his world, first of all in the sense that this is a poem about what ought to matter most of all in life. And then the moon appears, as a vision of completeness, in the far distance, highlighting by contrast the incompleteness – in Rose's alternative metaphor, the 'brokenness' – of the earthly, walled-in middle where he stands. That is: the whole structure of habits and prejudices framing his given identity.

To be situated in the middle is to be stranded between opposing pulls, here represented by 'east and west'. But the moon now mutates into the all-reconciling sun:

> when that sun arrives
> east and west arrive

They 'arrive' – all the opposing pulls 'arrive' – to be reconciled. The love of which the poem speaks is, surely, none other than the self-effacement of the ideal mediator. It is that self-effacement, inasmuch as it serves as a channel for the all-reconciling work of divine *agapé*.

In its ideal fulfilment

> love is the sea of not being
> and there intellect drowns

What Rumi speaks of as the 'sea' – is this not what Hegel means by 'absolute knowing'? In Hegelian terms, 'absolute knowing' overwhelms 'the understanding' (*Verstand*) in the sense that the latter is a mode of thinking entirely oriented towards abstract, propositional truth-as-correctness. For, again, what such 'knowing' knows is the absolute moral priority, far outranking any scholarly or dogmatic interest in pure truth-as-correctness, of truth-as-perfect-conversational-openness.

And is not Rumi's 'sea', also, a direct non-Christian anticipation of what Kierkegaard conceives as the true appropriation of the 'absolute paradox' at the heart of the gospel?

So too, one might compare St Paul's words about baptism: 'Do you not know that all of us who have been baptized into Christ Jesus were baptized into his death? Therefore we have been buried with him by baptism into death, so that, just as Christ was raised from the dead by the glory of the Father, so we too might walk in newness of life' (Romans 6.3–4). Where Rumi speaks of 'drowning', Paul speaks of 'dying with Christ' in the waters of baptism.

Notwithstanding the complete difference in context, is there not at least some analogy between the two ideas?

Meanwhile, Rose's meditation on the need for an unflinching recognition, and acceptance, of 'brokenness', right at the heart of things, may I think be seen very much as a fresh philosophic version of Rumi's poetic chiding and summons:

> you lift up your robe
> so as not to wet the hem;
> come! drown in this sea
> a thousand times

The urgent truth of her writing, I would argue, consists, above all, in the way it leaves the reader so profoundly all at sea, in this sense.

Notes

Epigraphs

1 Rowan Williams, *Remembering Jerusalem: Poems*, Oxford: Perpetua Press, 2001, p. 31.
2 Geoffrey Hill, *A Treatise of Civil Power*, London: Penguin, 2007, p. 35.

Chapter 1

1 See for instance the criticism of the then Archbishop's sermon in Martin Kavka, 'Saying Kaddish for Gillian Rose', in Clayton Crockett, ed., *Secular Theology: American Radical Theological Thought*, London and New York: Routledge, 2001, p. 105.

(There are, incidentally, two other minor inaccuracies in the Archbishop's account: her final illness lasted rather more than two years, more like two and a half from the time of the initial diagnosis; and she was in fact too sick to be confirmed, she was only baptized.)

2 See in particular his essay, 'Between Politics and Metaphysics: Reflections in the Wake of Gillian Rose', *Modern Theology* 11.1, 1995. For all its brevity, this is perhaps the most insightful discussion of Rose's thought, as a whole, that has yet appeared.

3 The little book *Paradiso*, edited from her papers by Howard Caygill, is also a sort of supplement to *Love's Work*.

4 Gillian Rose, *Love's Work*, London: Chatto & Windus, 1995, p. 77.

5 *Love's Work*, pp. 43–4. (It is a lively picture, but in fact somewhat fictional: they did not really speak either Russian or Hebrew, and only a minimal amount of French.)

6 *Love's Work*, p. 15. (Again, the bayonets, in this particular case, are actually fictional.)

7 *Love's Work*, pp. 39–40.

8 *Love's Work*, p. 53.

9 Jay, *The Dialectical Imagination: A History of the Frankfurt School and the*

Institute of Social Research, 1923–1950, revised edition, Berkeley: University of California Press, 1996; *Marxism and Totality: the Adventures of a Concept from Lukács to Habermas,* Berkeley: University of California Press, 1992; *Adorno,* London: Fontana, 1984.

10 Jay, 'The Conversion of the Rose', in *Refractions of Violence,* New York and London: Routledge, 2003, p. 62.

11 Jay, 'The Conversion of the Rose', p. 66.

12 Jay, 'The Conversion of the Rose', p. 67.

13 Jay, 'The Conversion of the Rose', p. 70.

14 *Love's Work,* p. 98.

15 *Love's Work,* p. 68. My italics.

16 *Love's Work,* pp. 15–16. The 'bayoneting' is just the most obvious example of poetic licence in this passage. *Love's Work,* in general, shows its author to have been someone who loved the flare of a good story rather more than she cared about strict factual accuracy. And who, moreover, does not seem to have rated tact, or discretion, as major virtues at all.

Her relationship with her mother appears here to have been fraught, but the fact is it was also very close. In her last days (although this is not registered in *Love's Work*) she became highly dependent upon her. And her mother having preceded her into the Church of England some years before was a significant factor in her own final decision to be baptized.

17 *Love's Work,* p. 70.

Chapter 2

1 'Athens and Jerusalem: A Tale of Three Cities', in *Mourning Becomes the Law: Philosophy and Representation,* Cambridge: Cambridge University Press, p. 30.

2 Since 1996, in Germany, 27 January has been a 'Memorial Day for the Victims of National Socialism'. Italy and Poland have also adopted the observance. And the UN General Assembly designated it an international day of remembrance in 2005.

3 Hegel, *Philosophy of Right,* English translation by T. M. Knox, Oxford: Oxford University Press, 1952, Preface, p. 13.

4 The book has been criticized for its 'glibness'. But she replies, 'If the book is "glib", it is because the story it tells is glib – the ironic, sustained glibness of the style is its integrity: it leaves the crisis to the reader.' 'Beginnings of the Day: Fascism and Representation', in *Mourning Becomes the Law,* p. 47. In this context, it is far better to be glib than to be sentimental.

5 *Mourning Becomes the Law,* pp. 47–8.

6 *Mourning Becomes the Law,* p. 43.

7 *The Broken Middle: Out of Our Ancient Society*, Oxford: Blackwell, 1992, pp. 294–6.

8 'Derrida's Spirit', in *Judaism and Modernity: Philosophical Essays*, Oxford: Blackwell, 1993. On what she sees as his misunderstanding of Benjamin, see especially pp. 81–7. Also: 'The Comedy of Hegel', in *Mourning Becomes the Law*, pp. 64–9.

9 Rose discusses Blanchot chiefly in 'Potter's Field: Death Worked and Unworked', and 'O! Untimely Death / Death!' in *Mourning Becomes the Law*.

10 *Mourning Becomes the Law*, pp. 55–8.

11 See 'The Comedy of Hegel' and 'Potters Field: Death Worked and Unworked', in *Mourning Becomes the Law*, and 'Walter Benjamin: Out of the Sources of Modern Judaism', in *Judaism and Modernity*.

12 *Mourning Becomes the Law*, p. 63. The reference is to Hegel, *Aesthetics: Lectures on Fine Art*, trans. T. M. Knox, Oxford: Clarendon Press, 1974–5, vol. 2, p. 1200.

13 *Mourning Becomes the Law*, p. 76.

14 Adorno was a major contributor to the great sociological research project into 'authoritarian' attitudes among the population of the USA, in the later 1940s: Adorno et al., *The Authoritarian Personality*, New York: W. W. Norton & Co., 1950.

15 *Mourning Becomes the Law*, pp. 48–9.

16 Primo Levi, *If This is a Man/The Truce*, trans. Stuart Woolf, Harmondsworth: Penguin, 1979.

17 Tadeusz Borowski, *This Way for the Gas, Ladies and Gentlemen*, English selection trans. Barbara Vedder, Harmondsworth: Penguin, 1976.

18 *Mourning Becomes the Law*, p. 50.

19 *Mourning Becomes the Law*, p. 50.

20 Gitta Sereny, *Into that Darkness: An Examination of Conscience*, London: André Deutsch, 1974.

21 *Mourning Becomes the Law*, p. 61.

Chapter 3

1 Undated letter to Simon Barrington-Ward, quoted in Anna Rowlands, 'Practical Theology in "The Third City"', Ph.D. thesis no. Th28503, Manchester University, 2007, p. 11.

2 This appears as a technical term in *Dialectic of Nihilism* – but in a sense it is the 'question' at the heart of her thought as a whole.

3 She probably derived the formula from her reading of Emil Fackenheim. It is perhaps an unconscious influence – she does not acknowledge it. But Fackenheim actually uses the precise phrase, 'the post-Hegelian broken middle' in *To Mend the World*, New York: Schocken Books, 1982,

p. 127. (I owe this reference to Nick Walker.) And the idea arises out of his extended discussion of the 'Hegelian middle' and its 'crisis' in the 'fragmentation' of the post-Hegelian world, in *The Religious Dimension in Hegel's Thought*, Bloomington, Ind.: Indiana University Press, 1967. Fackenheim here is talking specifically about the 'middle' between the two interpretative approaches of Right Hegelianism and Left Hegelianism; and he also wants to hold fast to this 'middle', just as Rose does.

As we shall see, however, she systematically extends the range of the idea.

4 Hegel, *Phenomenology of Spirit*, English translation by A. V. Miller, Oxford: Oxford University Press, 1977, p. 27.

5 Hegel, *Faith and Knowledge*, English translation by Walter Cerf and H. S. Harris, Albany, NY: SUNY Press, 1977, p. 191. In this famous passage, Hegel is suggesting that the underlying symbolic truth of the Good Friday story has, in principle, become clearer in his own day than ever before – due, albeit indirectly, to the legacy of the Enlightenment. So he speaks of the Enlightenment itself as a large-scale experience of the 'death of God'. Thank God, the old 'God' of rigidly un-negotiative pre-Enlightenment orthodox theology has died a death. Theology is now, as never before, being compelled to negotiate with radical critics. And as a result it is, at least potentially, being opened up to recognize the intrinsic sacredness of negotiative openness, as such. But this is just what Jesus, himself, at the deepest level symbolically represents: the Truth that is identical with the infinite openness of divine Love. The anti-theological, deistic or atheistic thought of the Enlightenment is, in itself, a dead end; and yet, just by virtue of the radicalism of its challenge, it prompts the sort of fresh approach to theology that Hegel himself wants to develop.

6 In what follows I have opted to stick with the Hegelian term *Sittlichkeit* – rather than the perhaps most obvious alternative, 'communitarian ethics' – for two reasons. Both because it is less cumbersome, and because of its relative unfamiliarity in an Anglophone context, which means that it does not have so many potentially misleading preconceptions clinging to it.

7 The threefold-ness of these three modes of innocence directly corresponds to the threefold-ness of the three primordial modes of theology, as analysed in Andrew Shanks, *Faith in Honesty*, Aldershot: Ashgate, 2005. For here, in raw, un-negotiative form, we have the three basic critical impulses which, I there argue, good theology is, systematically, meant to bring together into negotiation, and so open up to the threefold-ness of the Holy Trinity. Thus, the first mode of innocence is what is cancelled and transformed in Second-Person theology; the second mode, in First-Person theology; the third mode, in Third-Person theology.

8 There is evidence, among the papers left behind from her final illness, that at one point she seriously considered the alternative of Roman Catholicism. But she had a number of close Anglican friends, and she was following her mother.

Chapter 4

1 *Hegel contra Sociology*, London: Athlone, 1981, p. 159.

2 On the relationship between the trans-metaphysical argument of the *Phenomenology* and the new-model metaphysics of Hegel's *Logic*: see pp. 79–82.

3 Rose, *Hegel contra Sociology*, pp. 42, 92, 204, 208.

4 See pp. 84–7, 131–40.

5 Consider for example the crucial passage on the 'unhappy consciousness': Hegel, *Phenomenology of Spirit*, English translation by A. V. Miller, Oxford: Oxford University Press, 1977, chapter IV B. This is a classic case in point – with all the unmistakable implicit references, there, to Christian dogma and church history. Hence the most common misinterpretation of the passage, that it is 'really' all about Christianity, and especially the medieval Church. But, in fact, it is all about one of the most elementary obstacles hindering the progress of Spirit, on the way towards 'absolute knowing', in all civilizations, and every subculture within them, alike. Namely: where individuals are held back by a simple lack of the necessary self-confidence to think for themselves, having internalized the prevailing prejudices of the world around them in the form of an aggressively censorious super-ego. Hegel thinks that the essential, especially distinctive truth-potential of Christianity lies in its exceptional capacity to render the problematics of the unhappy consciousness, and the desirability of its overcoming, symbolically explicit. And, as a Christian himself, he is particularly interested in the way that the unhappy consciousness is nevertheless endlessly resurgent, even in Christian culture. However, the fact remains, he is by no means only talking about a phenomenon of Christian culture. And that is why he does not speak of the specifically Christian forms of it more explicitly, in this passage where the concept is first introduced; even though it would no doubt make it so much easier to read if he had. See Andrew Shanks, *Hegel's Political Theology*, Cambridge: Cambridge University Press, 1991, chapter 1.

6 At any rate, *The Melancholy Science* is subtitled *An Introduction to the Thought of Theodor W. Adorno*. But even this work is not really a very introductory introduction.

7 Her final verdict on Adorno is delivered in the essay, 'From Speculative to Dialectical Thinking – Hegel and Adorno', in *Judaism and Modernity*. Here she argues that Adorno misunderstands Hegel. In Hegel's own terms, he has retreated from Hegel's 'speculative thinking' to pure 'dialectical thinking', unmediated by the 'speculative'. 'Dialectical thinking' is pure, principled restlessness of thought. But 'speculative thinking' is just the ideal combination of such restlessness, precisely, with the sort of fixity required in order to provide a basis for effective *Sittlichkeit*.

8 Walter Kaufmann, 'The Hegel Myth and its Method', first published in

his book *The Owl and the Nightingale*, London: Faber & Faber, 1959; then republished in Jon Stewart, ed., *The Hegel Myths and Legends*, Evanston, Ill.: Northwestern University Press, 1996. Kaufmann's essay is a rumbustious critique, in the first instance, of Karl Popper's especially silly and malicious version of the 'myth'. Stewart's book is a collection of essays covering all the various misrepresentations.

9 This misreading always refers to Hegel's famous dictum, in the Preface to his *Philosophy of Right* (English translation by T. M. Knox, Oxford: Oxford University Press, 1952, p. 10), that 'what is rational is actual and what is actual is rational'. But the word 'actual', for Hegel, is a technical term, meaning in effect: what helps actualize 'absolute knowing', historically. It does not mean, as the 'myth' would have it, whatever historically prevails; but it means whatever, in history, most of all needs highlighting, as a contribution to the emergence of that ideal. What is rational is 'actual': in order to understand the demands of pure reason, which is 'absolute knowing', there is a story to be told. Thus, Hegel here is calling for a form of historiography systematically tracing the latent emergence of proper political rationality in the real world, to take us beyond the essentially a-historical approach of traditional natural law theory. And what is 'actual' is rational: if we are properly to understand the history of the human spirit, it needs teleological interpretation precisely as a progressive revelation of the demands of 'absolute knowing'.

Hegel indeed was already driven in his own lifetime to protest against the crude misreading of this densely compacted formulation of his: in section 6 of the third edition of his *Encyclopaedia* (1830); English translation by William Wallace, *Hegel's Logic*, Oxford: Oxford University Press, 1975, p. 9. And see Rose's discussion in *Hegel Contra Sociology*, p. 81.

10 Eric Voegelin is the critic who most aggressively attempts to centre the 'Hegel myth' on an ill-defined, impressionistic charge of 'Gnosticism'. But see Cyril O'Regan's measured remarks on Voegelin in *The Heterodox Hegel*, Albany, NY: SUNY Press, 1994, p. 19. O'Regan's book is, in general, a much more helpful guide to the issue.

As for 'pantheism': see Hegel's own exasperated comments in section 573 of the *Encyclopaedia*: English translation by William Wallace, *Hegel's Philosophy of Mind*, Oxford: Oxford University Press, 1971, pp. 302–13. Various friendly commentators have suggested that we speak of Hegel's thought as 'panenthe-ist': affirming that all is 'in' God. Well yes, although this is not his terminology, no doubt it is a valid enough characterization – but then all it actually says is that his thought is in fundamental continuity with the classic mainstream of Christian philosophy. Once again (and see pp. 79–82) what is truly *distinctive* about Hegel is, in fact, the decisive way he steps beyond this whole, still all too abstract level of discussion, with his basic methodological separation of trans-metaphysical philosophic theology (as in the *Phenomenology*) from trans-theological metaphysics (the *Logic*).

11 Cf. the discussion of Rose's attack on what she sees as the modern 'Gnosticism' of Thomas Mann and René Girard in Chapter 5.

12 Cf. Tony Gorman, 'Gillian Rose and the Project of a Critical Marxism', *Radical Philosophy* 105, January/February 2001. Gorman prefers the first 'phase' of her thought to the second. He thinks she should have stayed with Adorno's completely irreligious take on Hegel, and with Adorno's residual hankering, at least, after a revolutionary political movement. (I disagree: after all, it seems to me much more *politically realistic* for philosophy, as such, to try and work through religion . . .)

13 For the most sophisticated recent reworking of something like the Kierkegaardian critique, see William Desmond, *Hegel's God: A Counterfeit Double?*, Aldershot: Ashgate, 2003.

Desmond is impatient with Hegel for the very reason that Hegel, unlike Kierkegaard, is far more concerned with the potential contribution of religion to political rationality than he is with trying to do justice to pre-political experiences of self-expressive/self-transcendent prayer. The basic trouble, though, is that – like Kierkegaard – Desmond just does not want to see what Rose, by contrast, regards as the ultimately complementary nature of these two approaches. His whole argument appears to be premised on the, in fact, quite arbitrary mere *assumption* that they are incompatible. And then he approaches Hegel's work in the manner of a prosecuting counsel.

He is an expert one. But is this ever actually an appropriate type of approach to any serious thinker's work? I must say I do not think so.

14 Kierkegaard, *Either / Or* (*Enten-Eller*, ed. 'Victor Eremita', 1843), English translation by Howard V. Hong and Edna H. Hong, vols 3 and 4 of *Kierkegaard's Writings*, Princeton, NJ: Princeton University Press, 1987.

15 Kierkegaard, *Repetition* (*Gjentagelsen*, by 'Constantin Constantius', 1843), English translation by Howard V. Hong and Edna H. Hong in *Kierkegaard's Writings*, vol. 6: *Fear and Trembling / Repetition*, Princeton, NJ: Princeton University Press, 1983, pp. 148–9, 308, 321, 324.

16 Kierkegaard, *Philosophical Fragments* (*Philosophiske Smuler*, by 'Johannes Climacus', 1844), English translation by Howard V. Hong and Edna H. Hong, vol. 7 of *Kierkegaard's Writings*, Princeton, NJ: Princeton University Press, 1985.

17 'Vigilius Haufniensis' is the pseudonymous author of *The Concept of Anxiety* (*Begrebet Angest*, 1844), English translation by Reidar Thomas, vol. 8 of *Kierkegaard's Writings*, Princeton, NJ: Princeton University Press, 1980. 'Frater Taciturnus' is one of the pseudonyms at work in *Stages on Life's Way* (*Stadier paa Livets Vej*, ed. 'Hilarius Bogbinder', 1845), English translation by Howard V. Hong and Edna H. Hong, vol. 11 of *Kierkegaard's Writings*, Princeton, NJ: Princeton University Press, 1988. 'Anti-Climacus' is the pseudonymous author of *The Sickness Unto Death* (*Sygdommen til Døden*, 1849), English translations (a) by Howard V. Hong and Edna H. Hong, vol. 19 of

Kierkegaard's Writings, Princeton, NJ: Princeton University Press, 1983, (b) by Alastair Hannay, Harmondsworth: Penguin, 1989, and *Training in Christianity* (*Indøvelse i Christendom*, 1850), English translation by Howard V. Hong and Edna H. Hong, vol. 20 of *Kierkegaard's Writings*, Princeton, NJ: Princeton University Press, 1991.

18 Rose, *The Broken Middle*, pp. 164–70.

19 The most direct retellings are in *Repetition* and 'Quidam's Diary' in *Stages on Life's Way*.

20 Kafka, *Letters to Felice*, English translation by James Stern and Elizabeth Duckworth, Harmondsworth: Penguin, 1978; *Wedding Preparations in the Country, and Other Posthumous Prose Writings*, English translation by Ernst Kaiser and Eithne Wilkins, London: Secker & Warburg, 1973.

Kafka had also read Kierkegaard, on *his* broken engagement: see especially the letter to Max Brod, from March 1918, in *Letters to Friends, Family and Editors*, English translation by Richard and Clara Wilson, New York: Schocken, 1978, pp. 199–200.

21 English translation in *Wedding Preparations in the Country*, pp. 157–217.

22 *The Journals of Kierkegaard, 1835–1854*, a selection, translated into English by Alexander Dru, London: Fontana, 1969, p. 87, a page torn from the Journal:

> Had I not honoured her above myself, as my future wife, had I not been prouder of her honour than of mine, then I should have remained silent and have fulfilled her desire and mine, and have been married to her – there are so many marriages that conceal their little tale. That I did not want; in that way she would have become my concubine; I would rather have murdered her. – But if I had had to explain myself then I would have had to initiate her into terrible things: my relation to my father, his melancholy, the eternal darkness that broods deep within, my going astray, pleasures and excesses which in the eyes of God are not perhaps so terrible, for it was dread [or anxiety] that drove me to excess, and where was I to look for something to hold on to when I knew, or suspected that the one man I revered for his power and strength had wavered.

23 *Journals of Kierkegaard, 1835–1854*, p. 86.

24 *Frygt og Baeven*, 1843; *Kierkegaard's Writings*, vol. 6.

25 Blanchot, 'The Work's Space and Its Demand', in *The Space of Literature* (1955), English translation by Ann Smock, Lincoln, Nebr.: University of Nebraska Press, 1982, p. 61. She also cites Max Brod and Martin Buber as other representatives of this 'conventional wisdom'.

26 *Fear and Trembling*, in *Kierkegaard's Writings*, vol. 6, pp. 75–6.

27 Hegel, *Phenomenology of Spirit*, chapter V, C, a. See pp. 86–7.

28 'Johannes Climacus', *Concluding Unscientific Postscript* (*Afsluttende uvi-*

denskabelig Efterskrift, 1846), English translation by Howard V. Hong and Edna H. Hong in *Kierkegaard's Writings*, vol. 12.1, Princeton, NJ: Princeton University Press, 1992, pp. 186–7.

29 She criticizes Foucault in particular, there, for his dismissal of Freud: *Dialectic of Nihilism*, pp. 196–7.

30 English translation in *The Pelican Freud Library* (PFL), ed. James Strachey, Harmondsworth: Penguin, vol. 11: *On Metapsychology, The Theory of Psychoanalysis*, 1984.

31 English translations: 'Inhibitions, Symptoms and Anxiety', in PFL, vol. 10, *On Psychopathology*, 1979; 'Anxiety and Instinctual Life', in PFL, vol. 2, *New Introductory Lectures on Psychoanalysis*, 1973.

32 The new theory of anxiety was in fact partly prompted by the challenge of Otto Rank's argument, that all neurosis was essentially a recrudescence of the trauma of birth; an argument which Freud initially welcomed, but then came to repudiate as an over-simplification.

33 'Anxiety and Instinctual Life', in PFL, vol. 2, p. 118.

34 In relation to his hypothesis of the Oedipus Complex, Freud links the origins of such anxiety in boys very specifically to a repressed fear of castration.

35 *The Broken Middle*, p. 85.

36 'Inhibitions, Symptoms and Anxiety', XI, in PFL, vol. 10, pp. 318–20.

37 *The Ego and the Id*, in PFL, vol. 11, p. 391, n. 1. (The observation is relegated to a footnote, just because Freud does not know what else to do with it.)

38 *The Ego and the Id*, p. 391, n. 1.

39 *The Concept of Anxiety*, in *Kierkegaard's Writings*, vol. 8, p. 42.

40 *The Concept of Anxiety*, in *Kierkegaard's Writings*, vol. 8, p. 42.

41 *The Concept of Anxiety*, in *Kierkegaard's Writings*, vol. 8, p. 61.

42 *The Concept of Anxiety*, in *Kierkegaard's Writings*, vol. 8, p. 61.

43 *The Concept of Anxiety*, in *Kierkegaard's Writings*, vol. 8, p. 123. In chapter IV as a whole, the contrast is worked out as being between two forms of 'anxiety as the consequence of sin in the single individual'. On the one hand, there is 'anxiety about evil'; on the other hand, there is 'anxiety about the good'. The former is what belongs to a moral opening-up: so it is a guilty anxiety on the way towards faith, turning away from evil although not yet arrived at its overcoming. But the latter is the demonic – in that it is, on the contrary, a guiltily anxious turning away from the good. 'Virgilius Haufniensis' refers to the gospel portrayals of the possessed, those whom Jesus exorcized, as symbolic representations of this. However, he argues that we need to recognize the demonic not only in such spectacular manifestations, but also as a very much more widespread species of phenomenon.

44 *The Concept of Anxiety*, in *Kierkegaard's Writings*, vol. 8, chapter III.

45 *The Broken Middle*, pp. 99–101.

46 *The Sickness Unto Death*, in *Kierkegaard's Writings*, vol. 19, I C.B, pp. 49–74.

47 *The Broken Middle*, p. 108.

48 *The Broken Middle*, p. xiv.

49 Hegel, *Philosophy of Right*, para. 260; English translation by T. M. Knox, Oxford: Oxford University Press, 1952, p. 161.

50 At the time of the Napoleonic Wars, Hegel tended to take the side of the French, inasmuch as they stood, at any rate somewhat more than their German opponents, for constitutional restraints on arbitrary power, freedom of speech, religious liberty, open courts, trial by jury. This was the guiding principle of his journalism, as editor of the *Bamberger Zeitung* in 1807–8. And later on, in his time at Berlin, he was also a notable opponent of antisemitism. He became, in particular, a close friend and ally of the Jewish philosopher-jurist Eduard Gans, in Gans's protracted struggle, against fierce antisemitic resistance, to be admitted to a teaching post in the Faculty of Law. More generally, he fought constant battles against the often highly antisemitic new German nationalism represented, in philosophical terms, by figures like Jakob Friedrich Fries, and which was widespread especially within the *Burschenschaften*, student fraternities, of the day. This was also a major source of the tension in his relationship with Schleiermacher, who was much more sympathetic to the movement. In 1824–5, on the other hand, he was in alliance with Schleiermacher, as he played a key role in successfully defending the French liberal Victor Cousin, who had been arrested by the Saxon police as a suspected 'subversive'. The common element in all of Hegel's actual political activity was his commitment to the 'principle of subjectivity'.

51 Having been Fichte's successor as Professor of Philosophy at the University of Berlin, Hegel is actually laid side by side with him in the Dorotheenstädtische Cemetery there.

52 *Hegel contra Sociology*, p. 5.

53 Hegel's main tutor at the Tübingen Stift, Gottlob Christian Storr, was, as it happens, a prime example of this approach – to which Hegel, indeed, was just as allergic as Fichte was.

54 English translation by Garrett Green, Cambridge: Cambridge University Press, 1978.

55 Kant's own book with this title did not appear until the following year, 1793.

56 *Hegel contra Sociology*, p. 212.

57 Letter to the Danish poet Jens Baggesen, in H. Schulz, ed., *Fichtes Briefwechsel*, Leipzig, 1925, vol. 1, pp. 449–51.

Fichte, be it noted, was always very prone to speak of '*my* system' in this way. Hegel, even though he was just as self-consciously systematic a thinker, was never so possessive.

58 See for example the comparative discussion of both thinkers in George Armstrong Kelly, *Idealism, Politics and History*, Cambridge: Cambridge University Press, 1969.

59 Again, this is my terminology. See also Shanks, *Faith in Honesty*, Aldershot: Ashgate, 2005.

60 There is just one philosopher before Fichte who develops such a form of metaphysics: namely, Spinoza. Although of course Spinoza in his *Ethics* continues to use the term 'God', there is, again, nothing 'theological' about his argument here. And Fichte regarded Spinoza, very much, as his one great equal as a metaphysician, his great opponent.

61 Hegel, *Science of Logic*, English translation by A.V. Miller, Atlantic Highlands, NJ: Humanities Press International, 1989, Introduction, p. 50.

62 English translation by Peter Heath and John Lachs, in Fichte, *Science of Knowledge (Wissenschaftslehre) with First and Second Introductions*, New York: Meredith Corporation, 1970, p. 93.

63 Hegel, *Phenomenology of Spirit*, chapter VI, C, a.

64 *Hegel contra Sociology*, p. 211. The reference is to Georg Lukács, *History and Class Consciousness*, English translation by Rodney Livingstone, London: Merlin, 1971, p. 119.

65 See note 49, above.

66 Hegel, *Phenomenology of Spirit*, chapter V, B.

67 Hegel, *Phenomenology of Spirit*, chapter V, C, a.

68 Hegel, *Phenomenology of Spirit*, chapter VI, C, c. See also below, pp. 133–4.

69 *Hegel contra Sociology*, p. 202.

70 *Lectures on the Philosophy of Religion*, English translation edited by Peter C. Hodgson, translated by R. F. Brown, P. C. Hodgson and J. M. Stewart with the assistance of J. P. Fitzer and H. S. Harris, 3 vols, Berkeley: University of California Press, 1984–7, vol. 1, p. 452 (1831 series). Quoted by Rose (in her own translation) in *Hegel contra Sociology*, p. 48.

71 *Hegel contra Sociology*, p. 49.

72 *Hegel contra Sociology*, pp. 118–20. Cf. Fackenheim, *The Religious Dimension in Hegel's Thought*, Bloomington, Ind.: University of Indiana Press, 1967, pp. 233–5.

73 Hegel, *Lectures on the Philosophy of Religion*, vol. 3, p. 160.

74 Hegel, *Lectures on the Philosophy of Religion*, vol. 3, p. 162.

75 Hegel, *Lectures on the Philosophy of Religion*, vol. 3, p. 158.

76 This is not in fact something Rose herself observes. She was writing before the publication of the new edition of Hegel's *Lectures*, in which the various lecture series are clearly differentiated. (Neither does Fackenheim observe it.) And so she, for her part, rather misleadingly presents the 'discordant note' here as if it were Hegel's final word.

77 Nietzsche, *The Will to Power*, Preface, 3. English translation by Walter Kaufmann, New York: Vintage, 1968, p. 3.

78 Heidegger, *Identity and Difference*, English translation by Joan Stambaugh, New York: Harper & Row, 1969, p. 72.

79 *Dialectic of Nihilism*, p. 77.
80 *Identity and Difference*, pp. 49–52.
81 *Dialectic of Nihilism*, p. 80.

Chapter 5

1 *The Broken Middle*, p. 157; alluding to *Søren Kierkegaard's Journals and Papers*, English translation by Howard V. Hong and Edna H. Hong, vol. 3, Bloomington: Indiana University Press, 1876, 2550 p. 101, 2514 p. 80.

2 *The Broken Middle*, p. 157.

3 Matters are complicated by Dietrich Bonhoeffer's not at all 'Gnostic' advocacy of 'non-religious Christianity'. But when in common parlance, today, people oppose 'religion' to 'spirituality' they do not mean what Bonhoeffer means, in opposing 'religion' to 'faith'.

4 Besides the Prelude to the novel as a whole, there is also a second Prelude to Part 4, 'Joseph the Provider' – a continuation of the first. *Joseph and His Brothers*, English translation by H. T. Lowe-Porter, Harmondsworth: Penguin, 1978, pp. 3–34, 843–51.

5 Heller, *The Ironic German: A Study of Thomas Mann*, London: Secker & Warburg, 1958.

6 Mann's immediate inspiration was in fact an article on Islamic Gnosticism: Hans Heinrich Schaeder, 'Die islamische Lehre vom vollkommenen Menschen', *Zeitschrift der Deutschen Morgenländischen Gesellschaft*, 1925.

7 This is the central theme of the second Prelude.

8 Cf. *Paradiso*, p. 24: 'Gnosticism is our normal spiritual condition: premodern, modern, post-modern.' This is the broadest possible definition. 'Gnosticism' here has simply become a term for the 'normal', or default, condition of the 'spiritually' minded, but unchastened, intellectual as such, to the extent that they remain locked into the natural conceit of their class.

9 Rorty, *Contingency, Irony and Solidarity*, Cambridge: Cambridge University Press, 1989.

10 The best way in to Girard's understanding of Christianity is his late work, *I See Satan Fall Like Lightning*, Maryknoll: Orbis, 2001.

11 *The Broken Middle*, p. 147.

12 See for example James Alison, *The Joy of Being Wrong: Original Sin Through Easter Eyes*, New York: Crossroad, 1998, and *Faith Beyond Resentment: Fragments Catholic and Gay*, London: Darton, Longman & Todd, 2001.

Chapter 6

1 Rose, *Judaism and Modernity*, pp. 211–23. (And see also the discussion of the 'new ethics' in the Introduction to *Judaism and Modernity*.)

2 Weil, *Waiting on God*, English translation by Emma Craufurd, London: Collins, 1959, p. 21.

3 Levinas, *Difficult Freedom: Essays on Judaism*, English translation by Seán Hand, London: Athlone Press, 1990, pp. 133–41.

4 *Judaism and Modernity*, p. 213.

5 Levinas, *Difficult Freedom*, p. 138.

6 In fact, the texts in question were originally written to serve a metaphorical purpose – they are set in an extremely distant, legendary past, and had no direct application to the political realities of the world in which they were written.

7 Levinas, *Difficult Freedom*, p. 136.

8 Levinas, *Difficult Freedom*, p. 137.

9 Levinas, *Difficult Freedom*, p. 139.

10 The association between the 'face' of the Other and the proper 'infinity' of the 'ethical' is a theme of Levinas' book, *Totality and Infinity*, English translation by Alphonso Lingis, Dordrecht: Kluwer, 1991. His discussion of 'proximity', in relation to 'ethics', and the distinction between the 'saying' and the 'said' are to be found in *Otherwise Than Being Or Beyond Essence*, English translation by Alphonso Lingis, Dordrecht: Kluwer, 1991. These are, by general consensus, Levinas' two most important books.

11 Simone Weil, *The Need for Roots*, English translation by A. F. Wills, London: Routledge & Kegan Paul, 1952, p. 3.

12 *Totality and Infinity*, I.C, 'Truth and Justice', and Conclusions 11, 'Freedom Invested'.

13 In his essay, 'Hegel and the Jews', in *Difficult Freedom*, pp. 235–8, Levinas also accuses Hegel of antisemitism. He is thinking here of Hegel's earliest, only posthumously published, writings about the origins of Christianity. And it is true that these works do feature a caricature of first-century CE Judaism, not dissimilar to Weil's. As in Weil's case, though, the real, contemporary target of the polemic here is not Judaism, but corrupted forms of Christianity. Moreover, in the *Phenomenology of Spirit* (1807) Hegel has changed his mind. Thus, he no longer counterposes the essential truth of the gospel to the supposed errors, specifically, of Jewish religion. Rather, he counterposes it to a phenomenon, the 'unhappy consciousness', which is in principle a feature of all cultures without exception, in varying forms.

There is still a trace of conventional Christian prejudice against Jewish religion in the *Phenomenology* – it pops up, curiously, in the passage on the absurdities of phrenology. Here he cites the supposed intrinsic corruption of Jewish religion as an illustration of the general principle that sometimes, in the evolution of thought, the worse things are, the better the opportunity for creative new departures.

And, more fundamentally, he continues to stress what he sees as the unique capacity of the Christian gospel to articulate the proper overcoming of the 'unhappy consciousness' – he does not consider, as he might, how such an overcoming could also be articulated in rabbinic terms. In general, he never shows any particular interest in rabbinic tradition. This is certainly regrettable.

Yet, as I have said – see Chapter 4, note 50 – the fact remains that by the 1820s Hegel was clearly identified as a leading opponent of antisemitic German nationalism. And the treatment of Judaism in his Berlin *Lectures on the Philosophy of Religion* evolves: whereas in the 1821 lectures he is still chiefly interested in the gulf between Judaism and Christianity, by 1827 his attitude towards Jewish religion has become much more open. See Peter C. Hodgson, *Hegel and Christian Theology*, Oxford: Oxford University Press, 2005, pp. 228–37.

14 See Levinas, *Proper Names*, English translation by Michael B. Smith, Stanford, Cal.: Stanford University Press, 1996, chapters 8, 'Kierkegaard: Existence and Ethics', and 9, 'A Propos of "Kierkegaard vivant"'.

15 *The Broken Middle*, pp. 247–67.

16 Cited in Simone Pétrement, *Simone Weil: A Life*, English translation by Raymond Rosenthal, London: Mowbrays, 1976, p. 424.

17 *Judaism and Modernity*, p. 222.

18 Kierkegaard, *Fear and Trembling*, English translation by Walter Lowrie, Princeton, NJ: Princeton University Press, 1945, p. 53.

19 See Thibon's (generally affectionate) Introduction to Weil, *Gravity and Grace*, English translation by Emma Craufurd, London: Routledge, 1952, p. viii.

20 *Love's Work*, p. 134. And see also *Paradiso*, pp. 17–18. (As an item of actual self-portraiture, it must be said, this does seem rather odd! But then it is clear that the desire 'to pass unnoticed' did not altogether come naturally to Kierkegaard, either. Rather, it was a desire that he desired to feel; or that he at any rate believed in, as a supremely desirable gift of supernatural divine grace.)

21 *The Broken Middle*, pp. 216–28.

22 *The Broken Middle*, pp. 228–36.

23 Arendt, *On Revolution*, New York: Viking, 1963.

24 Arendt, 'On Humanity in Dark Times: Thoughts About Lessing', in *Men in Dark Times*, Harmondsworth: Penguin, 1973. See also the English version of Lessing's play, *Nathan the Wise*, translated by Edward Kemp, London: Nick Hern Books, 2003; and Rose's comments: *The Broken Middle*, pp. 234–5.

Lessing's play, first published in 1779, is set in Palestine at the time of the Crusades, and is a story about the development of friendship between individual Jews, Christians and Muslims, notwithstanding the violent enmity between their communities. He is the first Christian thinker to suggest that open-mindedness towards the adherents of other faith-traditions should be regarded as a major criterion of true Christian faith.

25 *The Broken Middle*, p. 230. (As she further points out, the 'public realm' is also a hybrid term in Arendt's work: sometimes referring to an ideal, but at other times more neutral. The two hybrids thus mirror one another.)

26 *Die Liebesbegriff bei Augustin* (1929); English translation by Arendt herself, *Love and Saint Augustine*, edited by Joanna Vecchiarelli Scott and Judith Chelius Stark, Chicago: University of Chicago Press, 1996.

27 Elizabeth Young-Bruehl, *Hannah Arendt: For Love of the World*, New Haven: Yale University Press, p. 498.

28 *The Broken Middle*, p. 216.

29 Augustine, *The City of God*, Book XIV, chapter 28. English translation by Henry Bettenson, Harmondsworth: Penguin, 1972.

30 This essay is in Arendt, *Between Past and Future*, New York: Viking, 1968.

31 Hannah Arendt, *Rahel Varnhagen: The Life of a Jewish Woman*, English translation from the original German by Richard and Clara Winston, New York: Harcourt Brace Jovanovich, 1974.

32 Letter to Heinrich Blücher, 7 July 1936, cited in Young-Bruehl, *Hannah Arendt: For Love of the World*, p. 56.

33 Hannah Arendt, 'Rosa Luxemburg: 1871–1919', in *Men in Dark Times*.

34 Rose, *The Broken Middle*, pp. 236–7.

35 Rose, *The Broken Middle*, p. 199.

36 Thomas Carlyle, 'Varnhagen von Ense's Memoirs', in *Critical and Miscellaneous Essays*, vol. 5, London: Chapman & Hall, 1869. (It was Carlyle who translated *Wilhelm Meister* into English.) And there is also a report that Goethe himself applied the term to Rahel. See the report by Franz Horn, following the letter from David Veit, 3 September 1795, in Rahel Varnhagen, *Gesammelte Werke*, eds Konrad Feilchenfeldt, Uwe Schweikert and Rahel E. Steiner, Matthes und Seitz, 1983, vol. 1, pp. 157–8.

37 Rose, *The Broken Middle*, p. 237.

38 For a satirical portrait of the type at its most 'beautifully' pretentious, see for instance Milan Kundera, *Life is Elsewhere*, English translation by Peter Kussi, London: Faber & Faber, 1986.

39 Rose, *The Broken Middle*, p. 237.

40 Hannah Arendt, *Eichmann in Jerusalem: A Report on the Banality of Evil*, Harmondsworth: Penguin, 2006. (Originally a series of articles in the *New Yorker*, 1963.)

41 Rose, *The Broken Middle*, p. 237.

42 Denis Diderot, *Rameau's Nephew and D'Alembert's Dream*, English translation by L. W. Tancock, Harmondsworth: Penguin, 1966, p. 65.

43 Rose, *The Broken Middle*, p. 237.

44 Rose, *The Broken Middle*, p. 235.

45 Rose, *The Broken Middle*, p. 234.

46 Hegel, *Phenomenology of Spirit*, English translation by A. V. Miller, Oxford: Oxford University Press, 1977, paras 656, 668.

47 He is also no doubt thinking of his friend Hölderlin's descent into schizophrenia, and Novalis's death from consumption. On the apparent tastelessness, or worse, of these allusions, see H. S. Harris, *Hegel's Ladder*, vol. 2: *The Odyssey of Spirit*, Indianapolis and Cambridge: Hackett, 1997, pp. 498–501. I would only add that it seems to me Hölderlin represents the standpoint of the beautiful soul – or that of the hard-heart, he fluctuates between the two – at its most poignant and genuinely challenging just by virtue of the combination, in his case, of lyrical genius with insanity.

Simone Weil, indeed, would clearly be another example of such a fate.

48 *Phenomenology of Spirit*, para. 664.

49 Hegel, *Phenomenology of Spirit*, paras. 489, 522, 545.

Chapter 7

1 *The Broken Middle*, p. 282, *Judaism and Modernity*, p. 14.

2 See for instance Emmanuel Levinas, *Totality and Infinity*, English Translation by Alphonso Lingis, Dordrecht: Kluwer, 1991, p. 28, where he speaks of Rosenzweig's *Star of Redemption* as 'a work too often present in this book to be cited'.

3 Strauss, 'Introductory Essay', in Cohen, *Religion of Reason out of the Sources of Judaism*, English translation by Simon Kaplan, Atlanta: Scholars Press, 1995, pp. xxiii–xxxviii.

4 Rosenzweig's first scholarly work was *Hegel und der Staat*, Munich and Berlin: R. Oldenbourg, 1920.

5 Nahum Glatzer, ed., *Franz Rosenzweig: His Life and Thought*, Indianapolis and Cambridge: Hackett, 3rd edn, 1998, p. 29.

6 Glatzer, *Franz Rosenzweig*, p. 58.

7 Glatzer, *Franz Rosenzweig*, pp. 68–9.

8 Hermann Cohen, 'Deutschtum und Judentum', reprinted in *Hermann Cohens Jüdische Schriften*, vol. 2, edited by Bruno Strauss, Berlin: C. A. Schwetschte und Sohn, 1924, pp. 237–301.

In *Judaism and Modernity*, pp. 81–4, Rose defends this essay of Cohen's against Jacques Derrida's critique in 'Interpretations at War: Kant, the Jew, the German', *New Literary History* 22 (1991). She certainly prefers Cohen to Derrida. Whereas Derrida is interested in the essay only as a pathological phenomenon, a 'hypernationalist' effusion, symptomatic of an all too typical German-Jewish over-anxiety to assimilate, Rose is at any rate concerned to be fair. Derrida, she argues, has unfairly ignored the way in which, for Cohen, socialism still takes precedence over patriotism; and *Judentum* over

Deutschtum. In 1916 he actually published a second article, with the same title, in response to complaints that, in the original, he had seemed to attribute everything good in German life to the 'spirit of Judaism', without remainder.

9 See Michael Mack, *German Idealism and the Jew: The Inner Anti-Semitism of Philosophy and German Jewish Responses,* Chicago: University of Chicago Press, 2003, p. 108.

10 *Judaism and Modernity,* pp. 121–3. (Here she is primarily discussing Cohen's 1910 essay on 'The Inner Relations of Kantian Philosophy to Judaism' – in vol. 1 of *Hermann Cohens Jüdische Schriften.* But the thesis developed in this essay also crucially underlies the argument of *Religion of Reason.*)

11 Cohen, *Religion of Reason,* pp. 239–41.

12 Cohen, *Religion of Reason,* pp. 329–33. Cohen here attacks Spinoza for misrepresenting the real views of Maimonides particularly, in this regard; and further blames Spinoza for having thereby misled Kant about Judaism in general.

13 Cohen, *Religion of Reason,* pp. 343–5.

14 Cohen, *Religion of Reason,* pp. 286–7, 439–40.

15 Although Hegel does not develop an explicit doctrine of 'anonymous Christianity', the notion is surely implicit in his thinking. So he understands the essence of gospel truth to lie in its symbolic overcoming of the inner servitude of the 'unhappy consciousness'. He thinks that the 'unhappy consciousness' is most vividly *articulated* in devoutly monotheistic cultures, as the servile worship of a tyrannical Lord God – hence the special liberating power of the gospel symbolism, as showing what St Paul calls the 'self-emptying' of the Lord God, incarnate 'in the form of a slave'. But this is not to say that the 'unhappy consciousness' – *in itself* – is confined to such cultures. On the contrary, it is a pervasive feature of the ordinary human condition in every culture. Again, Hegel's claim is that the gospel is uniquely well equipped to *articulate* the overcoming of the 'unhappy consciousness'; yet that does not mean it cannot be overcome, even if less articulately, elsewhere. And the Truth of salvation, for Hegel, consists in the actual overcoming of the 'unhappy consciousness'. It does not depend on any gift of articulacy, either religious or philosophical. The lived Truth that Christ, perfectly, represents can perfectly well be present without Christ being acknowledged by name.

Likewise, Kierkegaard is adamant in distinguishing the actual Truth of salvation from any form of 'objective' correctness, doctrinal or practical. Indeed, he insists that such Truth simply '*is* subjectivity': what Christ – the Way, the Truth, the Life – represents is just a maximum intensity of 'subjectivity', in the sense of pathos-laden, free-spirited inwardness.

Therefore, Cohen's accusation that Christian faith denies the proper trans-cultural universality of saving Truth has no real purchase against either of these approaches to Christian theology. They both set out to vindicate Christian faith precisely as an opening towards Truth understood in the most purely universal terms; in the end, absolutely transcending any sort of confessional particularism.

16 *Judaism and Modernity*, p. 150. (It should also be noted that Rosenzweig was himself very much an admirer of Goethe.)

17 *Judaism and Modernity*, pp. 128–9.

18 Franz Rosenzweig, *The Star of Redemption*, English translation by William W. Hallo, London: Routledge, 1971, p. 407.

19 Rose, *The Broken Middle*, pp. 278–87.

20 Mark C. Taylor, *Journeys to Selfhood: Hegel and Kierkegaard*, 2nd edn, New York: Fordham University Press, 2000. (He had previously published another, preparatory work on Kierkegaard: *Kierkegaard's Pseudonymous Authorship: A Study of Time and the Self*, Princeton, NJ: Princeton University Press, 1975.)

21 Nietzsche comes to the fore in Taylor, *Erring: A Postmodern A/theology*, Chicago: University of Chicago Press, 1984; Heidegger, and his French commentators, in *Altarity*, Chicago: University of Chicago Press, 1987.

22 Rose, *The Broken Middle*, p. 5, note 10.

23 Rose, *The Broken Middle*, p. 5, note 10.

24 Milbank, *Theology and Social Theory: Beyond Secular Reason*, Oxford: Blackwell, 1990, p. 9.

25 The other was Fergus Kerr.

26 *Dialectic of Nihilism*, pp. 104, 107. Heidegger began his academic career with a study of Scotus: *Die Kategorien- und Bedeutungslehre des Duns Scotus*, Freiburg Habilitationschrift, 1915. And Deleuze also acknowledges Scotus as the true founder of 'ontology' in *Difference and Repetition*, English translation by Paul Patton, New York: Columbia University Press, 1994, p. 35.

27 See Milbank, *Theology and Social Theory*, p. 302.

28 On the logic of Hegel's Christology, see Shanks, *Hegel's Political Theology*, Cambridge: Cambridge University Press, 1991.

29 Milbank, *Theology and Social Theory*, p. 170.

30 *Mourning Becomes the Law*, pp. 15–39.

31 See for instance Taylor, *Erring*, pp. 11–13, 70–1, 156–7; Milbank, *Theology and Social Theory*, p. 417.

32 *The Broken Middle*, p. 284.

33 *The Broken Middle*, p. 285.

Chapter 8

1 The one extended theological discussion, to date, is Anna Rowlands, 'Practical Theology in the "Third City"', Ph.D. thesis no. Th28503, Manchester University; to which I am indebted.

2 'O! untimely death. / Death!', in *Mourning Becomes the Law*, pp. 127–8.

3 Translation by Daniel Liebert, in *Rumi – Fragments, Ecstasies*, Santa Fe, NM: Source Books, 1981.

Bibliography

Works by Gillian Rose

'How Is Critical Theory Possible?', *Political Studies* 24, March 1976.
The Melancholy Science: An Introduction to the Thought of Theodor W. Adorno, London: Macmillan, 1978.
Hegel contra Sociology, London: Athlone, 1981.
Dialectic of Nihilism: Post-Structuralism and Law, Oxford: Blackwell, 1984.
The Broken Middle: Out of Our Ancient Society, Oxford: Blackwell, 1992.
Judaism and Modernity: Philosophical Essays, Oxford: Blackwell, 1993.
Love's Work, London: Chatto & Windus, 1995.
Mourning Becomes the Law: Philosophy and Representation, Cambridge: C.U.P., 1996.
'The Final Notebooks of Gillian Rose', ed. Howard Caygill, *Women: A Cultural Review*, 9. 1, 1998.
Paradiso, ed. Howard Caygill, London: Menard Press, 1999.

Secondary literature, on Gillian Rose's work

Avrahami, Einat, '"Keep Your Mind in Hell and Despair Not": Illness as Life Affair in Gillian Rose's *Love's Work*', *Narrative* 9.3, 2001.
Ayres, Lewis, 'Representation, Theology, and Faith', *Modern Theology*, 11.1, 1995.
Barnes, Michael, *Theology and the Dialogue of Religions*, Cambridge: C.U.P., 2002.
Barrington-Ward, Simon, '"Forgiven, Forgiving", "Failing Towards…" – The Goal and the Journey', paper given at the Symposium on the Life and Work of Gillian Rose, The Social Theory Centre, University of Warwick, December, 2000.
Bernstein, Jay, 'Philosophy Among the Ruins', *Prospect Magazine*, 6, 1996.
Caygill, Howard, 'The Broken Hegel: Gillian Rose's Retrieval of Speculative Philosophy', *Women: A Cultural Review*, 9.1, 1998.

Cohen, Josh, 'Phenomenologies of Mourning: Gillian Rose and Walter Benjamin', *Women: A Cultural Review*, 9.1, 1998.

'Dialectic of Entanglement: Adorno, Auschwitz and the Contradictions of Representation', in Holger Briel and Andreas Kramer, eds, *In Practice: Adorno, Critical Theory and Cultural Studies*, Oxford: Peter Lang, 2001.

Ellis, Marc, 'Questioning Conversion: Gillian Rose, George Steiner, and Christianity', in *Revolutionary Forgiveness: Essays on Judaism, Christianity, and the Future of Religious Life*, Baylor University Press, 2000.

Evans, Mary, 'De-constructing Death: In Memory of Gillian Rose', *Women: A Cultural Review*, 9.1, 1998.

Gorman, Tony, 'Gillian Rose and the Project of a Critical Marxism', *Radical Philosophy*, 105, 2001.

— 'Nihilism and Faith: Rose, Bernstein and the Future of Critical Theory', *Radical Philosophy*, 134, 2005.

Jarvis, Simon, 'Idle Tears: A Response to Gillian Rose', in G. K. Browning, ed., *Hegel's Phenomenology of Spirit: A Reappraisal*, Dordrecht: Kluwer, 1997.

Jay, Martin, 'The Conversion of the Rose', in *Refractions of Violence*, New York & London: Routledge, 2003.

Kavka, Martin, 'Saying Kaddish for Gillian Rose', in Clayton Crockett, ed., *Secular Theology: American Radical Theological Thought*, London & New York: Routledge, 2001.

Kilminster, Richard, 'From the Standpoint of Eternity: A Commentary on Rose's Hegel Contra Sociology', *Theory, Culture and Society*, 2.1, 1983.

Kolbrenner, William, 'The Hermeneutics of Mourning: Multiplicity and Authority in Jewish Law', *College Literature* 30.4, 2003.

Lathangue, Robin, 'Yielding Actuality: Trust and Reason in Gillian Rose's Vision of Community', *Southern Journal of Philosophy*, 45.1, 2007.

Lloyd, Vincent, 'On the Use of Gillian Rose', *Heythrop Journal*, 48.5, 2007.

— 'On Gillian Rose and Love', *Telos*, forthcoming.

— *Law and Transcendence: On the Unfinished Project of Gillian Rose*, forthcoming.

Marcus, Laura, 'The Work of Gillian Rose', *Women: A Cultural Review*, 9.1, 1998.

Osborne, Peter, 'Hegelian Phenomenology and the Critique of Reason and Society', *Radical Philosophy*, 32, 1982.

Parkinson, Anna, '"Mourning Rationalism without Reason?" Affectual Surplus in the Wake of Poststructuralism', *REAL: The Yearbook of Research in English and American Literature*, 16, 2000.

Parry, Ann, '"... To give... death a place": Rejecting the "ineffability" of the Holocaust: the Work of Gillian Rose and Anne Michaels', *Journal of European Studies*, 30.4, 2000.

Ratekin, Tom, 'Working through the Four Discourses: Gillian Rose and the Products of Love's Work', *Prose Studies*, 28.1, 2006.

Rose, Jacqueline, 'On Gillian Rose', in *The Last Resistance*, London: Verso, 2007.

Rose, Lynn, *A Journey Together?*, unpublished memoir.

Rowlands, Anna, *Practical Theology in 'The Third City'*, Ph. D. thesis no. Th28503, Manchester University, 2007.

Stanley, Liz, 'Mourning Becomes…: The Work of Feminism in the Spaces between Lives Lived and Lives Written', *Women's Studies International Forum*, 25.1, 2002.

Stone, Alison, 'Hegel's Dialectic and the Recognition of Feminine Difference', *Philosophy Today*, Supplement 47.5, 2003.

Tubbs, Nigel, *Contradiction of Enlightenment: Hegel and the Broken Middle*, Aldershot: Ashgate, 1997.

— 'What is Love's Work?' *Women: A Cultural Review*, 9.1, 1998

— 'Mind the Gap: The Philosophy of Gillian Rose', *Thesis Eleven*, no. 60, 2000.

— *The Philosophy of the Teacher*, Oxford: Blackwell, 2005.

Williams, Rowan, 'Between Politics and Metaphysics: Reflections in the Wake of Gillian Rose', *Modern Theology*, 11.1, 1995.

Wolf, Arnold Jacob, 'The Tragedy of Gillian Rose', *Judaism*, Fall edition, 1997.

Conferences

'Philosophy as Radical Thought: A Tribute to the Philosopher Gillian Rose', The London Consortium and the Institute of Contemporary Arts, December 9, 2005.

'Symposium on the Life and Work of Gillian Rose', University of Warwick, December 8, 2000.

Acknowledgements

The author and publisher acknowledge with thanks the following copyright material.

Rowan Williams, 'Afternoon', *Remembering Jerusalem: Poems*, Oxford: Perpetua Press, 2001, p. 31.

Geoffrey Hill, 'In Memoriam: Gillian Rose', *A Treatise of Silver Power*, London: Penguin, 2007, p. 35.

Rumi, 'Subtle Degrees', trans. Daniel Liebert, *Rumi – Fragments, Ecstasies*, Santa Fe, NM: Source Books, 1981.

Index